KILLERS

WORLD SERIAL KILLERS

GORDON KERR

Futura

FUTURA

First published in Great Britain in 2010 by Futura

A CIP catalogue record for this book
is available from the British Library.

ISBN 978-0-7088-6401-2

Typeset in Great Britain by Omnipress Limited
Printed and bound in Great Britain by CPI Mackays, Chatham ME5 8TD

Futura
An imprint of
Little, Brown Book Group
100 Victoria Embankment
London EC4Y 0DY

An Hachette UK Company
www.hachette.co.uk

www.littlebrown.co.uk

Photo credits: Getty Images

The views expressed in this publication are those of the author.
The information and the interpretation of that information are
presented in good faith. Readers are advised that where ethical
issues are involved, and often highly controversial ethical issues
at that, they have a personal responsibility for making their own
assessments and their own ethical judgements.

CONTENTS

PART THREE: SOUTH AMERICA

PART FOUR: AFRICA

PART FIVE: AUSTRALIA

PART SIX: ASIA

INTRODUCTION

Murder. It stalks the streets at night waiting to pounce, lying within the most innocent request. When a man wearing a plastercast introduces himself as 'Ted' and asks if you would mind helping him carry some books to his car, how are you to know that he is Ted Bundy, killer of anywhere between thirty and one hundred young women, and that hidden about his person is a crowbar that he will bring crashing down on your head as soon as you reach the vehicle? His handsome, smiling face will be the last thing you see before everything goes dark. When a man bids you good evening as you walk in a quiet country lane, how are you to know that he is in reality Peter Kürten, the infamous Vampire of Düsseldorf and as soon as he is a few paces past you, he will be lunging at your back with a knife trying to kill you? If you were an elderly lady and you were offered help to carry your groceries by a pleasant-looking man, you would surely say thank you, not realizing that he was John Wayne Glover, the 'Granny Killer', the 'Monster of Mosman', and that tucked in his belt was a hammer that he was going to bring down on your head as soon as you were in the secluded foyer of your retirement home.

Murder also lurks in ordinary places, in a semi-detached, three-storey house in Cromwell Street in Gloucester, the 'house of horrors' where Fred and Rose West acted out their depraved fantasies on innocent victims, amongst them their own children. Or in a disused bank in the small town of Snowtown, north of Melbourne in Australia, where a welfare scam resulted in bodies being dissolved in vats of chemicals. A respectable bungalow in High Burnside, on the outskirts of Glasgow, hid the bodies of Marion Watt, her sixteen-year-old daughter Vivienne and her sister, Margaret Brown, killed by Peter Manuel, burglar and rapist turned serial killer, a charmer who became a monster. And you could also find murder in the serenity of your own north of England sitting room. A visit by the doctor just to check up on you and give you a little injection to make you feel better. The only problem is that the doctor's name is Harold Shipman and he has already given that injection to a couple of hundred people, all of whom died as a result.

Murder also thrives on every continent around the world. Australia has had its share of serial killers, men like serial sex offender, Peter Dupas, convicted of the murder of three women in Melbourne in the

1990s and suspected of killing at least another three. Catherine and David Birnie were the Australian version of the British Moors Murderers, Myra Hindley and Ian Brady. They stalked young women, abducting them and taking them home to work out their sexual perversions on them before murdering them. South Africa, too, can boast horrific killers such as Moses Sithole, a mass murderer of around forty women whom he killed with relentless regularity, tempting them with the possibility of work and then extinguishing their young lives.

Serial killers are, of course, a breed apart, the doyens of the murder world, people who have stepped over the imaginary boundary that separates men from beasts. They are often deranged, bitter, vengeful people taking their revenge on the world. The South Korean killer Yoo Young Cheoi, for instance, was angry at the world, especially the rich, and resolved to kill as many of them as possible. He then switched his anger to women, especially prostitutes, and set about disposing of as many of them as he could. The Pakistani mass murderer, Javed Iqbal, killer of one hundred young boys in an astonishing five-month killing spree in 1999, is presumed to have launched his attack on the street urchins of Lahore after being beaten up by a gang of them. He may also have been taking revenge on society for the death of his mother who passed away as a result of her distress at his situation.

But serial killers are also, unlike Javed Iqbal, mother-haters. Ed Kemper loathed his mother, Clarnell, with such a passion that every one of the eight women he murdered, had sex with and dismembered, was a representation of her. When eventually he did kill her, he displayed his fantastic contempt for her by using her severed head as a dartboard. Pedro Alonso López, the Colombian slayer of hundreds of little girls in Colombia, Peru and Ecuador in the 1970s and 1980s, was another mother-hater. His mother had thrown him out of her house at the age of eight – he had been raping his younger sister, after all – and he took revenge on womankind for several decades afterwards. African serial killer Stuart Wilken also hated the mother who had abandoned him to a life of unrelenting brutality. To make matters worse, his adoptive mother also rejected him. Seven people, boys and women, paid for all the wrongs he perceived had been done to him. One-eyed mass killer Henry Lee Lucas hated his mother so much he killed her in the middle of a furious argument. She had been the cause of him losing an eye and, earning money as a prostitute, had had no hesitation in conducting her business in front of her eight children and her legless husband.

But serial killers can also be coldly calculating and manipulative. The Japanese murderer Futoshi Matsunaga, for instance, was a person with an astonishing power to make people do his bidding, a man around whom a kind of cult was formed. Although he never actually murdered anyone, he was responsible for the deaths of seven people, including two children. He persuaded his cohorts to actually do the deed, but there is no doubt who was really behind the murders. Charles Manson, too, leader of the murderous hippie clan known as the Family, was a manipulator of minds who, like Matsunaga, never actually killed anyone but was certainly responsible for the horrific actions of his followers, often runaway girls whose minds had been addled by drugs and his poisonous outpourings about society. French killer, Henri Landru, also preyed on gullible women. A modern-day Bluebeard, he lured a number of them to his house at Gambais where he stripped them of their savings and their clothes before killing them and burning them in a large stove.

Like Landru, there have been numerous serial killers who were in it for financial gain. South African nurse Daisy de Melker inherited a substantial sum when a well-off fiancé died and proceeded to hasten the deaths of several of her husbands in order to benefit from their kindness to her in their wills.

She paid for it with her life at the end of a rope, of course. The horrific H. H. Holmes, America's first serial killer, killed in order to benefit from insurance scams, but how he enjoyed it, constructing a block-long killing factory in Chicago in which he tortured and murdered countless women, constantly improvising and experimenting with his methods. The infamous Edinburgh bodysnatchers Burke and Hare also found killing to be a lucrative pastime, certainly easier than actually working for a living, and many people ended up on the dissecting slab at Edinburgh University's medical school as a direct result of their nefarious activities. French Dr Marcel Petiot exploited Jews trying to get out of Paris after the Nazi invasion of France during the Second World War, killing them horrifically and taking their money and valuables.

Sex is, of course, often a motivation for killing. The 'Butcher of Hanover', Fritz Haarmann, killed young boys, dozens of them, and sold their flesh in the markets of Hanover. Another German killer, Joachim Kroll, the 'Ruhr Hunter', raped his victims and ghoulishly also ate their flesh, a perversion he shared with the American Albert Fish who killed in the 1920s and 1930s and who cooked the flesh of his victims like a Michelin-starred chef.

Of course, there are also the natural-born killers,

the ones that just cannot help themselves, men such as the American Tommy Lynn Sells, the 'Cross-Country Killer', an itinerant killer, like Henry Lee Lucas, who claimed to have killed as many as seventy people in his travels across the United States. Luis Garavito may have raped and killed as many as three hundred young boys in Colombia in the late 1990s, travelling the length and breadth of the country. Another born killer was Eric Edgar Cooke, who created panic in the sleepy Western Australian city of Perth in the early 1960s, killing randomly and at will. He did it, as many others did, because he had the urge … and, quite frankly, because he enjoyed it.

The serial killer is amongst us, going about his business, seething with discontent, raging in private about his mother, his job, his wife, his boss and vowing to take revenge against whatever segment of society takes his fancy.

All you have to do is hope that you never meet him.

PART ONE

EUROPE

BURKE AND HARE

In the nineteenth century, as medical science flourished and new teaching institutions opened, there was a growing demand for corpses on which medical students could learn anatomy. Executions had always provided a ready supply of cadavers but with changes to the Bloody Code, the system of law and punishment in England, resulting in only five crimes being punishable by death, as opposed to the dozens that had previously warranted that penalty, the availability of bodies for study was drastically reduced.

The gap between demand and supply was filled by criminal elements who were willing to provide bodies obtained by any means. These men, feared and reviled by a general public that believed redemption was impossible if the body was not left intact, became known as body-snatchers or resurrectionists. Two of the most infamous of their number were the Irishmen William Burke and William Hare.

Burke and Hare were Irish immigrants, originating in Ulster and coming to Scotland in the early 1820s to work as labourers on the New Union Canal being built between Edinburgh and Falkirk where it joined up with the Forth and Clyde Canal. Burke was thirty-six years old and had spent much of his adult life in the army. He had a wife back in Ireland, but had soon hooked up with a Scottish woman, Helen MacDougal, with whom he travelled to Edinburgh, leaving MacDougal's two young children behind.

William Hare did not meet Burke during his time working on the canal, but following its completion, he, too, was in Edinburgh, lodging in the area known as the West Port at a cheap boarding house owned by a man named Logue and his wife Margaret. Logue died in 1826 and Hare was soon living with Margaret as her common-law husband while running the lodging house with her.

Burke and MacDougal, also living in the West Port, met Margaret Logue one day by chance and an introduction to Hare followed. They moved into the boarding house and became friends, sharing a liking for whisky and a desire to make money as easily as possible.

In November 1827, one of the lodgers of the boarding house, an elderly man named Donald, became ill and died. The man owed Hare rent and he was not best pleased to realise that he would never be paid. He and Burke dreamt up a plan to sell Donald's body to a medical school. They filled his coffin with tree bark to give it adequate weight and sold the body to an ambitious anatomist, Professor Robert Knox, who taught at Edinburgh University. Knox paid them £7 10s for it and Burke and Hare were in business.

Another lodger became ill a few days later and they decided also to help him on his way. They gave him whisky until he passed out and then suffocated him. Handing the body over to the medical school, they said he had died of drink.

The next victim was a woman who had been brought back to the boarding house by Margaret who, like Helen MacDougal, was in on their money-making scheme. The woman was again fed a quantity of whisky until she was senseless. She was suffocated and next day was on the dissecting table at the university.

In February 1828, an elderly woman, Abigail Simpson, had come to Edinburgh to collect some pension money. As she was walking back home, Hare met her and suggested she go to the boarding house for a dram and to rest before continuing her journey. The whisky flowed until it was so late that she was persuaded to stay the night. The trouble was, however, that Burke and Hare had also, by this time, consumed a large amount of whisky and they were incapable of taking action that night. Next morning, however, they plied her with more until she was incapable of fighting back. They held her down and suffocated her. Her body was with Knox by the evening and they were delighted to receive a bonus because the cadaver was so fresh.

Burke and Hare could not believe their luck at finding such an easy way to make money. They began to hang around inns like the White Hart in the Grassmarket, trying to spot waifs, strays and runaways, people no one would miss. They would then lure them away and strangle or suffocate them before taking them to Professor Knox.

On the morning of 9 April 1828, William Burke met two eighteen-year-old West Port prostitutes, Mary Paterson and Janet Brown, in a local tavern. He invited them to have breakfast with him, escorting them to the boarding house where they ate and carried on drinking. Eventually, however, Burke's woman, Helen, walked in and lost her temper when she saw Burke with the two women. A violent argument ensued and Burke threw Helen out. Mary was asleep throughout and remained thus when Janet left. Later, when Janet returned to fetch her friend, she was told she had gone out with Burke. Mary Paterson was never seen again.

A few weeks later Burke murdered Elizabeth Haldane, a former lodger who had fallen on hard times and who he had allowed to sleep in his stable.

He would murder her daughter Peggy a few weeks later.

Not long after dispatching Elizabeth Haldane, Burke watched the police take a very drunk woman into custody and spotted an opportunity. He approached the constables and told them he knew the woman and was happy to take her home. The officers were delighted to have her taken off their hands. Needless to say, however, Burke had never seen the woman before and she was dead before the day was out.

An old woman and her deaf grandson were next in their sights. Burke and Hare used the familiar tactic of inviting them back to the boarding house for drinks and once there, suffocated the old woman. They were unsure what to do with the boy but it did not take them long to come up with an idea. With his customary callous disregard for human life, Hare seized the young man and held him over Burke's knee, pushing down on him and breaking his back. They got £8 for each body.

But soon, greed would come between the deadly duo. Burke learned that Hare was working on his own, killing and selling the victims without sharing the spoils with his erstwhile partner. He was furious and after loud arguments he moved out. Nonetheless, they continued to work together and it did not matter who the victim was. Even an old friend who visited Burke was soon being dissected by eager students.

They began to get careless, however. For instance, on one occasion they delivered an eighteen-year-old boy to the university. Known as 'Daft Jamie', he was a well-known local character who lived on the streets and entertained children with jokes and riddles. Jamie's mother located his body at the university and her identification was confirmed by several of the students who also knew him. There was public outrage, although Burke and Hare denied that it was Jamie and Professor Knox began to dissect the face as soon as possible to conceal the boy's identity.

They killed for the last time on Halloween morning, 1828. Burke met an old Irish woman, Mary Docherty, in a tavern. He told her that his mother's name was also Docherty and that she came from the same town as the woman. Therefore, he smiled, they must be related. He persuaded her to return with him to his house where he introduced her to Helen and a couple, James and Ann Gray, who were lodging there. Mary was persuaded to stay the night while the Grays were to be lodged for that night at Hare's boarding house.

That night there was a great deal of noise from

Burke's house and, around midnight, a neighbour passing the door heard a woman's voice shout 'Murder! Get the police, there is murder here!' The man tried to locate a police officer but there were none around. He listened at the door again, however, and hearing nothing, assumed everything was alright.

When the Grays returned the following morning for breakfast there was no sign of Mary Docherty. Helen told them that she had asked the woman to leave because she was paying a little too much attention to Burke. Ann Gray went towards a spare bed in the room in order to get some socks. Suddenly Burke screamed at her to stay away from the bed. She found this very strange, especially when he shouted at her again later on when she went close to it. Alone in the room a little later, she decided to have a look. Lifting the bedcover she found Mary Docherty's lifeless eyes staring back at her.

The Grays fled but bumped into Helen MacDougal who asked them where they were going. When they told her they had found the body and asked her what she knew about it, Helen panicked and offered them £10 a week for their silence. They were not to be bought, however. They went straight to the police.

Helen found Margaret and they ran off to inform Burke and Hare of this disastrous development.

The two men managed to get Mary's body out of the house before the arrival of the police although they were spotted by neighbours manhandling a tea chest.

Burke and Hare arrived back at the house to find the police waiting for them, but they had worked out alibis, informing the officers that Mary Docherty had left the house at seven the previous evening. They were not believed, however, and were taken in for questioning.

It all became academic when an anonymous tip-off led police to Professor Knox's lecture theatre where Mary Docherty's body was discovered, not yet dissected.

Evidence against Burke and Hare started to pile up as the authorities began to investigate the spate of disappearances that had occurred in West Port during the last twelve months. The culprits turned on each other but it was still proving difficult to pin the murders on them. There had been no witnesses to the actual killings, after all, and the evidence was mostly circumstantial. The Lord Advocate approached William Hare and offered him a deal. If he would testify against Burke, he would be given immunity from prosecution. Hare did not hesitate and a short while later William Burke and Helen MacDougal were charged with the murder of Mary Docherty, while Burke alone was charged with the murders of Daft Jamie and the prostitute Mary Paterson.

Their trial began on Christmas Eve and by Christmas Day the jury was already out. When they returned they pronounced William Burke guilty and Helen not proven, a unique Scottish verdict that falls between guilty and innocent. She was free to go.

William Burke was hanged in 1829 amidst demands that Professor Knox should face the same fate. Although Knox was never charged, his reputation was damaged to such an extent that for the remainder of his career, he was rejected for every position for which he applied.

William Hare was released and there are stories of him as a blind beggar on the streets of London. The last reported sighting of him was in Carlisle.

JACK THE RIPPER

What is it about Jack the Ripper that still fascinates us, more than a hundred years after he stalked the dingy streets of Whitechapel? After all, compared with the monsters who have entered the annals of crime in the years since, he is small time. Ted Bundy murdered thirty-five women and Gerald Stano confessed to forty-one. The Ripper only killed five. Perhaps the reason for our enduring interest is the fact that we still do not know who Jack the Ripper was. Every year, it seems, there is another theory and an entire industry has grown up around him, with more books having been written about him than have been written about all of the United States presidents put together.

There are at least twenty-seven suspects, amongst whom is Montague John Druitt, a doctor, who was described by his own family as 'sexually insane'. They believed him to be the Ripper. Coincidentally, he disappeared around the time that the murders ceased and his body was fished out of the Thames on 31 December 1892, just over a month after the last murder.

Some claim, on the other hand, that the Polish Jew Aaron Kosminski, was the Ripper. Kosminski, who hated all women but especially prostitutes, lived in Whitechapel and had homicidal tendencies. In 1889, he was declared insane and sent to an asylum.

Russian doctor Michael Ostrog was another asylum inmate who possessed homicidal tendencies. His whereabouts at the time of each murder was never established.

Amongst the other suspects are some surprising names. Prince Albert Victor, Duke of Clarence, popularly known as 'Eddie', was Queen Victoria's grandson. One theory suggests that a shop girl who was carrying his baby had been institutionalised for the remainder of her life by the queen's doctor, Sir William Gull. The prostitutes who were murdered, it is suggested, all knew the shop girl and were aware of what had happened to her. To maintain silence on the matter, Sir William had killed them, making it look like the work of a madman. There are a couple of elements of this story that make it unlikely, however. Firstly, Sir William was a man of over seventy years of age at the time of the murders and it would have been difficult for a man of that age to commit such murders. Secondly, Eddie's sexual preferences leaned more in the direction of men than women.

The artist Walter Sickert has recently become a suspect. He painted prostitutes he met on the streets of London's East End and his pictures sometimes replicate photographs of the Ripper's victims. Furthermore, some of the letters allegedly written by Jack the Ripper contain phrases used by the American painter James McNeill Whistler. Whistler was Sickert's teacher.

Whoever he was – and it is unlikely that we will ever know for sure – he launched his brief eighteen-month reign of terror towards the end of August 1888. Charles Cross was walking through Buck Row in Whitechapel at around four in the morning when he spotted what he thought at first was a bundle of clothing lying on the ground at the entrance to a stable yard. As he got closer, he saw that it was actually a woman lying on her back. His initial thought was that she was drunk. After all, it was not unusual in those times to find someone dead drunk on the street. Whitechapel was a rough area, populated mostly by the poor and the unemployed and serviced by around 1,200 prostitutes.

Seeing another man walking along the street, Cross called to him for help. They knelt beside her but realised there was nothing they could do for her. For the sake of decency they pulled down her skirt which had been lifted up over her waist. When

Constable John Neil arrived on the scene, he noted that her throat had been cut from ear to ear. He shone his lamp in her face and saw it reflected dully in eyes that were wide open and staring. A doctor and ambulance were summoned, but, of course, there was nothing for them to do but confirm that she was dead and remove her from the scene.

She had been dead for not more than thirty minutes, Dr Rees Llewellyn surmised, and had died as a result of the devastating wound to the throat. Her throat had, in fact, been slashed twice, but on further examination at the mortuary, it emerged that she had also received a stab wound to the abdomen and several other long, deep cuts. The killer had mutilated her as she lay on the ground, it appeared. A police surgeon is reported to have said of this mutilation, 'I have never seen so horrible a case. She was ripped about in a manner that only a person skilled in the use of a knife could have achieved.' Perhaps that was the beginning of the legend of the Ripper and the beginning of the speculation about who he was.

The victim was identified as Mary Ann Nichols, a forty-two-year-old prostitute known as 'Pretty Polly'. Mother of five children, she had been married to a printer but her excessive drinking had brought the marriage to an end. A veteran of the police force,

Frederick Abberline, was put in charge of the case but he had little to go on. There had been no witnesses and the killer had left no clues. He wondered if Mary Ann's death was connected with the murder of thirty-nine-year-old prostitute, Martha Tabram, a few weeks previously. She had been stabbed thirty-nine times in the body, neck and private parts, but crucially, her throat had not been cut and there was no mutilation of her abdomen. Furthermore, Mary Ann had been killed with a long-bladed knife; Martha's killer had used a penknife.

Several months before that another prostitute had been seriously injured in a vicious attack during which her assailant had rammed a blunt instrument into her vagina. These incidents, however, seemed to Abberline to be unrelated to the murder he was now investigating.

The next Ripper victim was Annie Chapman, known on the streets as 'Dark Annie', who was found in Hanbury Street by a porter from Spitalfields Market. Forty-seven years old and ravaged by tuberculosis, she had been thrown out of her lodgings in the early hours of 8 September and ordered to earn some money to pay her rent. Her body presented a grim spectacle. Her skirt was hoisted up over her waist but this time the killer had cut out her small intestine and other internal organs and they lay on the ground beside her. Her throat had been cut after she had been strangled just enough to render her unconscious. Her pathetic few possessions also lay, neatly arranged, by her feet. To their horror, doctors examining the body realised that her uterus, part of her bladder and the upper part of her vagina had been removed and were not at the scene. The killer had taken them home with him.

Investigating officers began to think, from the way in which her internal organs had been removed and from the type of knife he had used, that the killer might have been a medical man or someone with anatomical knowledge.

Whoever he was, he was a maniac who had killed twice and was likely to strike again.

Panic began to stalk the streets of the East End and Whitechapel's large Jewish community came under suspicion. In response, Jewish traders banded together to create the Mile End Vigilance Committee, a kind of neighbourhood watch. Suspects were rounded up – drunks, eccentrics and people who were insane. However, the men they were bringing in either had alibis for the times of the killings or were incapable of wielding a knife as precisely as the Ripper. No progress was made.

He struck again on the last day of September. Forty-five-year-old Elizabeth Stride, known as

'Long Liz', had left her lodgings early the previous evening and was found dead at one the following morning in Dutfield's Yard, just off Berner Street. Liz, a part-time prostitute who also earned a living from sewing and cleaning, was estimated to have died between 12.36 and 12.56 am. Her skirt was not pulled up as in the other cases, but her throat was cut with such force that the knife had sliced through her windpipe.

She had been seen around 12.30 am by a policeman, talking to a man aged about thirty, with dark hair and a moustache, wearing a deerstalker hat, a black cutaway coat, a white shirt and a dark tie. In his hand he was carrying a bundle. Was this the first sighting of Jack the Ripper? Another witness who spotted her at 12.45 am said that she was arguing with a man when she screamed and he threw her to the ground in anger. This witness said that there was a second man across the road lighting a pipe, to whom the first man called out, 'Lipsky!' He followed the first man as he left the scene of the argument. However, Long Liz talked to numerous men that night.

As they examined the body of Elizabeth Stride, just a quarter of a mile away a constable found another body. At 1.30 am, Constable Edward Watkins had passed through Mitre Square and had seen nothing untoward. Fifteen minutes later, on his return, he found the body of a woman whose throat had been cut and whose internal organs protruded from the gaping wound that had been made in her stomach.

Forty-year-old Catherine Eddowes' right ear had been cut off, as had the tip of her nose, and her eyelids had been sliced through. A trail of blood led from her body to a message scrawled in chalk on a nearby wall. Poorly spelt, it read, 'The Juwes are The men That Will not be Blamed For Nothing.'

This was a significant piece of evidence, but, astonishingly, Metropolitan Police Commissioner Sir Charles Warren ordered that it be washed off. He took it as a deliberate attempt to put the blame on the Jews and was worried that it might provoke an attack on Jews living in the area.

One witness came forward, saying that he had seen Eddowes earlier, at around 1.35 am talking to a young man with a fair moustache who was wearing a deerstalker. She had actually been in police custody earlier that night, having been put in a cell at Bishopsgate police station after she was arrested for being drunk and disorderly. They had let her out at 12.30 am. Shortly afterwards she had encountered Jack the Ripper.

The murders were on everyone's lips and hundreds of letters arrived at Scotland Yard, at newspaper offices and even at the homes of the detectives involved in the case. One particular letter gave the name to the anonymous murderer that has gone down in the annals of crime. It was sent on 25 September to the Central News Agency and read:

Dear Boss

I keep on hearing the police have caught me but they won't fix me just yet. I have laughed when they look so clever and talk about being on the right track. That joke about Leather Apron gave me real fits. I am down on whores and I shan't quit ripping them till I do get buckled. Grand work the last job was. I gave the lady no time to squeal. How can they catch me now. I love my work and want to start again. You will soon hear of me with my funny little games. I saved some proper red stuff in a ginger beer bottle over the last job to write with but it went thick like glue and I can't use it. Red ink is fit enough I hope ha. ha. The next job I do I shall clip the lady's ears off and send to the Police officers just for jolly wouldn't you. Keep this letter back till I do a bit more work then give it out straight. My knife's so nice and sharp I want to get to work right away if I get a chance. Good luck.

Yours truly Jack the Ripper.

Don't mind me giving the trade name.

The recipient of the letter at first failed to take it seriously. After a couple of days, however, he decided to pass it to the police. The night after they received it, Catherine Eddowes and Liz Stride were killed.

On 1 October, another letter in the same handwriting arrived at the news agency. 'I wasn't codding dear old Boss when I gave you the tip,' it said,

You'll hear about saucy Jacky's work tomorrow double event this time number one squealed a bit couldn't finish straight off. Had not time to get ears for police thanks for keeping last letter back till I got to work again. Jack the Ripper.

Copies of the letters were posted up outside every police station in London in the hope that the handwriting would be recognised, but no one came forward. On 16 October a third letter was sent, this time to George Lusk who was head of the Mile End Vigilance Committee. It was in different handwriting to the previous two and read:

From hell.
Mr Lusk Sor I send you half the kidne I took from one women prasarved it for you tother piece I fried and ate it was very nise I may send you the bloody knif that took it out if you only wate a whil longer.

Signed Catch me when You can
Mishter Lusk.

Accompanying it was a piece of flesh. It turned out to be a human kidney.

It is impossible to say whether any of these letters were genuine. Some said that the one predicting the double murder must have been genuine, but by the time it had been sent, on the night of 31 September, news had already broken about the killing of Eddowes and Stride.

Londoners became hysterical and the streets of Whitechapel emptied as soon as darkness fell. Extra police patrolled and bloodhounds were brought in. Still, there were no new developments.

Neither were there any new murders and as autumn turned to winter, people began to take to the streets again after dark. Prostitutes returned to their old stamping grounds and resumed their trade.

The Ripper was not finished yet, however.

On 9 November, a landlord sent an employee out to collect overdue rent from a twenty-five-year-old prostitute named Mary Kelly. When John Bowyer knocked at the door of number 13 Miller's Court, however, he got no reply. He went to a window, reached in through a broken window pane and drew aside the grubby curtain, revealing a scene of horror that would remain with him for the rest of his life. On the bed lay Mary Kelly, her face horrifically mutilated and her throat cut right through to her spinal column. This time the Ripper had excelled himself. The top layer of her abdomen and thighs had been removed and her abdominal cavity had been 'emptied of its viscera' as the doctor's report put it. He had cut off her breasts and placed one under her head, along with her uterus and kidney, and the other by her right foot. Her liver lay between her feet, her intestines by her right side and her spleen by her left side. The flesh he had sliced off her abdomen and thighs lay on the table. Her heart was missing. That had gone home with him.

There was a kind of mass hysteria in Whitechapel at the news. Mobs turned on strangers or anyone who was at all suspicious. Even Queen Victoria became involved, criticising the standard of policing in Whitechapel and the lack of lighting in the area.

Still, however, no one was arrested and no clues were found. And it remains that way a hundred years later. Mary Kelly was believed to be the last victim of Jack the Ripper. He vanished into the dimly lit shadows just as quickly as he had arrived, but, of course, he remains ever-present in books, films and newspapers, stalking our imaginations just as he used to stalk the streets of Whitechapel.

HENRI LANDRU

He was not a handsome man. Short, and bald, with a luxuriant dark beard and bushy eyebrows over dark penetrating eyes, he in no way gave the appearance of being a ladies' man. Nonetheless, with his intelligence, wit and silver tongue, Henri Désiré Landru was seemingly able to sweep women off their feet and, at the same time, divest them of considerable sums of money. In the early years of the twentieth century, he enjoyed a series of liaisons with generally vulnerable women that usually ended with their disappearance and the enrichment of his bank balance, earning him a reputation for being a real-life Bluebeard.

Born in Paris in 1869, Landru was the son of a fireman. He showed intelligence as a child and after school attended the School of Mechanical Engineering before enlisting in the army, remaining a soldier for four years during which he achieved the rank of sergeant.

While a soldier, he seduced his cousin, a Mademoiselle Remy, and when she announced she was pregnant, he was forced to marry her. Their daughter was born in 1893, a year before his return to civilian life. Around this time, however, towards the end of the nineteenth century, Landru served two years in prison for fraud, the first of seven prison sentences he received during his life.

While incarcerated, Landru launched his career as a modern-day Bluebeard when he placed a matrimonial advert in a Lille newspaper. As a result a forty-year-old widow made contact with him and, on his release, he absconded with a 15,000-franc dowry with which the woman provided him.

By the outbreak of the First World War, Landru was being sought by the police on a number of counts and in his absence he had actually been sentenced to four years imprisonment and deportation to New Caledonia. His parents, meanwhile, had both died, his father having committed suicide, unable to live with the shame of his son's crimes.

In 1914, Landru placed an advert in a paper that read:

Widower with two children, aged forty-three, with comfortable income, serious and moving in good society, desires to meet widow with a view to matrimony.

It was decorous and very plausible. Above all, its tone gave promise of exactly what a lonely widow or spinster might be hoping for. It was answered by Jeanne Cuchet, a thirty-nine-year-old with a sixteen-year-old son André, who earned her living by working in a Paris lingerie shop. Monsieur Diard, as Landru styled himself when he met her, seemed just the sort of respectable and prosperous man to lift her out of the life of drudgery she had been living.

They began a relationship, but it did not always go smoothly. On one such occasion, Jeanne turned up at his house with her brother-in-law to try to sort matters out. Landru was not at home but they went into his house anyway and had a look round. Her brother-in-law opened a chest and to his surprise discovered a pile of letters to 'Monsieur Diard' from various women. Horrified, he attempted to persuade Jeanne that this 'Monsieur Diard' was a fraud, as he had suspected. Tragically, she would have none of it.

Eventually, given a choice between 'Diard' and her family, she chose 'Diard'. She would never see her family again. She and Landru moved to a villa outside Paris and soon after she and her son disappeared. In January 1915, Landru deposited 5,000 francs in his bank account and there is little doubt where it had come from. He also later gave his wife – he was still married – Jeanne Cuchet's gold watch.

His next victim was a Madame Laborde-Laline, widow of an Argentinian hotelier. She announced to friends and family that she was going to marry a Brazilian engineer, as Landru was presenting himself, but when the wedding began to take too long to organise, she moved in with him anyway. After her arrival at the Vernouillet villa of her engineer fiancé, she was never seen again. A short while later, Landru brazenly appeared at her house to collect her furniture.

Not wasting any time, he struck up a relationship just a month later with Marie Guillin, a fifty-one-year-old widow who had answered one of his adverts and made the journey to his villa at Vernouillet, never to be seen again. He arrived at her house not long after, to collect her furniture, claiming to be her brother-in-law. To anyone who asked, he explained that she had fallen ill and was paralysed. She had asked him to look after her affairs, he added solicitously.

Meanwhile, he sold her bonds and forged documents that enabled him to empty her bank account of the tidy sum of 12,000 francs.

In December 1916, Landru relocated to the northern French village of Gambais where he had a huge cast-iron oven installed and ominously ordered a large stock of coal. He took the name Dupont and acquainted himself with a widow nine years older than himself, Madame Heon. Nine months later, he was selling her furniture. She, of course, had vanished, although friends continued to receive postcards from her, all delivered via Landru.

A Madame Collomb believed that she was meeting a Monsieur Cuchet. Initially, the relationship failed and they separated for a year. When they reunited, she introduced him to her family who hated him on sight. Undeterred, however, she moved in with him. By the time Christmas had come and gone, so had she, never to be seen again.

In 1917, he picked up a nineteen-year-old servant girl, Andrée Babelay, whom he found crying on a Metro platform after a fight with her mother. She was also about to lose her job and did not know where to turn. Landru took her back to his room in Rue de Mauberge and within a couple of months she was telling her mother that she was going to be married. She travelled out to Gambais and soon the stove was belching smoke from its chimney. No one saw her or heard from her again.

Celestine Buisson was a rich prospect, a wealthy widow who had been in correspondence with Landru for two years before they finally met. He was posing as Monsieur Fremyet at this time and succeeded in persuading her to abandon her family, including her son, and travel to Gambais. Madame Buisson was never seen again after April 1917, around which time Landru deposited 1,000 francs in his bank account. When Louise Leopoldine vanished in September 1917, benefiting him to the tune of almost 2,000 francs, neighbours began to complain to Landru about the thick, acrid smoke that often billowed from his chimney. He ignored them, however, giving them the chance to renew their complaints when Ann Marie Pascal moved in with him and then disappeared a short while later.

Marie Therese Marchadier, who had enjoyed a successful stage career as 'La Belle Mythese' before retiring, moved to Gambais after selling the Paris guesthouse she owned for 7,000 francs. She and her two dogs disappeared not long after a large order of coal was delivered to the house.

Landru persisted, meanwhile, with an extraordinary and complex pretense that his victims were still alive, sending postcards and letters to their families and friends. In one case, that of Madame Jaume, he announced that she had appointed him as her lawyer and proceeded to begin divorce proceedings against her husband and liquidate her bank accounts.

It all began to unravel when the son of Celestine Buisson – she had left the boy behind when she moved to Gambais – died, and the family wanted to inform his mother. Aware only that she had moved to Gambais to live with a Monsieur Guillet, Madame

Buisson's sister, Mademoiselle Lacoste, wrote to the mayor of the village asking for his assistance in finding either of the two. The mayor, of course, had never heard of a Monsieur Guillet but, having also been contacted by the family of Madame Collomb enquiring about her whereabouts, he suggested she speak to them. The families compared notes and, before long, the police were informed. By the time they arrived at Landru's estate, however, Bluebeard was long gone.

Mademoiselle Lacoste was nothing if not persistent and, having once met Landru in the company of her sister, was certain she would recognise him if she saw him again. She began searching the streets near where he used to live, finally catching sight of him coming out of a dry goods shop with twenty-seven-year-old Fernande Segret on his arm. Madamoiselle Lacoste lost him in the crowds but learned from the shopkeeper that his name was indeed Guillet and that he lived on the Rue de Rochechouart. The police were informed and Landru was arrested at his apartment. Conveniently, they found a notebook listing all his victims.

His trial, which began on 7 November 1921, was one of the most sensational in French legal history. Landru resolutely maintained his innocence throughout and, although admittedly no bodies or human remains had been recovered from his estate at Gambais, copious amounts of legal documents relating to his victims had been uncovered. He claimed that the women had been no more than business clients of his. His neighbours, however, told of the putrid smoke that emerged periodically from his chimney and one suggested that while fishing he had hooked what looked like a piece of human flesh. Landru stoically answered all questions and accusations with 'I have nothing to say.'

Needless to say, such an attitude antagonised the jury and they took just two hours to find him guilty of the murders of eleven women. He was sentenced to death by guillotine.

In February 1922, Henri Landru was executed in Paris. He proved to be one of the most callous killers in French history, never admitting his crimes or explaining how he did them. He expressed no remorse whatsoever to the horrified families of his victims.

Just before he was executed, Landru gave a member of his legal team a drawing he had done while awaiting execution. Forty years later, as she examined the picture which had hung on the wall of her father's office ever since, the man's daughter spotted some words scribbled on its frame. They read, 'I did it. I burned their bodies in the kitchen stove'.

It seems that he had confessed, after all.

FRITZ HAARMANN
THE 'BUTCHER OF HANOVER'

I'd make two cuts in the abdomen and put the intestines in a bucket, then soak up the blood and crush the bones until the shoulders broke. Now I could get the heart, lungs and kidneys and chop them up and put them in my bucket. I'd take the flesh off the bones and put it in my waxcloth bag. It would take me five or six trips to take everything and throw it down the toilet or into the river. I always hated doing this, but I couldn't help it – my passion was so much stronger than the horror of the cutting and chopping.

Hanover, in the Lower Saxony region of Germany, was ravaged by terrible hunger and harrowing poverty following the disaster of the First World War. There was unparalleled crime, a surge in black market activity, and prostitution – particularly male prostitution – was rife. At the same time, in the years following the armistice, there was a sharp increase in sex crime, and in Germany several serial killers launched their murderous careers. None was more prolific than Fritz Haarmann, the 'Butcher of Hanover', who would become Germany's most notorious serial killer.

He was born in 1879, the youngest of six children to a heavy-drinking locomotive stoker and his wife who was seven years older than her husband. Pampered as a child, young Fritz played with dolls and harboured a hatred for his father that would remain with him throughout his entire life. However, his loathing for his father and the violent arguments that characterised their relationship did not prevent them from joining forces in criminal activity and they would work together on swindles, often popping up in court to provide alibis for each other.

It was, indeed, a strange family. Fritz's mother was left weak and ailing by his birth and spent most of the remaining twelve years of her life in bed. Meanwhile, of his siblings, one brother went to prison while still young for a sexual offence, while at least three of his sisters could only be described as very odd.

Following a failed locksmith apprenticeship, in 1895 Fritz attended a school for non-commissioned army officers at Nau-Breisach but when, soon after enrolling, he began to display signs of epilepsy, his college career was over. He dismissed himself from the college to work for his father.

Haarmann's sexual offending had begun at an early age, but back in Hanover it got so out of hand that shortly before his eighteenth birthday he was sent to an asylum. This would be a terrifying experience for him and for the remainder of his life he said that he would rather be hanged than return there. Unable to stand it, he escaped and fled to Switzerland before returning to Hanover in 1899, making an attempt at stability by marrying. Staid normality was not for Fritz, however, and he had soon enlisted in the army, leaving behind his new wife and their unborn child. Army life was good for a while – one of the happiest times of his life – but hospitalisation after a collapse during an exercise, put paid to his military career and he was soon back in the bosom of his dysfunctional family.

The next twenty years were interrupted by spells in prison as he embarked on a life of burglary and confidence trickery. In 1918, after a five-year stretch for burglary, he became a smuggler, but was also employed as a police spy which helped to keep him out of jail on a number of occasions. His sexual offending continued throughout these years, of course, but he was rarely caught and when he was, nothing happened.

On 17 May 1924, some children who were playing by a river in Hanover made a gruesome discovery. On the banks of the river they found the skull of a young man. Twelve days later, another was found, washed up on the riverbank. A fortnight later, a couple more turned up. On examination, it was clear that the heads had been separated from their torsos by a sharp instrument and that it had been done fairly recently.

Hysteria mounted in Hanover, especially when a sack containing human bones was found. There had been an unusual number of disappearances of boys and young men in the area in the last few years – in 1923, almost six hundred had been reported missing – and grim rumours began to circulate that the flesh from these boys had been on sale in Hanover's meat market. Talk was that a 'werewolf' or a 'man-eater' was at large.

On Sunday 8 June 1924, a huge crowd gathered in the old part of the city where the remains had been found, in order to carry out a thorough search. They found a large quantity of human bones and when they dammed the river so that the riverbed could be searched, the remains of at least twenty-two people were uncovered.

The authorities had one main suspect – Fritz Haarmann. He was openly homosexual, which the killer certainly was, and he was regularly to be seen in the company of young men at the railway station.

One report even had him being seen tossing a heavy sack into the river one night. However, his work for the police during the past five years caused some consternation and not a little embarrassment. He was known to some as 'Detective Haarmann' and had even opened a private detective agency with a police official as his partner.

Nonetheless, they put together a plan to trap him. Two good-looking young policemen from Berlin would arrive at the station and entrap him. However, before they could put the plan into action, there was a new development. On 23 June a fifteen-year-old boy was arrested on a charge of travelling with forged papers. At the police station, he told them how he had spent the last two nights at the apartment of Fritz Haarmann and that Haarmann had raped him, at one point holding a knife to his throat. They went to Haarmann's house where they discovered blood stains and a good deal of old clothing. The smooth-talking killer still managed to charm his way out of arrest, however, by claiming that the blood came from his work as a butcher and the clothes were part of his work as a merchant dealing in old clothing. With no evidence to the contrary, they had to let him go.

He was finally caught by pure chance. The parents of a missing boy, Robert Witzel, had been particularly persistent in their search for their son. Robert had visited the local circus on the evening of 26 April 1924 with another boy, Fritz Kahlmeyer. Kahlmeyer, who knew Haarman, and had been sexually abused by him, introduced Witzel to him. The boy was never seen again. Amongst the skulls discovered at the river was one with an irregularly shaped jawbone which Herr Witzel identified as belonging to his son.

Seated outside the Chief Commissioner's office at the police station, Frau Witzel recognised a jacket being worn by a man who, coincidentally, was walking past in the company of Haarmann's landlady. The man admitted that he had bought the jacket from Fritz Haarmann and showed them a card that he had found in the pocket. The name on the card was Robert Witzel.

Faced with such overwhelming evidence of his guilt, Haarmann had no choice but to confess. It made harrowing listening and a tour that he took the police on through Hanover uncovered still more remains hidden in bushes in alleyways and in lakes.

It had begun in 1918, not long after Haarmann had emerged from his latest spell behind bars. Friedel Roth had fallen out with his mother and had run away from home. Investigations at the time had led to Haarmann's house and when police burst in they found him in bed with a young boy, not Roth. He was sent back to prison for nine months for seducing a juvenile, but what the arresting officers had not discovered was Roth's head, hidden behind Haarmann's stove, neatly wrapped in newspaper.

In 1919, Haarmann met Hans Grans, who was working as a rent boy at Hanover railway station. Grans would go on to become not only his lover but also his partner in crime. Haarmann described their relationship as based on 'madness and spiritual parasitism'. They became a respected, well-dressed pair of gentlemen to locals, but behind their air of respectability lay murderous intent.

They were making good money, however, selling clothes and bringing in supplementary income from an invalidity pension Haarmann received.

In 1923, he killed again. Pretending to be an officer inspecting the waiting rooms at the station, he took a runaway called Fritz Franke home, sexually assaulted him and killed him by biting him through the windpipe as he sodomised him. It was the beginning of an extraordinary year-long killing spree during which twelve more boys died in that room.

The method was always the same and there were even witness reports stating that Haarmann and often Grans had been seen leaving the station with the missing boy in question, but they were never questioned, such was the respect the two men had earned by this time. On one occasion, Haarmann is even said to have replied to an advert in a newspaper asking for information about a missing boy. He turned up at the door of the missing boy's parents, claiming to be a criminologist, and is reported to have laughed hysterically throughout his meeting with them.

Throughout the early months of 1924, Haarmann continued to prey on young men and murder them at the rate of two a month. By the time distraught parents had realised that their sons, often runaways, had disappeared, Haarmann and Grans had long since distributed the clothing and the meat throughout the city. The evidence was long gone.

Fritz Haarmann was convicted of the murder of twenty-four people between September 1918 and June 1924. He conducted his own defence, taking the stand himself to explain that it had been beauty and sexuality that had driven him to kill, not sex or financial gain. He claimed that it was easier to kill someone you love – in that way you could bring them peace. As if to confirm these points, he denied killing one young man, saying that he was far too ugly to have interested him.

He was given twenty-four death sentences. Hans Grans, meanwhile, was sentenced to twelve years' imprisonment. On hearing the verdict, Haarmann announced that he wanted to be executed in Hanover's market place and on his tombstone he wanted inscribed the legend, 'Here Lies Mass-Murderer Haarmann'. The court refused his request, however. He was guillotined at Hanover prison on 15 April 1925.

Dr Marcel Petiot

After he killed his victims, he decapitated them before adroitly cutting off their limbs – he was a doctor, after all – and mutilating the severed heads. He then scalped them and sliced off the eyebrows, lips and ears. The torsos were then disembowelled, the remains being disposed of with fire and quicklime.

Dr Marcel Petiot was France's most prolific serial killer, the murderer of at least twenty-seven people, but probably more, some estimates claiming that he may have been responsible for more than two hundred deaths.

Born Marcel André Henri Félix Petiot on 17 January 1897, in Auxerre in Burgundy, he was his parents' first child and for thirteen years, until the arrival of his brother Maurice in 1910, their only child. Both parents were postal workers and Monsieur Petiot often worked away from home, installing telephone exchanges. When Marcel, an attractive child with dark wavy hair, was two years old, his mother decided that she would like to accompany her husband on his trips and little Marcel was put into the care of his aunt, Henriette Bourdon, a spinster who lived with her maid, Marie Gaston.

The two women had no idea how to bring up a child and Marcel was soon out of control, throwing terrible tantrums and sulking; he bit them and, when angry, would take revenge on them by trampling all the flowers in their well-manicured garden. Worryingly, however, he also began to display sadistic tendencies, impaling insects on needles and imprisoning birds and watching them die of hunger. Of course, he did not let all of them die of hunger. Occasionally, he would let one go free, but not before he had stuck needles in its eyes, blinding it. He also smothered his cat after it had survived immersion in boiling water.

When he had misbehaved, he was dragged off to Mass, inducing in him a lifelong aversion to religion; he even refused the last rites before his execution. The front gate was always locked at the two women's house and for the remainder of his life he only locked one door – the front door of his Paris townhouse, behind which he carried out his murders.

Two years after his mother's death from cancer at the age of only thirty-six, Petiot first fell foul of the law when he was caught stealing letters from letterboxes using a stick with glue daubed on the end. He was hoping to find cash or money orders in the envelopes. Examined by a child psychologist, he was described as having hereditary mental problems. His indignant father retorted that there was no insanity on either side of the family. Nonetheless, the diagnosis saved him from serving time in a reform school but he could not avoid expulsion from school. He studied at home and eventually, having done well in his school-leaving exams, announced to his incredulous father that he wanted to become a doctor. His plans were interrupted by the First World War. To his credit, he enlisted immediately but his mental health problems resurfaced and he spent a great deal of the war in asylums.

Returning to Auxerre in 1922, he announced to the great surprise of everyone that he was now Doctor Petiot. How he had done this, when he had spent the last few years in and out of asylums, was a mystery, but he launched a medical practice in the village of Villeneuve-sur-Yonne, twenty-seven miles from Auxerre, a town of some two thousand people. The new doctor, with his dashing good looks, was an instant hit and he was soon establishing a reputation as a good doctor.

He began seeing a woman, Louise Delaveau, but when she fell pregnant, she told a friend in confidence that Petiot wanted to perform an abortion on her.

Not long after, she disappeared and when the headless body of a woman was found in the Yonne river, it was surmised that it was her. The members of the local gendarmerie claimed that as there was no evidence there was no point in launching an investigation into the death.

Of course, there were whispers that Petiot had been involved in his lover's disappearance but that did not prevent people from voting for him to become mayor. When the new mayor felt it only fitting that he should have a mayoress to share his duties, he married twenty-three-year-old Georgette Lablais whose father was a successful Paris restaurateur. In April 1929, aged thirty-one, Dr Petiot became a father when his son Gerhardt was born.

Not long after, there was another suspicious death in the town. A fire had broken out at the local dairy and when firefighters eventually entered the building, they found the body of the dairy owner's wife lying in the kitchen with her skull smashed. Once again, however, the murderer got away with it when the local gendarmerie once again declined to investigate.

The next to die was the owner of the town's bistro, Monsieur Frascot, who collapsed after being given a shot for his rheumatoid arthritis by Petiot. Interestingly, Frascot had been telling anyone who would listen that Petiot had been responsible for the death of the dairy owner's wife.

Eventually Villeneuve-sur-Yonne became too hot for Petiot. He had been embezzling from the town's finances for some time and a string of summonses had been delivered to him. He moved his family to Paris where he established a successful practice by distributing leaflets promising miracle cures and revolutionary new methods. He claimed to have a string of ambulances and the most modern medical equipment – all lies of course. Nevertheless, his waiting room was always full and his bank account grew. Before long, he had bought an apartment building and was earning even more money from that.

When the Germans occupied Paris shortly after the outbreak of the Second World War, the Petiots did not join those who fled the capital. Instead Dr Petiot purchased a large townhouse at 21 Rue le Sueur in Paris's wealthy sixteenth arrondissement; property was cheap as the owners hastened to sell up and get out of the city. He converted an outhouse into a surgery and had a great deal of other work done, including the conversion of another outhouse into a small, triangular-shaped room. One of the walls had a fake, padded door and another had large metal rings fastened to it. A third had a peephole inserted. He told the builders he planned to use it as a mental clinic and the padded door would soundproof the room. The rings, he said, were for hanging equipment from and the peephole was so that he could keep an eye on his patients.

Of course, it was not going to be a mental clinic. It was going to be a charnel house where he could act out his depraved fantasies in private.

On 11 March 1944, police were called to the house by neighbours complaining of a foul smell emanating from smoke that had been billowing from Petiot's chimney for the past five days. Two officers and a few firefighters gained entry to the house through a window on the ground floor and found a scene of sheer horror. Human remains were being burned in an old water boiler in the basement of the house. In the triangular chamber – Petiot's 'mental clinic' – still more body parts were being dissolved in a pit filled with quicklime. The Petiots had, of course, fled but Madame Petiot was swiftly located and arrested, having returned to Auxerre. She continued to stand up for her husband, 'the most loving husband, father and doctor', as she described him.

It was seven months before Petiot was apprehended, but in the meantime the horrific story of 21 Rue le Sueur slowly emerged. Neighbours told how a man had been visiting the house for short periods over the past two years. He arrived on foot or riding a bicycle and was often accompanied by other people who never re-emerged from the building. Noises had been heard, however, crying and a great deal of banging. Someone said he had once heard the word 'Help!' being shouted as he walked past. The man who came and went from the building was its owner, Dr Marcel Petiot.

It had been another of Petiot's money-making schemes. He had already made a considerable amount of money from illegal abortions and drug-dealing but now, with the Germans in occupation, he realised there was a lot of cash to be made from people desperate to flee France. He pretended he was a member of the French Resistance, with the *nom de guerre* 'Dr Eugène', and offered his services to those people, charging them considerable sums of money. For good measure, he also requested that they bring with them all their valuables so that they would be able to establish themselves in their new country which he named as Argentina. Of course, they got no further than 21 Rue le Sueur. He began to make so much money that he recruited his barber and other associates to find clients and shared the considerable spoils with them. Frightened people, many of them Jews, terrified of the prospect of the concentration camps, queued up to meet Dr Eugène.

It all came to an abrupt end in May 1943 when an informer told the Jewish Affairs Department that a certain 'Dr Eugène' was helping people to flee France. Two of Petiot's co-conspirators were arrested and Petiot was picked up after they revealed his identity to the Gestapo. The three men were held for seven months before being released without charge after Petiot's brother Maurice had bribed someone in the Jewish Affairs Department.

On his release, Petiot and his brother tried to clean up the townhouse but Maurice had made the fatal mistake of telling a friend about the bodies that he had discovered there while his brother was being held and word soon spread. Soon, even Petiot's wife Georgette learned the terrible truth.

Petiot was arrested on the last day of October 1944, a couple of months after the liberation of Paris, and for nine months he insisted that the people he had killed had all been Germans and collaborators. Then he suddenly went silent, saying nothing at all for the next two months.

Due to the turmoil of the times, it can only be surmised how much money he made and how many died at his hands. It is believed that he first drugged his victims before dictating letters to their families that he forced them to write in their stupour. The letters reassured the people at home that they had made it safely to Argentina. It is thought he then killed them with a lethal injection but the decomposition of the bodies made it impossible to say what chemical had been used.

At his trial, when the death penalty was announced, Marcel Petiot showed no emotion and he remained stoic right up to 25 May 1946; the day he mounted the scaffold to face the guillotine. He said to the small assembly of witnesses, 'Gentlemen, don't look, this won't be pretty'.

Asked if he had any last words, the man the press had dubbed 'Dr Death' replied simply, 'No, I am one traveller who is taking all his baggage with him'.

PETER KÜRTEN

Few killers have been responsible for as much terror and outrage as that created by Peter Kürten in the German city of Düsseldorf between February and November 1929. His ten-month murder spree, in which eight people were killed in a variety of ways while fourteen others were the victims of savage attacks, created panic and hysteria in the city and news of it spread around the world. A staggering 900,000 names were given to police by the public as potential suspects as they struggled to find the killer they called the 'Vampire of Düsseldorf'.

A small-time crook from an early age, Peter Kürten claimed to have killed for the first time at the age of only nine, drowning two young friends while playing on a raft on the River Rhine. Their deaths were treated as accidents. His childhood was relentlessly brutal. His father was a drunk who abused his wife and thirteen children, raping Kürten's mother and daughters in front of them. He was eventually sent to prison for incest with his thirteen-year-old daughter, leaving Kürten to pick up where he had left off, imitating his father's abuse of his sisters.

By this time, he was also torturing dogs for fun and as he grew older, his sexual perversions knew no bounds. He committed acts of bestiality on sheep and goats and discovered that the intensity of his sexual experience was heightened by stabbing the creature during the act.

By the age of sixteen, he had been in and out of prison a number of times, mostly for the theft of clothing or food. While incarcerated, he had lots of time to think and to imagine. He trained himself to achieve orgasm just by enacting brutal sex acts in his imagination. He intentionally broke prison regulations in order to be sent to solitary confinement where he was free to be alone with such thoughts. Released once again, he moved in with a masochistic prostitute more than twice his age and was at last able to satisfy his intense sexual urges with a human being.

His first attack took place not long after one of his frequent periods in prison. He had picked up a girl and taken her for a walk in a wooded area. While having sexual intercourse with her, he attacked her and left her for dead. As her body was never found, however, and no one was reported missing at the time, it is almost certain that she survived the attack. She was most probably too ashamed to report it to the police.

On 25 May 1913, he did kill, however. He was twenty years old and had been making a living by breaking into bars and inns where the owner lived above the premises. While they were working downstairs, he was free to steal whatever he could find upstairs. On this particular night he broke into an inn in Cologne owned by a man called Peter Klein. He went from room to room on the first floor but was disappointed with his haul. Opening a bedroom door, however, he found a little girl, ten-year-old Christine Klein, in bed asleep. He smiled, went over to the bed, bent down and, wrapping his hands around the sleeping girl's tiny neck, strangled her. He then sexually molested her before taking out a penknife he always carried and slitting her throat. It had taken less than three minutes and he later described with relish how the blood spurted from the gaping wound 'in an arch, right over my hand'.

The authorities believed they had found the culprit when they arrested Otto Klein, the dead girl's uncle. Otto had threatened his brother when he had refused to lend him a sum of money, saying that he would do something that Peter would 'remember for the rest of his life'. They charged him with the murder of his niece, but he was later acquitted due to lack of evidence.

Kürten's criminal career entered an eight-year

hiatus when he was sent to prison in 1913 and for once, prison seems to have had the desired effect. When he was released in 1921, he resolved to begin a new life, moving to the town of Altenburg and marrying a prostitute. He began to lead a fairly normal, law-abiding life, becoming active in trade unionism.

It lasted just four years. By 1925, he was back in Düsseldorf, living in a city-centre apartment and immersing himself in the criminal life he knew so well. He was involved in petty crime and carried out numerous arson attacks in the city. He was also responsible for a growing number of horrific random attacks, using knives or scissors. On one occasion, he described sucking blood from the head of one of his victims.

It was in 1929 that he gave vent to the full horror of his imagination, killing and attacking with rare ferocity. He attacked men, women and children indiscriminately, making the job of the police even more difficult. The press spoke of a maniac being on the loose; headlines screamed that a vampire was stalking the streets of Düsseldorf. The impact on the city was astonishing. The streets emptied as darkness approached and some even moved out to the countryside.

The first attack that dreadful year took place on

8 February when Kürten pounced on a woman, stabbing her repeatedly. He ran off leaving her bleeding from twenty-four stab wounds. He returned, however, as he often did, to the scene of this crime later that evening. 'In doing so,' he said, 'I sometimes had an orgasm.'

The body of eight-year-old Rosa Ohliger was discovered under a hedge the following day. She had died from thirteen vicious stab wounds, some in her vagina. Semen stains were found in her underwear, but in those days before DNA testing, they were of little use other than to confirm to police the sexual nature of the attack. When he had finished with her, he poured petrol over her body and set it alight. He became so excited by the flames, he later confessed, that he had another orgasm.

On 13 February, he murdered a middle-aged mechanic, stabbing him twenty times and returning later to gloat as police officers investigated the scene. He even brazenly engaged one detective in conversation.

A man called Stausberg, with learning difficulties, was arrested. He had recently assaulted a couple of women using a noose, leading detectives to feel certain that he must also be responsible for the February murders. He confessed and the killings seemed to have come to a halt with Stausberg locked up. It looked as if he was the vampire. But hopes were dashed on 21 August when the killer re-emerged in a savage knifing spree, stabbing three people in separate attacks. They all walked past a man on a country lane who bade them good evening and then lunged at them from behind, stabbing them in the back.

Two days later, he struck again while attending the annual fair in the Düsseldorf area of Flehe. He followed two young girls who were walking home from the fair, two sisters aged five and fourteen. As they walked through some allotments, he stopped them and asked one of them, whose name was Louise, to return to the fair to buy some cigarettes for him. As soon as she was out of sight, he picked up the other girl, Gertrude, and strangled her. He then cut her throat. When Louise returned, he strangled her before decapitating her.

The following day, he accosted a woman and asked if she would have sex with him. When she responded 'I'd rather die!' he snarled back 'Die then!' and plunged his knife into her. He ran off, but the woman survived the attack and for the first time police officers had a description of the Vampire of Düsseldorf.

Kürten was rampant. In September he committed a rape and a murder and also savagely beat a girl with a hammer. He utilised the hammer again in October when he attacked two women with it. On 7 November, he strangled a five-year-old girl, stabbing her thirty-six times with a pair of scissors. He even felt bold enough to send a map showing the location of the girl's body to a local newspaper.

The city seethed with rumour and counter-rumour and police were inundated with tip-offs, but all went quiet until February and March 1930 when Kürten carried out numerous hammer attacks, none of which proved fatal.

The authorities were stumped. The randomness of the attacks in terms of the type of victim, the locations and even the manner in which they were carried out, made it almost impossible to come up with any real leads.

It was an accident, however, that finally brought his murderous campaign to an end.

In May, a man picked up a homeless domestic servant, Maria Budlick, at Düsseldorf station, promising to show her the way to a hostel where she could spend the night. As he led her into a poorly lit park, however, the story of the maniac who was on the loose came into her head. She refused to go any further and the two argued. Another man, hearing the argument, approached and asked her if everything was alright. At this the first man left, leaving her alone with the second. Unfortunately for her, it was Peter Kürten.

He took her to his room on Mettmannerstrasse but she was reluctant to have sex with him and asked if he could take her to a hostel or a hotel. He agreed and they jumped on a tram. Leaving the tram and walking through a secluded, wooded area, he suddenly grabbed the unfortunate girl by the neck and told her he was going to have sex with her whether she liked it or not. He raped her but afterwards took her back to the tram instead of killing her. He let her go, doubting that she would remember where his flat was.

He was wrong, however. A few days later, she was waiting there for him, with the police. Spotting them, Kürten had time to escape. He knew that it would soon be over, but reasoned that he would be charged only with the rape of Maria Budlick which would bring a maximum sentence of fifteen years. But, he was still married and became concerned that his wife would be left destitute if he went to prison. Making sure that he wasn't being followed, Kürten went home and told his wife everything, telling her to go to the police and claim the substantial reward that had been put on his head. A few days later, she went to the nearest police station and passed on what he had told her to say, also informing them that she had arranged to meet her husband that afternoon outside a Düsseldorf church. At three that afternoon, the area around the church was filled with police officers. When Kürten arrived, he put his hands up to the officers approaching him, smiled and said, 'There is no need to be afraid'.

His trial was awaited with huge anticipation. They had built a special shoulder-high cage for him both to prevent his escape and to stop any member of the public from attacking him. But when he finally appeared, there was a gasp of astonishment around the courtroom. Instead of the monster in human form they had been expecting, they saw an immaculately dressed, ordinary-looking man. He had the air of a successful businessman and spoke in a calm, quiet voice. He recanted the confession he had made to police and pleaded not guilty.

The most striking thing about Peter Kürten was his complete lack of remorse for what he had done. He demonstrated all the narcissistic characteristics of a truly pathological personality, killing purely for his own gratification. Asked by the judge whether he had a conscience, he replied:

I have none. Never have I felt any misgiving in my soul; never did I think to myself that what I did was bad, even though human society condemns it.

My blood and the blood of my victims will be on the heads of my torturers. There must be a Higher Being who gave in the first place the first vital spark to life. That Higher Being would deem my actions good since I revenged injustice. The punishments I have suffered have destroyed all my feelings as a human being. That was why I had no pity for my victims.'

He described to the court the thoughts he had about devising methods of killing thousands of people in accidents: 'I derived the sort of pleasure from these visions that other people would get from thinking about a naked woman.'

On 2 July 1931, as he climbed the steps to the guillotine in Klingelputz prison, Kürten turned to the prison psychiatrist and asked him whether, after his head had been chopped off, he would still be able to hear, at least for a few seconds, the sound of his own blood gushing from his neck. 'That would be a pleasure to end all pleasures,' he added, a faraway look in his eyes.

PETER MANUEL

In autumn 1956, people in the towns and villages to the south of Glasgow slept in fear, pushing heavy furniture against their bedroom doors and nervously making sure that all doors and windows were closed and firmly locked. A killer walked the streets, a heartless murderer who killed for pleasure and seemed to be unconcerned as to the sex or age of his victims.

Peter Thomas Anthony Manuel was an unsuccessful small-time crook and burglar, a serial offender who had been in and out of court since the age of twelve. At this tender age he was sent to approved school for housebreaking only five weeks after his first appearance before the authorities for burgling a cycle shop.

He had been born in Manhattan in 1927 to British parents who moved back to Britain in 1932, eventually settling first in Motherwell and then in Coventry. His true home, however, was the approved school, or at least it was when he was not on the run from it. He escaped no fewer than eleven times, each time being rearrested, usually in the course of breaking into a house. He soon graduated to borstal, having indecently assaulted the wife of a school employee at the age of fifteen.

On his release, he moved to Scotland where his parents were now living but was arrested once again for burglary in 1946. Released on bail, he carried out three sex attacks in the next two weeks. In the first, he attacked a woman with a three-year-old child. She struggled with Manuel, screaming so loudly that he ran off. A nurse he attacked shortly after was saved when a cyclist passed, interrupting the attack. The third, a married woman, was attacked on a quiet road after dark. She had been in hospital and did not have the strength to resist him. He dragged her to a nearby railway embankment, beat her and then raped her.

Unfortunately for Manuel, however, a police officer named Muncie, who had arrested him for the burglary, recognised him from the description given by his victims. He was identified by two of his victims in an identity parade, found guilty and sentenced to eight years in prison.

In 1953, released from prison and living back with his family, he found work first with the Gas Board and then British Rail. He seemed to be settling down, becoming engaged for almost a year to a bus conductress. Around this time, Manuel demonstrated just how much of an attention-seeker he was by writing a letter to his girlfriend that he pretended had come from someone else. The letter stated that he had been in the Secret Service. Manuel claimed that it had been written by someone who did not like him but it was no more than an attempt to make himself appear to be more than he actually was. As it was, the girl later terminated the engagement, anyway.

It was 1954 and he tried to obtain American citizenship, bizarrely offering the American authorities information about certain crimes of which he claimed to have inside knowledge as well as information he said was about US national security. Needless to say, the Americans wanted nothing to do with him and his bid for citizenship failed.

He attempted rape once more on the night of 30 July 1955. He pulled a knife on a girl, Mary McLaughlin, and forced her to accompany him into a field. She screamed loudly, however, and people came out of their houses to see what was going on. Manuel pushed her down and hid while the searchers passed and eventually gave up. He put his hand inside her underwear, but did not rape her. It was later suggested that Manuel sometimes did not rape his victims because he climaxed before getting to that point. Instead of raping her, then, he talked to her, telling her about his engagement and that today was actually the day on which he should have been getting married. After talking for about an hour, they walked back across the fields and when she promised she would not go to the police, he let her go.

She did, of course, and Manuel was immediately identified from her description. He was arrested but when the case came to court, he defended himself well, proving to be an intelligent and articulate young man. He was so plausible, in fact, spinning the jury a story about having been courting Mary McLaughlin, that a verdict of 'not proven' was passed.

It was a verdict that the authorities would regret, however, because his next attack would lead to the loss of a young woman's life.

Seventeen-year-old Anne Knielands left her house in the new town of East Kilbride on 3 January 1956 to meet her boyfriend. To his eternal regret, he had forgotten about their date and was, instead, out with friends. As Anne walked home, she was attacked from behind. She tried to escape, running across a field, losing both her shoes in the process and cutting herself climbing over a barbed wire fence. Her attacker finally caught up with her, however, hitting her on the back of the head with a length of iron and breaking her skull into fifteen pieces. When found by a man out walking his dog the following day, her underwear and one stocking were missing.

When it was learned that Peter Manuel was working at the time on a site near to where the body was found, he was immediately brought in for questioning. He had scratches on his face that he explained away as having been acquired in a fight. He said that he had been at home on the night in question, an alibi confirmed by his father. The police had no choice but to let him go.

He was in trouble again two months later after a break-in at a colliery in Blantyre. A piece of clothing was found on a barbed wire fence that matched an item of his clothing. He was charged and released on bail.

In September that year, the month before his case was due to come to court, there were three burglaries in Lanarkshire. On 12 September someone broke into an empty house in Bothwell, scattered soup on the floor, left dirty boot-prints on a bedcover and slashed the mattress and quilt. The burglar had opened a tin of pears and drunk the juice, pouring the pieces of canned pear over the floor. He had taken a watch, an electric razor and some tools, but other valuable items had not been taken.

On 15 September there was a similar break-in at High Burnside, a well-off suburb on the outskirts of

Glasgow. Again, tins had been opened, soup and spaghetti were scattered on the carpet and there were footprints on the bed. Four pairs of nylon stockings and a couple of gold rings had been taken.

A lot worse was to follow, however.

On 17 September, a cleaner, arriving at the home of baker William Watt – 5 Fennsbank Avenue – and his family, walked into a scene of horror. Three women lay dead, all shot in the head at almost point-blank range. Mrs Marion Watt, her sister Margaret Brown and her sixteen-year-old daughter Vivienne, were all clad in their nightclothes. Marion's pyjama bottoms had been ripped and Vivienne's had been taken off and a brassiere had been torn from her body. Although Vivienne had a large bruise on her chin, there was no other sign of assault. The killer had stubbed a cigarette out on the carpet.

William Watt was immediately the prime suspect in the killings and was arrested. He had been away on a fishing trip, but could easily have travelled back to High Burnside during the night. Furthermore, the arresting officer felt that Watt did not behave like a man whose family had just been massacred.

A burglary further along Fennsbank Avenue, at number eighteen, made police also consider Peter Manuel a suspect. Again soup had been poured on the floor and a cigarette had been stubbed out on the carpet. On a chair in the lounge they found a pair of nylon stockings. A bizarre story about a dead cow also made police consider Manuel a suspect. An informant told them that Manuel had planned to use a revolver in the robbery of what he called 'a Jew's house'. He had tested the gun, he told the informant, by firing it up the nose of a cow. By the time they found the farmer who owned the cow, however, it had been removed to a local slaughterhouse. The police spent days trying to find the bullet amidst piles of offal – an unpleasant task – but they failed to do so.

Manuel was questioned, his father now angrily accusing officers of harassing his son. He refused to tell them where he had been on the evening the Watts were murdered, and the police had nothing to link him to the killings. A couple of weeks later, however, he was sentenced to eighteen months' imprisonment for the colliery break-in.

Peter Manuel now did a very odd thing. He contacted William Watt's lawyer, telling him that Watt was innocent and that he could tell him who had actually killed the three women. He tried to give credence to his claims by describing in detail the furnishings of the Watt home, saying that he had been given this information by the killer. He also claimed that the killer had given him the gun to dispose of. Despite this obvious knowledge of the inside of the Watt home, the police still could not pin the murders on Manuel, however, and with no further evidence to charge William Watt, he was released from custody after sixty-seven days.

When he was released a year later, Manuel met Watt and gave the name of the killer as a man called Tallis. Watt could not help having the uneasy feeling that the man he was talking to was the cold-blooded murderer of his wife, daughter and sister-in-law.

On 8 December 1957, Manuel was in Newcastle. He hired a taxi driven by Sidney Dunn. Near the village of Edmundbyers in County Durham, he suddenly shot Dunn in the back of the head and slit his throat. He smashed the windows and headlights of the vehicle and left Dunn's body on moorland. He left Dunn's wallet untouched. Peter Manuel was killing for pleasure, not for financial gain.

Just under three weeks later, he struck again. Isabelle Cooke had left her home in Mount Vernon in Glasgow to go to a dance. She never arrived, but while police searched for her body, Manuel killed yet again. The Smart family lived in Uddingston. Peter Smart was a forty-five-year-old civil engineer and he lived at Sheepburn Road with his wife and ten-year-old son. It was New Year and he had been expected to pay a visit to relatives living nearby but when he failed to turn up and then, on 6 January, failed to arrive at work, people became concerned. Furthermore, his car had been found abandoned in the Gorbals area of Glasgow, not far from the city centre. Police went to the house and getting no reply to their knocks, broke in, finding the three Smarts dead in their beds, all shot in the head at point-blank range. A neighbouring family turned out to have had a narrow escape. When a burglar had appeared at their bedroom door, Mr McMunn had quick-wittedly said to his wife, 'Where's the gun?' and she had replied, 'Here it is'. The intruder had taken to his heels.

Manuel was the prime suspect, especially when it transpired that after complaining of having no money on New Year's Eve, he had been spending freely the following day. Peter Smart had made a withdrawal of £35 from the bank just before the holiday, all in new notes. When police traced the serial numbers, they found some of the notes in the pubs in which Manuel had been carousing. On 13 January, they raided the Manuel house, to the deep irritation of Manuel's father who again complained about police harassment. However, they found items that had been taken from a house in Mount Vernon that had been broken into on Christmas Day. Manuel was charged with burglary and taken into custody.

Manuel immediately began to spin a story that he had been given the Smart banknotes by a man called Samuel Mackay as payment for giving him a tour of the area in which the Smarts lived, so that Mackay could find suitable houses to burgle. Mackay was furious when he was told and responded by giving the police the vital information that Manuel had obtained a Beretta pistol just before Christmas.

Suddenly, however, it all became academic. The mercurial killer decided to confess, admitting killing Anne Knielands, Isabelle Cooke, the Watts and the Smarts. He repeated his confession to his parents when they were brought to the police station. He led police to the place where he had buried Isabelle Cooke's body and showed them the spot in the River Clyde where he had disposed of the pistol. It was recovered by a police diver.

As ever, Manuel relished the spotlight provided by his trial which began on 12 May 1958. He began sensationally by dismissing his defence team and electing to defend himself. He announced that his confessions had been obtained under duress, declaring that William Watt had indeed killed his own family. He put his mother on the stand, but she did him no favours, telling the jury that when he had spoken to her at the police station he had said, 'I don't know what makes me do these things'. It was an acknowledgement from his own mother that her son had confessed to the murders of his own free will and, try as he might in court, she would not retract the statement.

The jury took a mere two hours and twenty-one minutes to reach a verdict of guilty on all counts, apart from the murder of Anne Knielands. The judge had instructed the jury that there was insufficient evidence to enable a verdict to be reached on that particular case. Peter Manuel was sentenced to death.

He was unpopular in prison – rapists and child killers always have to be kept away from other prisoners because of the danger of them being harmed. Steps were even taken to ensure that he was not poisoned. As anticipated, his appeal was rejected and Manuel reacted by ceasing to speak and giving up smoking. For three weeks he uttered not a single word. Two days before the execution date, when his last appeal to the Home Secretary for clemency was rejected, he started to speak again.

On 11 July 1958, Manuel made his last confession to a priest, ate breakfast, washing it down with a large measure of whisky, and went to the gallows, claiming to the last that he had been framed.

JOACHIM KROLL
THE 'RUHR HUNTER'

The local children knew him as 'Uncle Joachim'. He was a slight man in his early forties, with large ears and thinning hair, who lived alone and was always nice to them, filling their pockets with sweets and keeping dolls in his apartment for the little girls to whom he was particularly attracted. They did not see the other dolls he kept in that apartment, though, inflatable sex dolls that he used to gratify himself, especially after returning home from strangling and raping his latest victim. It was a special bonus and while he did that, a pot would be simmering on the stove in the kitchen. Inside would be a stew consisting of a few vegetables and the main ingredient – pieces of buttock or shoulder sliced from his victim while her body was still warm.

Germany has had its share of killers who were also driven to eat the flesh of their victims. Karl Denke, an organist at his local church, was more interested in other types of organs, killing and consuming the body parts of more than thirty people; Georg

Grossman is thought to have consumed the flesh of perhaps fifty women and Fritz Haarmann is thought to have sold the meat of some of the forty or so young men he is believed to have murdered. In the 1950s and 1960s, to the ranks of the cannibal killers was added the name of Joachim Kroll.

Born in 1933, the son of a miner in Upper Silesia, Kroll was the youngest of eight children, a delicate child of very low IQ who frequently wet the bed. He was brought up by his mother, his father having been captured and either imprisoned or killed by the Russians during the Second World War. Frau Kroll moved her large brood to the North Rhine region of West Germany after the war and at least the young Joachim got some education there, but sadly not enough to enable him to make anything of himself.

The defining moment of Joachim Kroll's life appears to have occurred in 1955 when his mother died. To Kroll, twenty-two at the time and still living at home, it seems likely that the passing of his mother was a traumatic event. But it could also be viewed as a liberating one for him because just three weeks later, he raped and murdered his first victim – nineteen-year-old Irmgard Strehl, whom he stabbed to death and horrifically disembowelled in a barn close to the town of Lüdinghausen.

Thus began the series of killings committed in the Ruhr Valley by the man who came to be known by several gruesome nicknames, such as the 'Ruhr Hunter', the 'Ruhr Cannibal' and the 'Duisburg Man-Eater'.

Irmgard Strehl, Kroll later recalled, had been a blond, a runaway he had met as he was out walking. He had struck up a conversation with her and when he suggested that they walk together in the woods, she naively agreed. Out of sight amongst the trees, he clumsily tried to kiss her and she struggled. He fought back, succeeding eventually in dragging her into a barn. There he plunged the folding, long-bladed knife he had been carrying into her neck and, consumed by a sexual frenzy, raped her lifeless body. He wanted to make sure she was dead – she could identify him after all – so he strangled her. He then used the knife to disembowel her and left her bloody corpse there to be found five days later.

It would be a year before he struck again, establishing a pattern of intervals between his killings. His second victim was twelve-year-old Erika Schuletter, killed in the town of Kirchhellen. Again, an innocent encounter on the street led to her rape and murder.

In 1957, Kroll moved to the large, industrial town of Duisburg where he found a job as a toilet attendant for the Mannesmann company and then for Thyssen Industries. He rented an apartment at 11 Friesenstrasse in the suburb of Laar and spent his spare time on trips to nearby towns and villages, walking in wooded areas, hunting for victims on whom he could try out his sexually violent fantasies.

There was a gap until 1959 when, according to some sources, Kroll's urge to kill seems to have reached new heights. In March he is said to have murdered a twenty-three-year-old homeless woman called Erika. He knocked her unconscious after following her from a tavern in Duisburg to the Rheinbrücke in the Rheinhausen district. He left her for dead in a meadow beside the Rhine, but she survived the encounter – one of the very few who did. After that, he is said to have killed two women in different towns in the space of five weeks, but these have not been proved definitely to have been his work.

Two months after he had killed Erika, he found another victim, twenty-four-year-old Klara Frieda Tesmer. He grabbed her by the arm but she instantly pulled away from him. He struck her hard on the head, stunning her momentarily, but she began to struggle, pulling him down the river embankment. At the bottom, he put his hands around her throat as she kicked and punched and gradually throttled her, her struggles becoming quiet as the life drained from her. He undressed her and raped her before leaving her to be found by some boys playing by the river the following day.

Kroll had vented his sexual urges for the moment, but it was not enough. He would take his fantasies to new depths of depravity with his next victim.

Sixteen-year-old Manuela Knodt was strangled and raped in a wooded area of Essen, but this time, after he had raped her, he used his long-bladed knife to slice off strips of flesh from her buttocks. His sexual urge still not sated, or perhaps rekindled by removing her flesh, he then masturbated over her dead body. The semen deposits on her face and pubic area were such that police were led to believe that she had been attacked by a gang of deranged killers rather than just one lone pervert.

The removal of her flesh was horror enough for anyone, but what the police did not know was that Kroll had not taken it for fun; he took it because he wanted to cook and eat it. Later, he would claim that he had been driven to eat human flesh because he had been going hungry due to the scarcity of meat supplies, but it seems more likely that he took it simply because he wanted to experience the perverse thrill of tasting human flesh.

Bizarrely, six months after the murder of Manuela Knodt, a young man came forward and confessed to the crime. Shortly after, he withdrew his confession, but the authorities, relieved to have someone on whom to pin the blame, refused to accept his with-drawal, sentencing him to eight years in prison, of which he served five years. It would not be the last time an innocent man confessed to one of Kroll's murders.

He was now confident in his ability to get away with murder whenever he felt the urge and settled into a pattern of taking a train or bus to an isolated area where he would walk in the hope of coming upon an unaccompanied female. The only element that did not follow a pattern was the timing of his killings. He sought to confuse the police by leaving uneven gaps between each, although it has also been suggested that the gaps are only between the murders that are known, and that he did in fact kill more often than has been thought. There were a number of child-killers operating in the area at the time and it is hard to attribute all the deaths to the correct perpetrator.

The body of Kroll's next victim, twelve-year-old Barbara Bruder, has never been found, but when he was arrested fourteen years after the incident, he did indeed confess to killing her. She was dragged into a field near her home at Burscheid-Klein-Hamberg, raped and killed.

That same year, 1962, two thirteen-year-old girls, Petra Giese and Monika Tafel, also fell victim to his murderous instincts. At Easter, Kroll used Petra Giese's own scarf to strangle her, before sexually assaulting her. Once again, he sliced flesh from her body, taking it from her buttocks, her left forearm and hand. The authorities once again got their man – the wrong one, unfortunately – when Vinzenz Kuenh was arrested and sent to prison.

Kroll also took flesh from the buttocks and thighs of Monika Tafel, killed and raped on 4 June in Walsum as she walked to school. It has been suggested that he may even have eaten some of this material raw at the scene of the crime.

As had become the norm with Kroll's crimes, another man, Walter Quicker, became a suspect and was arrested. There was insufficient evidence to convict Quicker, but the suspicion was enough to turn his neighbours against him. Faced with accusations and rumours, he hanged himself in the woods in Walsum that October. His action convinced everyone that he had indeed been the murderer and the case was closed.

Kroll waited three years before claiming another victim and this time his modus operandi was radically different. On 22 August 1965, as he walked in a beauty spot close to a lake near Duisburg, he spotted a Volkswagen parked in an isolated spot often used by couples. Inside the vehicle were twenty-five-year-old Hermann Schmitz and his girlfriend Marion Veen. Kroll jabbed his trusty knife into one of the car's tyres and Schmitz emerged from the vehicle to see what was going on. Kroll pounced on the man at once and drove the knife several times straight into his heart. Marion watched in horror but was quick-witted enough to leap into the driver's seat. She pressed hard on the horn and tried to start the car, pushing her foot down hard on the accelerator. As the vehicle lurched forward, it almost hit Kroll. He turned on his heel and fled deep into the woods. She survived, but her boyfriend had become a grisly statistic – the Ruhr Hunter's only male victim.

The authorities were stumped, in spite of the excellent description of her attacker provided by Marion Veen. Kroll was himself very disturbed by the incident, realising that if the car had hit him, his life would have been over, one way or another.

He stayed out of trouble for a year but could not resist the urge to kill again. Twenty-year-old Ursula Rohling had spent the evening of 15 September 1966 with her boyfriend, Adolf Schickel, eating ice cream and enjoying herself in the early autumn sunshine, near Duisburg. The couple were planning to get married and they had discussed wedding plans. At the end of the evening, after they kissed goodnight, Adolf watched her head towards a park through which she had to walk to get home. She would never arrive, however. Instead, Joachim Kroll was waiting for her. He strangled her, raped her and left her lifeless body in the bushes.

Once again, the tragedy did not end with the death of Kroll's latest victim. Her boyfriend Schickel was immediately suspected of her murder and the stress of being a suspect and being ostracised by his friends and neighbours, coupled with his fiancée's horrific death, proved too much for him. He drowned after throwing himself off a bridge across the River Maine.

Three months later when the body of five-year-old Ilona Harke was discovered in an icy stream in Wuppertal, it was initially thought that her death was nothing more than a tragic accident. A post-mortem soon showed, however, that the girl had been raped and that her death had been no accident. Horrifically, Kroll had drowned her as an experiment – he had simply wanted to know what it would be like to drown someone. She was easily overpowered after he had taken her by train from Essen to Wuppertal and he had forced her head down under the water in a ditch. He removed pieces of flesh from her corpse, wondering if the meat of a child might taste better than that of an older body.

After a couple of failed attempts, Kroll killed again in 1969 and 1970. Maria Hettgen became his oldest victim when she was strangled and raped in a tourist area of Essen, and a year later, thirteen-year-old Jutta Rahn was attacked and killed after getting off a train in Breitscheid and starting to walk through a wood. Once again, her boyfriend, Peter Schay, was suspected of killing her and was arrested and questioned before being released.

The last year of Joachim Kroll's twenty-one-year murder career was 1976. That year he raped and strangled ten-year-old Karin Toepfer in Voerde before dispatching four-year-old Marion Ketter. Marion had disappeared from a playground in Duisburg on 3 July, failing to return home that evening. Her mother and father reported her disappearance to the police and the following day officers began a door-to-door investigation.

That day, however, at 11 Friesenstrasse where Kroll lived, a neighbour, making his way to the building's only toilet, encountered the killer. Kroll advised him that the toilet was blocked and could not be used, oddly adding that it was filled with 'guts'. The neighbour investigated, finding that the bowl was filled with blood-red water. There was also a horrendous stench coming from it. Looking closer, he noticed some tissue-like matter floating just below the surface. He thought once again about Kroll's use of the word 'guts' and a chill ran down his spine. He decided to go to the police. Outside, however, he bumped into one of the officers investigating Marion Ketter's disappearance and explained what he had seen. It soon became apparent that the matter in the toilet was flesh and that the water had been turned red by blood. With a child missing in the area, they immediately feared the worst and climbed the stairs to speak to Kroll.

He told them that he was indeed responsible for the blockage but it was only the internal organs of a rabbit he had skinned to make a stew. The officers pushed past him, asking if they could enter his apartment and have a look around. One walked into the kitchen where a pot was indeed simmering on the stove. It did not contain rabbbit, however. Putting a spoon into the broth, the policeman lifted out a large piece of what was cooking. To his horror, he found himself staring at a tiny hand. Packages of human flesh were discovered in the refrigerator, neatly wrapped and ready for the pot in the future.

Kroll confessed and stated that he hoped to receive treatment that might cure him of his deviant urges and get on with his life, naively forgetting that he had to be punished. Convicted of nine murders, he was given a life sentence for each in April 1982.

The Ruhr Hunter died of a heart attack in prison nine years later.

IAN BRADY AND MYRA HINDLEY
THE MOORS MURDERERS

Forty years after their horrific crimes, the names Ian Brady and Myra Hindley still evoke revulsion in the minds of British people. Described by the House of Lords when Hindley's appeal was rejected as 'uniquely evil', they shocked the world with their callous disregard for young lives and their depraved pursuit of their deviant sexual urges.

They met as the swinging sixties were just gearing up. The Beatles were about to take over the world of music and fashion, and the war and rationing were fading into history. It was January 1961 and twenty-one-year-old Ian Brady was working as a stock clerk at Millwards, a chemical company in Manchester. Brady was a strange, embittered young man who had an unhealthy fascination for Nazi memorabilia. His favourite lunchtime reading was Hitler's autobiography, *Mein Kampf*, and at home he relaxed to recordings of the Führer's speeches.

Brady's upbringing had not been easy. Born in the slum area of the Gorbals in Glasgow, he had immediately been given up for adoption, growing into an angry child and often becoming so frustrated during his regular tantrums that he would bang his head on the floor. Needless to say, at school other pupils gave him a wide berth and he became a loner. He was no fool, however, and at the age of eleven gained entry to Shawlands Academy, one of Glasgow's better schools. He was always in trouble, however, both at school and, increasingly, out of school. Between the ages of thirteen and sixteen he was arrested three times for house-breaking and was eventually presented with the choice of leaving the city to live with his birth-mother, or receiving a custodial sentence. He moved in with his mother in the rough Manchester area of Moss Side.

He was even more of an outsider there, especially with his alien Glasgow accent. He took the name of his stepfather and started working as a market porter before finding better work at a brewery. It was not long, however, before he returned to his old habits and, arrested for stealing lead seals from his employers, he was sent to a young offenders institution for two years. As the young offenders facility was full, however, he had to spend the first few months of his sentence in Strangeways,

Manchester's adult prison. It was a harsh introduction to institutional life and Brady had to grow up fast.

On his release, he was taken on by Millwards. Working there was a young woman called Myra Hindley. Hindley's background was almost as unstable as his. Born in Gorton in Manchester, she had been brought up by her grandmother. She was a reliable girl, but not considered bright enough to take O Levels; she left school at fifteen and worked as a clerk. She became engaged at seventeen, but called the wedding off, worried about the drudgery of married life and dreaming of something more exciting.

Brady immediately impressed Hindley. He dressed well and rode a motorbike. Where others found him sullen and distant, she saw him as quiet and aloof, an enigma who was different from all the other men around her. She wrote about him in the diary she kept, recording her disappointment when he seemed not to be interested in her. For a year he did not even speak to her, but in December 1961 he finally asked her out. Her diary records the moment: 'Eureka! Today we have our first date. We are going to the cinema.' He took her to see *Judgement at Nuremberg*, a fictional account of the Nuremberg trials that took place at the end of the Second World War.

Soon, they were sleeping together and he was inducting her into his world of perverted sex, persuading her to be photographed as they had intercourse and introducing her to sex games and sex toys. He encouraged her to dress differently and she took to wearing high boots and leather skirts. She also began bleaching her hair blonde. His pet name for her was 'Myra Hess' or 'Hessie' after the infamous, sadistic concentration camp guard, Irma Grese. She read his favourite books – *Mein Kampf, Crime and Punishment,* and the works of the Marquis de Sade – and when he told her there was no God, she stopped going to church. Her devotion to him was total. 'I hope Ian and I love each other all our lives,' she gushed in her diary, 'and get married and are happy ever after.'

They were futile hopes.

Six months after their first date, Brady moved in with Hindley at her grandmother's house on the south-eastern outskirts of Manchester. They had the place more or less to themselves as the elderly owner of the house was bedridden. By this time she was completely controlled by Brady. She was besotted with him and would do anything to please him, as she was about to prove.

On the night of 12 July 1963, sixteen-year-old Pauline Read set out for a dance. By the end of the evening she was in a shallow grave on bleak Saddleworth Moor in the Peak District National

Park after encountering Hindley who asked for her help in finding a glove she claimed to have lost on the moor. Once they were on the moor, Brady arrived on his motorbike. He took Pauline off and while Hindley waited, he raped the girl and cut her throat. He came back and asked Hindley to help bury the body. Brady disagrees with this story, claiming that Hindley played a full part in the sexual molestation.

Pauline's frantic parents and friends searched for her all night after she failed to come home and in the morning the police were informed.

Four months later, on 11 November, Hindley hired a car and they abducted twelve-year-old John Kilbride who had spent the afternoon with a friend at the cinema in Ashton-under-Lyme before going to the town's market. Boys could often earn some cash helping stallholders to pack up there at the end of the day. The friend had taken a bus home, leaving John at the market. It was the last time he was seen alive.

When Hindley and Brady read in the newspapers about the massive search that had been launched, the two killers laughed. It all seemed so amusing to them.

In May 1964, Hindley purchased a white Mini van. It would come in useful. Just over a month later, on

16 June, twelve-year-old Keith Bennett disappeared. Keith usually stayed at his grandmother's house on Tuesday evenings while his mother went to a local hall to play bingo. That night he failed to turn up, but his grandmother simply presumed that his mother had decided not to go to bingo on that particular night. Next morning, when it was learned that he had gone missing somewhere between the two houses, yet another massive and ultimately futile search was launched.

Around this time, Hindley persuaded Brady to enrol at the local gun club. He bought pistols for them and they would practise on the moors. They would also pay visits to the graves of their victims. Chilling photographs of them kneeling over their victims' graves were later found.

The killing of Lesley Ann Downey took Brady's and Hindley's depravity to new, repulsive depths. On Boxing Day, 1964, ten-year-old Lesley Ann Downey went to a local fair with her two brothers and some friends. When the others decided to return home, Lesley Ann wanted to stay behind. She was last seen by a schoolfriend standing beside one of the rides.

She was abducted by Brady and Hindley and taken back to the house. They photographed her naked and bound and, as they tortured her to death, recorded her screams. Their voices can be heard on the tape, threatening and abusing her. She was buried, like the others, on Saddleworth Moor.

Brady began to think he was all-powerful and, deciding to recruit someone else to their evil gang, he approached Hindley's teenage brother-in-law, David Smith, and tried to corrupt him. He made Smith read his beloved books and forced him to write in a notebook ghoulish phrases such as 'Murder is a hobby and supreme pleasure' and 'People are like maggots – small, blind, worthless fish-bait'. He showed him his guns and talked to him about carrying out a bank robbery. Finally, he told him that he and Hindley were responsible for the disappearances and deaths of the four children who had recently gone missing. He told Smith he wanted him to take part in one of their murders. It was a big mistake.

On 7 October 1965, a visibly shaken David Smith walked into Hyde police station with an amazing story. He explained that his sister-in-law, Myra Hindley, had asked him to walk her home the previous night but while he waited in the kitchen at her house, he heard a loud scream coming from the living room. Then he heard Myra shout 'Help him Dave' and he went through. When he walked into the room, he saw Brady holding what appeared at first glance to be a life-size doll, but, on closer inspection, turned out to be the body of a young man. He was a seventeen-year-old homosexual named Edward Evans whom Brady and Hindley had picked up in a Manchester pub and had brought home with them. Brady stood up, straddling the body, an axe in his hand. As the young man on the floor moaned, Brady raised the axe and brought it crashing down on the man's head. The man's groans became fainter, turning to gurgles as Brady dealt blow after shuddering blow with the axe. He then threw a piece of material over the man's head and wrapped a piece of electrical cord around his neck, pulling it tight and uttering the words, 'You fucking dirty bastard' again and again as he strained at the cord. The body went silent and Brady turned to Hindley, saying casually, 'That's it, the messiest yet'. He handed the axe to Smith, cleverly incriminating him by getting his fingerprints on the murder weapon.

Terrified, Smith helped them clean up. The body was wrapped in a plastic sheet as Brady and Hindley cracked jokes about what had just taken place. It was carried up to a bedroom and Hindley calmly put the kettle on.

Incredulous police officers went to Hindley's house at 8.40 in the morning to check, just in case this crazy story was true. In the back bedroom they discovered

Edward Evans' corpse, as Smith had said.

Brady confessed to killing Evans but said it was the result of an argument that had turned violent. He tried consistently to implicate Smith. Meanwhile, Hindley was not arrested for four days. It was only when a document was found in her car detailing how they were going to carry out the murder and clean up afterwards that her involvement became clear. Curiously, the police also found a left-luggage ticket hidden in the pages of her prayer book. In the corresponding locker at Manchester Piccadilly station, amongst pornographic magazines and books, were horrific pictures of Lesley Ann Downey, naked and gagged. They also found the tape of her dying screams. There were photographs of Hindley on Saddleworth Moor, pictures that helped the police locate the bodies of John Kilbride and Lesley Ann.

When Hindley was arrested, she merely said, 'My story is the same as Ian's…Whatever he did, I did'. The only time she showed any emotion was when her dog was destroyed. 'You fucking murderers,' she screamed at the police, without irony.

The true nature of the couple's perversions emerged at their trial at Chester Assizes. It was disclosed to a stunned court that dog hairs were found around Edward Evans' anus; John Kilbride's trousers and underpants were described as being down around his knees. It emerged that Hindley was sexually aroused by Brady committing homosexual acts, and the court heard how they were both naked as they tortured Lesley Ann Downey.

Throughout the trial, however, they neither talked nor showed any remorse.

They were sentenced to life imprisonment. Brady did not appeal, but Hindley did and, needless to say, the appeal was rejected. They were also banned from seeing each other, although they were allowed to exchange letters and did so for seven years until Hindley abruptly stopped writing. She took a university degree and helped police with information as to the whereabouts of their victims' bodies, hoping it would help in her petitions to be released. Meanwhile, Brady revealed more and more information about her involvement in the murders, countering her every attempt to get out.

Myra Hindley died in prison, aged sixty, on 15 November 2002, of bronchial pneumonia brought on by heart disease. Twenty undertakers refused to handle her funeral, but eventually she was cremated following a short service at Cambridge crematorium.

Following his conviction Ian Brady asked to be kept in solitary confinement and he remains locked up, the longest-serving prisoner in England and

Wales. Declared criminally insane in 1985, he was confined to Ashworth Psychiatric Hospital where he remains. Having gone on hunger strike in 1999, he was force-fed, but in 2000 he asked for a judicial review of the decision to force-feed him, saying, 'I have had enough. I want nothing, my objective is to die and release myself from this once and for all … I'm eager to leave this cesspit in a coffin'.

Forty-six years after his murder, the body of Keith Bennett remains undiscovered in a shallow grave on windswept Saddleworth Moor.

FRED AND ROSEMARY WEST

It was just an ordinary three-storey house in central Gloucester but its address – 25 Cromwell Street – would become one of the most infamous in British criminal history, justifiably described by the media as 'the house of horrors'.

It was a knock on the door on 24 February 1994 that brought it all to an end. The police asked to speak to Fred West, the owner of the property, but he was out and they had to deal with his sullen, overweight, forty-one-year-old wife, Rosemary. They handed her a warrant, telling her they were looking for their daughter, Heather, who had disappeared in 1987, and wanted to dig up the back garden. Rose got on the phone to Fred as they went round the back and told him to get home as fast as he could.

After denying everything and claiming that Heather was probably working somewhere as a prostitute, Fred reconsidered his situation overnight and next day confessed that he had killed her. He described cutting her body into three pieces and burying them. He added that Rose had nothing to do with it. Twenty minutes later, however, he changed his tune and denied it all again.

Three human bones were found in the garden of number 25, but they were not Heather's. Fred confessed again and said that they were Heather's, no one else's. He told how he had accidentally strangled her during a furious argument. He had tried to revive her, putting her in the bath and running cold water over her, but when that failed, he took her tights and strangled her with them to make sure she was dead. He did not want to start cutting her up if she was still alive.

He told how he had cut off her head, describing the unpleasant 'scrunching' noise as he did so, and had left her in the dustbin. That night, he had buried her in the garden. She had lain there ever since.

Fred West was born in the village of Much Marcle in Herefordshire in 1941, into a family of farm labourers. He was brought up in grinding poverty but was very close to his mother and of her seven children was by far the favourite. He grew up into a scruffy, unkempt young man with curly hair and an unattractive face. A failure as a student, and barely literate, he left school at fifteen and found work as a farm labourer.

By sixteen, Fred was chasing anything in a skirt. He would later claim that his father committed incest with his daughters and that he had made his own sister pregnant, but it is uncertain whether these facts are true or just examples of Fred's pathological lying.

At seventeen, he was involved in a serious motorcycle accident that left him in a coma for a week and resulted in a metal plate being inserted in his head. Afterwards one leg would always be shorter than the other. His head injury seemed to change his character, rendering him prone to mood swings and sudden outbursts of anger. This may have been exacerbated when he was pushed off a fire escape a little later by a girl after sticking his hand up her skirt. Again he suffered a head injury.

His troubles began to escalate. He was arrested and fined for shoplifting at the age of twenty, and a few months later was accused of getting a thirteen-year-old girl pregnant. His upbringing led him to believe there was nothing wrong with this. 'Well, doesn't everyone do it?' he asked. He got off with underage sex without a jail sentence. But, he was thrown out of the West family home and went to work on building sites where he was arrested for stealing.

He moved back home in 1962, beginning a relationship with a Scottish prostitue, Rena Costello, who had a criminal record for breaking and entering. They married secretly in November 1962 and moved to Scotland. Rena was pregnant and Fred's parents thought the baby was Fred's, but the father was actually an Asian bus driver. When the baby, called Charmaine, was born, Fred led his parents to believe that their baby had died and that they had adopted a mixed-race baby.

Fred West had a minimal interest in 'normal' sex. Instead, he satisfied his voracious sexual appetite with bondage, sodomy and oral sex. Rena, however, was not always inclined to comply with his more perverse desires, especially as he constantly wanted to have sex. He found plenty of other willing young women, however, as he drove an ice cream van. Despite difficulties in the marriage and frequent separations, Rena gave birth to Fred's first child in 1964, a girl they named Anne-Marie.

Around this time, Fred and Rena made the acquaintance of Anna McFall whose boyfriend had recently died in an accident.

Anna would become his first victim.

Fred himself had been involved in an accident in his ice cream van, in which a boy had been killed. Although he had not been to blame, he was worried that he was going to lose his job because of it. He and Rena moved with Anna McFall to Gloucester where he found work in a slaughterhouse. Some suggest that at this point West developed an unhealthy obsession with corpses, blood and dismemberment. He certainly became very interested in necrophilia and the mutilation of corpses.

Meanwhile, his marriage was falling apart. Rena returned to Glasgow, leaving the children with Fred, and when she returned to visit them, she found Fred and Anna living together in a caravan near Much Marcle.

When Anna became pregnant in 1967, she wanted Fred to divorce Rena and marry her. Tiring of her demands, he murdered her and buried her body in Letterbox Field in Much Marcle. Before burying her, however, he dismembered her body, removing the foetus of his own unborn baby and burying it beside McFall. When McFall's body was found in 1994, her fingers and toes were missing. This would become a trademark of Fred West's murders.

With Anna gone, Rena moved back in with him and life returned to normal, Rena earning money as a prostitute. Soon, however, Fred was sexually molesting his stepdaughter, Charmaine.

On 5 January 1968, fifteen-year-old Mary Bastholm disappeared from a bus stop in Gloucester where she was waiting for a bus to take her to her boyfriend's house. Fred West denied killing Mary, but he certainly knew her. He was a customer at the cafe where she worked, she had known Anna McFall, and one witness claims to have seen her in Fred's car.

Fred was working as a delivery driver for a bakery when he met the love of his life, the fifteen-year-old girl who would become his second wife and his accomplice in murder.

Rosemary Letts had been born in 1953 in Devon to a violent, abusive father and a mother who could also be violent. Her mother had suffered from severe depression and in 1953, when she was pregnant with Rosemary, she had been treated with a course of electroshock therapy. It is thought that this treatment affected the unborn child and Rosemary was certainly very different from her siblings. While still a baby, she developed a habit of rocking violently in her cot or her pram. As she got older, she rocked only her head, but she did it for hours at a time. She was slow and the family nicknamed her 'Dozy Rosey'. However, she became sexually active at an early age and was known to climb into bed with her younger brother and fondle him. Grossly overweight, she grew into a sullen, aggressive loner who had sex with older men in her village.

When Rose met Fred, her father tried to keep them apart, reporting him to social services and threatening him. Before she was sixteen, however, she was pregnant with West's child. She moved into the caravan to look after Rena's two daughters, Rena having returned to Scotland.

Their baby, born in 1970, was named Heather. When she was born, however, Fred was in jail for non-payment of fines and Rose found it hard to cope, treating the children very badly. Eventually, Charmaine disappeared, Rose telling Anne-Marie that her mother had collected her and taken her to Scotland. She was lying, of course; she had simply lost her temper and killed her.

When Fred got out of prison, he helped her bury the girl's body under the kitchen floor of a house at 25 Midland Road, Gloucester, into which they had recently moved. Once again, there were no fingers or toes on the body when it was dug up in 1994.

In the 1960s, Rose whiled away her evenings having sex with many of the West Indian immigrants who lived and worked in Gloucester. Fred got a kick from watching them through a peephole, happy that Rose was earning good money.

Rena turned up again one day in 1971, and started asking questions about Charmaine. Fred decided that she would have to be killed to keep her quiet. He got her drunk in the house at Midland Road and strangled her. Her dismembered body, minus her fingers and toes of course, was buried in a field near Much Marcle.

By this time, Fred and Rose had found a new way of indulging their numerous perversions. They had started to cruise around the local area looking for young girls to abduct and rape, Rose accompanying Fred principally because the girls were more likely to get into the car if there was a woman in it. They explained this to a neighbour, Elizabeth Agius, who Fred later drugged and raped.

Rose became Mrs West when they married in January 1972 and five months later she gave birth to another girl, Mae. With the Midland Road house getting small for their growing family and also for Rose's growing prostitution business, they moved into 25 Cromwell Street, a bigger house on three storeys with a large basement where they thought Rose could entertain her clients. Alternatively, Fred said, he could soundproof it and convert it to a torture chamber. Sadly, he was not joking.

His eight-year-old daughter Anne-Marie was the torture chamber's first occupant. She was told that they were going to teach her how to satisfy her husband sexually when eventually she married. She was stripped naked, her hands were tied behind her back and Rose held her down while her father raped her. The rapes continued and she was threatened with a beating if she told anyone about them.

Towards the end of 1972, Fred and Rose picked

up seventeen-year-old Caroline Owens during one of their cruises. They offered her a job as a live-in nanny and she accepted. An attractive girl, Caroline rejected the advances of both Fred and Rose but when she decided to leave, she was stripped and raped. He threatened to keep her in the basement as a sex slave and then kill her if she told anyone. She remained silent about her ordeal until her mother noticed the bruises on her body and got the truth out of her. They went to the police but in court Fred convinced the magistrate that she had agreed to have sex with him. Incredibly, the story was believed, in spite of Fred West's long record of sex crimes. He was fined and given a slap on the wrists.

Seamstress Lynda Gough moved in as nanny. She was soon dead, dismembered and buried under the garage floor, minus fingers, toes and this time, for some reason, her kneecaps. She was missed briefly by her family but no one called the police. In August 1973, Fred's son Stephen was born.

Fifteen-year-old schoolgirl Carol Ann Cooper was next. In November 1973, they kept her for their own amusement for a week and then killed her, burying her under the house.

In December, twenty-one-year-old student Lucy Partington climbed into Fred's car before spending a horrific week at 25 Cromwell Road, during which she was raped and tortured before being killed. Again, she was buried under the house.

Fred now embarked on a series of home improvements, making the basement bigger and turning the garage into an extension of the house. Unsurprisingly, the work was all carried out at night, under cover of darkness. He needed to extend the basement space in order to house three more bodies under its floor – fifteen-year-old Shirley Hubbard, nineteen-year-old Juanita Mott and twenty-one-year-old Swiss hitchhiker, Therese Siegenthaler. Sometimes girls were brought back and there were other victims still alive in the basement. One girl who survived, saw two naked girls being held prisoner before she was raped by Fred West. One of the girls was probably Anne-Marie whom Fred was not only raping on a regular basis but also bringing home other men to have sex with her.

A lodger they had, a former prostitute by the name of Shirley Robinson, got pregnant by Fred, making Rose jealous enough to kill her in July 1977. The following December, Rose gave birth to a baby, Tara, whose father was one of her West Indian clients. Then, in November 1978, she gave birth to another daughter, Louise, who was Fred's child. There were now six children in the house and when Anne-Marie moved out, Fred started raping Heather and Mae.

In summer 1979, a seventeen-year-old Swansea girl, Alison Chambers, was abducted, raped, tortured and murdered. She was interred in the back garden.

A year later, Rose gave birth to another son for Fred whom they named Barry, and in April 1982, Rosemary Junior was born – again she was not Fred's child. July 1983 saw the arrival of Lucyanna, a child of mixed race, fathered by a client.

The children were all aware of what was going on in the house and when Heather told one of her friends, word got back to Fred. He killed her.

Eventually, the Wests' luck, which had held for twenty-five years of rape, torture and murder, ran out when one of their young victims told a girlfriend what had happened when she had been abducted. The girl went to the police. Fred and Rose were arrested, Fred being charged with the rape and sodomy of a minor, while Rose was charged with being an accessory.

An exhaustive investigation of the Wests was launched and the children were all taken into care. When they joked that Heather was under the patio, the investigating officers decided to take a look.

On 13 December 1994, Fred West was charged with twelve murders. In the dock, when he tried to comfort Rose she pulled away from him, a rejection that devastated him. He wrote to her later, 'We will always be in love … You will always be Mrs West, all over the world. That is important to me and you.' Rose did not write back.

On New Year's Day 1995, Fred West hanged himself with strips of his bedsheet in his cell at Winson Green Prison in Birmingham. Rose, meanwhile, was found guilty of the murders of all ten girls found at 25 Cromwell Street and sentenced to life imprisonment.

In October 1996, Gloucester City Council demolished 25 Cromwell Street and turned the space it had occupied into a landscaped footpath.

DR HAROLD SHIPMAN

Vera Shipman was well known to her neighbours as a snob. She seemed to think she was better than them and, even though she lived in a working-class red-brick terrace house just like them, had airs and graces that most found irritating. She fussed over her precious children – Pauline, the oldest and her two boys, Harold Frederick and his younger brother, Clive. There were some local children she would not let hers play with, as if somehow they were not up to scratch in some way. The favourite of her children, however, was never in doubt. The middle child, Freddy, seemed to her to be the one with the most potential to get on in life. She pushed him to ensure that he fulfilled that potential, always dressing him in a collar and tie, while his friends dressed casually. In return Freddy rewarded her with an unhealthy devotion, even though he was not quite as intelligent as she thought. He was something of a plodder at school and only just gained entry to Leeds University Medical School, having to resit the entrance exams to do so.

Vera did not live to see her dreams for Freddy come to fruition. She was diagnosed with terminal lung cancer while he was still at school and died on 21 June 1963, aged forty-three. While she was ill, however, her beloved Freddy devoted all the time when he was not at school to her, running home to make her a cup of tea and remaining by her bedside chatting into the evening. Vera's only respite from the intense pain she was suffering came from the shots of morphine administered by the family doctor on his daily visits to the Shipman house. What ran through young Freddy's mind as he watched the doctor prepare and administer these injections we will never know.

Freddy had few friends as a youngster, even though he took part in sports and was good at them, usually a ticket to social success at school. He had inherited Vera's inate sense of superiority and this made him unpopular amongst his classmates. In fact, few of his teachers or schoolmates even remember him or if they do, they recall a loner who, as one describes, '… tolerated us. If someone told a joke, he would smile patiently, but Fred never wanted to join in'.

Initially at medical school, he remained distant, even taking his sister to dances in the absence of any female friendships. He began to mellow, however, and at the age of nineteen, met a girl, sixteen-year-old Primrose, daughter of his landlord. She had come from a similarly sheltered background and it seemed as if they were made for each other. A year later, with Primrose five months pregnant, they were married.

By the age of twenty-eight, Harold Shipman was established as a family man and a GP, having joined a medical practice at Todmorden in Calderdale in West Yorkshire. It is feared, however, that even by that time, he had killed many people. When he had finally graduated from medical school, after resitting a number of his exams, he had become a junior house doctor at Pontefract General Infirmary where it is believed that he embarked on his murderous career, killing at least ten patients, one of whom was a four-year-old girl.

As a doctor, he was a changed man, much more outgoing than when younger, and he was well liked and respected by his patients and colleagues at the practice. His air of superiority had not completely deserted him, however, and those working for him found him to be rude and overbearing. They also found him to be manipulative and controlling.

Everything seemed fine until Shipman suddenly began to experience blackouts. He told colleagues that he suffered from epilepsy, but he was lying. Practice receptionist Marjorie Walker uncovered discrepancies in the narcotics ledgers of the local chemists. Against Shipman's name were large amounts of the drug pethidine, a morphine-like analgesic. An investigation launched by one of the other doctors at the practice revealed that Shipman had been prescribing the drug for patients who never received it. Instead, he was taking it himself.

Confronted with the evidence at a staff meeting, Shipman lost his temper but, faced with the evidence of his wrongdoing, was forced to resign from the practice and attend a drug treatment centre in York. The case was reported to the police and he was fined £600 for forgery and prescription fraud. Nonetheless, the British Medical Council did not strike him off its register and he was free to practise medicine, probably because he submitted himself for treatment.

Of course, the question remains as to whether Shipman had actually been using all the drug on himself. It may have been used to kill patients in Todmorden.

He returned to medicine at the Donnybrook Medical Centre in Hyde, Greater Manchester, two years later. Once again, he seemed to his colleagues and patients to be a diligent and caring doctor, but was loathed by his juniors whom he treated with disdain. He would remain there, however, for sixteen years before leaving to establish his own practice, with Primrose working for him as a part-time receptionist. He was so well liked in Hyde that a number of patients followed him to the new practice from Donnybrook. Some of them would pay for that decision with their lives.

It was local undertaker, Alan Massey, who first began to suspect something was amiss with Dr Harold Shipman. He observed a curious pattern with the patients of Shipman's whom he had to deal with. Firstly, there were a lot of them; Shipman's patients seemed to be dying at an unusually high rate. What was even stranger, however, was that the dead patients were mostly female, always died in a chair or lying on a settee and they were almost always fully clothed. There was nothing to suggest that they had been ill. It seemed odd.

Massey went to see Shipman but the doctor reassured him that everything was as it should be, showing him the book from which he issued death certificates. He seemed to be completely at ease and Massey decided that he had been worrying over nothing. The fears of his daughter Debbie Brambroffe, also a funeral director, were not so easily assuaged, however, and she told Dr Susan Boothe who worked at a different practice to Shipman, about her suspicions. Dr Boothe told her colleagues, and one of them, Dr Linda Reynolds, passed on the suspicions to coroner John Pollard who alerted the police. Shipman's records were inspected secretly but no irregularities were found.

They were unaware, however, that Shipman had been amending patient records after the patients had passed away.

In 1998, the death of Kathleen Grundy marked the beginning of the end for Dr Harold Shipman.

The death of the sprightly eighty-one-year-old on 24 July was unexpected and a shock to her friends and family. A well-off former mayoress of Hyde, she was well known and respected in the local community, and even at the age of eighty-one still devoted her energies to working for local charities. That day, she was due to help serve meals to fellow pensioners at a local Age Concern Club but had failed to turn up. Usually punctilious in her timekeeping, her friends became worried and went round to her house to see what was wrong. They found her lying on a sofa in her living room. She was fully clothed and she was dead. They called her doctor, Harold Shipman.

Shipman had paid her a house call earlier that morning and was actually the last person to see Mrs Grundy alive. He said he had visited her in order to take blood samples for studies on ageing that he was involved in.

Mrs Grundy's daughter, Angela Woodruff, was informed of her mother's death, but then, after the funeral, was in receipt of a call from her mother's solicitors informing her that they were in possession of a copy of her mother's will. This seemed odd to Mrs Woodruff as she was, in fact, a solicitor and naturally had always handled her mother's affairs. Her law firm had held Mrs Grundy's will since 1986. She asked to see the new document.

As soon as she saw it, she knew it was a fake. Badly worded, poorly typed, it left £386,000 to Dr Harold Shipman. There could only be one grim conclusion; Shipman had murdered her mother for her money. She called in the police.

The amateurish nature of the will convinced Detective Superintendent Bernard Postles that there was, indeed, something amiss. A post-mortem was requested which meant that Mrs Grundy's body would have to be exhumed, a rare and very serious undertaking. It was not such a rare occurrence, however, by the time the investigation into Harold Shipman's activities was over.

As Mrs Grundy's body was being exhumed, and before Shipman knew that it was happening, police raided his home and offices, giving him no opportunity to destroy or amend his records. Throughout, he maintained his customary air of arrogance and superiority. One vital piece of evidence was his ancient Brother portable typewriter, the one on which Mrs Grundy's will had probably been typed. He spun them an unlikely story about the elderly lady having often borrowed it from him. Police also found some jewellery and medical records. Unusually for a doctor, the house was messy and filled with dirty clothes and old newspapers.

The toxicology test on Kathleen Grundy found that she had been killed by an overdose of morphine, administered several hours before her death. This was a serious error by Shipman. As a doctor, he would have known that morphine is one of the few poisons that remains in the body tissue for a long time after death. Had he wanted to be caught, or was it just his usual contempt for everyone else that led him to believe he would get away with it? Confronted with the evidence, Shipman claimed, somewhat ridiculously, that Kathleen Grundy had been a junky.

It soon became grimly obvious that Mrs Grundy was probably not Harold Shipman's only victim. A massive investigation was launched, initially targeting those of his patients who had died immediately after he had made a house call on them. Of course, those who had been cremated presented the investigators with a problem and, unsurprisingly, Shipman had always urged relatives to cremate their loved ones.

His computer was examined. It emerged that he had altered computerised records to make the patients' symptoms match the treatment that had killed them, often making these changes only hours after their deaths. Something of a technophobe, he was unaware that his computer's hard drive contained records of every change he had made.

During interrogation, Shipman remained true to character, arrogant and supercilious He was uncooperative but was constantly faced with conclusive evidence to which he had no answer. Eventually he was charged with fifteen counts of murder and one of forgery of Kathleen Grundy's will.

When the case went to court on 5 October 1999, it was the prosecution case that Shipman killed simply because he enjoyed exercising the ultimate power of controlling life and death. He repeated the act so often, they claimed, that he must have found the drama of taking life to his taste. They explained the way in which he normally went about the business of killing.

He would obtain large quantities of morphine and, on a house visit on some pretext or other, inject his elderly patient with it. Within a few hours, with the patient close to death, he would pretend to anyone present to call an ambulance before pretending to cancel it when the patient died. When telephone records were checked during the later investigation, no record of these calls was found.

Of the blood samples he claimed he had taken from Kathleen Grundy on the day of her death, there was absolutely no trace. Initially, he told police he had sent them off for analysis, but then he said he had actually mislaid them and had to throw them away when he rediscovered them under a pile of papers on his desk because they were no longer any use. He claimed that he never carried morphine, but this was found to be a lie when a woman came forward to say that she had been given a morphine injection by him during a house visit.

It emerged that he was extraordinarily callous in his treatment of the families of his victims. Rather than just tell people that their relative had passed away, he seemed intent all the time on manipulating their emotions until they eventually realised that their wife, mother, aunt or grandmother had died. It was cruel and an extra piece of control for him to play with, adding to his overwhelming belief that he was better than everyone else.

The stories that were emerging were dreadful, but there were also some – not many – narrow escapes. The story was told of Jim King who had been diagnosed by Shipman as having cancer. Jim was given huge doses of morphine and when he suddenly got worse, Shipman told him he had pneumonia and wanted to give him another injection. Jim and his wife had resisted, however. They were wary of Shipman because both Jim's aunt and father had died after visits and injections from him. On this occasion Shipman failed to get his victim.

On 31 January 2000, Dr Harold Shipman was found guilty of all charges, receiving fifteen life sentences and an additional four years for the forgery of Kathleen Grundy's will.

His life sentence did not last long, however. On 13 January 2004, he was found hanged in his cell at Wakefield prison. He did it so that Primrose would be eligible for his NHS pension. If he had lived until sixty she would have lost it. It was his last piece of control. Harold Shipman is now listed in the annals of crime as possibly the most prolific serial killer of the modern age. The official number of murders he committed stands at 215, but the Shipman Inquiry, held after his trial, examined the cases of 500 patients and accepted that the death tally may well be much higher. It reported that it was likely that he had killed another forty-five people and it may be possible that another thirty-eight cases could be attributed to him. Some sources suggest that the number of people killed by Shipman could be as high as one thousand.

PART TWO

NORTH AMERICA

HERMAN MUDGETT
AKA H. H. HOLMES

It was a death factory, a building fashioned solely for the purpose of killing. Built on three storeys with a hundred windowless rooms, he called it his 'castle'. There were soundproof chambers with peepholes through which the process of dying could be closely followed, its every dreadful nuance savoured. Walls were padded and could be slid across, partitioning a room and making it larger or smaller, depending on his mood. Gas pipes fed a slow, choking death into the rooms and there were trapdoors and ladders leading to rooms above and below. There were false doors and secret passages known only to him, and behind the doors of a number of the rooms were metal, leather and rubber implements of pain. One room had been made into a specially equipped surgery. Its function was not to heal people, however, and the suffering that went on inside its walls can only be imagined.

He was fascinated by the process of dying, and liked to watch people in their death throes and in particular to experiment with different methods. He would set fire to the gas for a little more excitement, for instance. He liked to use the 'elasticity determinator', a kind of rack on which he would strap an unfortunate victim and stretch her until her muscles tore and her limbs snapped out of their sockets. Efficiency was all, however. When he had finished with someone, the corpse was placed on a chute with the sides nicely greased for smoother dispatch, and slid down to the two-level basement where he would always have a good fire going in the furnace. Down there, he had vats of acid and other chemicals that made short work of flesh and bones. Sometimes, if he was short of cash, he would strip a corpse down to its bones and sell the skeleton to the local medical school. They never asked any questions.

Holmes was born Herman Webster Mudgett in Gilmonton, New Hampshire, the son of a strict disciplinarian. As a child, he was bullied and it was as a result of one incident of bullying that he developed an interest in medical matters. A gang of school friends, knowing that he was afraid of the local doctor's surgery, forced him to look at, and touch, a human skeleton. However, rather than frighten him, the experience fascinated him and he resolved to become a doctor.

In 1884, Holmes graduated from the University of Michigan Medical School, but he had already begun his career of crime while enrolled there. He had been involved in an insurance scam, stealing bodies, disfiguring the corpses so they were unrecognisable and fooling insurance companies into believing they were people who had died in accidents. He had, of course, taken insurance policies out on them.

After graduation, he moved to Chicago where he worked in a medical practice for a while and then in an asylum, an experience that haunted him for the remainder of his life. He was also involved in a number of shady business ventures, using the name under which he would become notorious – H. H. Holmes, the initials standing for Harry Howard.

He married Clara Lovering in 1878, a fact that did not prevent him from bigamously marrying again in 1887, to Myrta Belknap. He would marry a third woman, Georgina Yorke, in 1894.

When he arrived in Chicago during the summer of 1886, Holmes stumbled on a drugstore in Englewood where he got a job as a prescription clerk. Within three years the owner, a Mrs Holton, had disappeared and he had taken it over. Holmes answered enquiries about her with the information that she had moved to California. He had, of course, killed her.

Across the street from the drugstore sat an empty piece of land. Using money he earned from insurance policies taken out on the women he employed in the drugstore and then murdered – the insurance was a condition of employment – Holmes bought it and built his block-long castle, relocating the drugstore there. He repeatedly changed builders during its construction so that only he knew the layout and design of the building.

It was opened as a hotel for the 1894 opening of the Chicago World's Fair that would bring a staggering twenty-seven million people to the city during the six months that it ran. It would also bring unprecedented opportunity for a psychopath such as Holmes to prey on the many vulnerable single women who would be in town.

He was no stranger to murder, having killed a former school friend, whom he had dispatched with a dose of laudanum, in order to make a claim against an insurance policy he had taken out on him. A second had been an accident. He had killed a man in a fight over money he claimed had been owed to him. Following that, he had killed a number of people whose bodies were sold to medical schools for anything between $25 and $45. He killed by beating to death, gassing in vaults and asphyxia, and it was a miracle he avoided detection for so long.

On one memorable occasion, he had attempted to kill three young women at the same time, using chloroform. When they escaped and reported him to the police, he was arrested but, astonishingly, was not prosecuted.

It is not known how many Holmes killed in his castle, but it is likely to run into double figures. In a confession he later wrote for the *Philadelphia Inquirer,* he claimed to have murdered more than one hundred people, but he later retracted that figure, reducing his tally to twenty-seven.

Holmes seduced the wife of a jeweller named Connor who rented space in the drugstore. Both the wife, Julia, and her eighteen-year-old daughter, Gertie, became his mistresses. When Gertie became pregnant, however, she became surplus to requirements and one day vanished, never to be seen again. A good-looking, sixteen-year-old girl, Emily van Tassell, who was a frequent customer in the shop, also disappeared. When Holmes took on a new secretary, Emily Cigrand, Julia Connor became jealous. She disappeared, too. She should have kept quiet, however, because the secretary soon also vanished. The following year it was the turn of Emily Williams and her sister, Nannie. Emily replaced Emily Cigrand as his secretary, but when her sister arrived on the scene, she became jealous, fearing that Holmes liked her more. According to Holmes, Emily hit Nannie on the head with a stool and killed her. She and Holmes dumped the body in Lake Michigan.

After the World's Fair, Holmes, now in financial trouble and with creditors closing in, travelled to Fort Worth in Texas where he owned property that had been left to him by two sisters who were wealthy heiresses. Naturally, he had murdered both of them but not before they had included him in their wills. He initially planned to build another castle in Texas, but found that the Texan police were a little too diligent. He took to the road, travelling around the United States and Canada, undoubtedly killing as he went, although the number of his victims from this period is unknown.

In July 1894, while he was briefly imprisoned for his involvement in a fraud, he met a well-known train robber named Marion Hedgepeth. The two dreamed up an insurance fraud in which Holmes would take a policy out on himself and then fake his own death. The plan did not succeed, however, and Holmes decided to put a similar plan into motion, but this time faking the death of an associate, Benjamin Pitezel.

Pitezel was supposed to be killed in an accidental explosion in a laboratory. Holmes would then substitute a corpse stolen from a medical school for Pitezel's. However, Holmes decided just to ignore the part about the substitute body, realising it would be easier just to kill Pitezel. One night he got him very drunk, laid him on his bed, tied him up, poured benzene over him and set fire to him. Pitezel came to, screaming horrifically as he died an agonising death. When he was dead and the fire had gone out, Holmes untied him and poured chloroform into his stomach to make it look like he had tried to kill himself. Holmes would later ghoulishly visit Pitezel's grave, pretending to be taking some samples for analysis. He later described how 'inordinately satisfying' it was to cut into the decomposing corpse with a knife.

He next began to wipe out the entire Pitezel family. Informing Mrs Pitezel that her husband was hiding out in South America and would be coming back soon, he persuaded her to let him have custody of her three children, two girls and a boy. He had soon poisoned nine-year-old Howard Pitezel, dissecting the body into pieces and burning them in a stove.

He took the eleven- and fifteen-year-old girls to Chicago, Detroit and Toronto, telling them that they were soon going to be reunited with their mother. Instead, he killed them by locking them in a large trunk and pumping gas into it. He buried them in shallow graves, feeling not a scintilla of remorse.

But it was almost the end of the line for Holmes. Having not received her share of the insurance money, the angry Marion Hedgepeth informed the insurance company about what Holmes had done. Pinkerton's Detective Agency were engaged to find him and they finally caught up with him in Boston in November 1894. With Holmes in custody, they gained entry to the castle in Chicago and the full horror of his murderous activities became clear. Intact skeletons were discovered and countless human bone fragments, amongst which was the pelvis of a fourteen-year-old.

The press went mad. 'The Castle is a Tomb!' screamed the headline in the *Chicago Tribune*. The *Philadelphia Inquirer* called it a 'charnel house'. True crime writers made it a staple of the genre. In Philadelphia, a Holmes Museum opened. As for the narcissistic Holmes, he wrote a memoir, *Holmes' Own Story, in which the Alleged Multimurderer and Arch Conspirator Tells of the Twenty-two Tragic Deaths and Disappearances in which he is Said to be Implicated.* 'My sole object in this publication is to vindicate my name from the horrible aspersions cast upon it,' he wrote, 'and to appeal to a fair-minded American public for a suspension of judgement.'

In the book he attempted to make himself seem completely normal and, typical of the narcissistic tendency of the psychopath, saw the book as having literary merit.

At his trial, he was the first murderer in American legal history to defend himself and, according to one newspaper of the time, his performance in court was remarkable. He claimed that Pitezel had committed suicide, but failed to convince the jury.

He was, unsurprisingly, found guilty and sentenced to death by hanging.

On the day of his execution in Philadelphia, 17 May 1896, H. H. Holmes was still spinning his story on the gallows, claiming now that he had only killed two people. He was about to say something else, but at that moment the trapdoor opened and he plunged to his death. There was some consolation for his many victims in the fact that his death was not easy – it took him fifteen minutes to die on the end of the rope. He was then buried in cement to deter souvenir hunters and bodysnatchers.

H. H. Holmes's castle did not last much longer than its owner, America's first serial killer. On 19 August 1895, it was destroyed by a mysterious fire.

ALBERT FISH

A recipe from the Albert Fish Cookbook, should he ever have compiled such a thing:

Take the body of a child, slicing off the ear, nose and belly and putting aside. Slice through the legs about two inches below the behind; put to one side.

Roast the behind and genitals in the oven and make a stew out of the ears, nose, pieces of face and belly; add onions, carrots, turnips and celery and salt to taste.

Split the cheeks of his behind and cover each with strips of bacon; roast in an oven for about fifteen minutes before adding onions and water for gravy, basting at regular intervals with a wooden spoon; cook for two hours until brown.

Serve.

Albert Fish was one of the most deranged child killers who ever lived; a cold, calculating pervert concerned only for the satisfaction of his own repulsive urges.

A strangely mild-looking man with a thin face and empty, watery eyes, he plied his cruel trade for many years and we can only speculate as to the exact number of murders for which he was responsible. Some sources claim fifteen, with hundreds of assaults over the decades, but that number may only be the tip of a very bloody iceberg.

One killing that has been well documented, even by Fish himself, is that of ten-year-old Grace Budd. On 28 May 1928, there was a knock at the door of the Manhattan basement in which the Budd family lived. When the door was opened, the visitor, introducing himself as Frank Howard, although, of course, it was none other than Albert Fish, explained that he had come after seeing an advertisement placed in the *New York World* newspaper by eighteen-year-old Edward Budd. The ad had read:

Young man, 18, wishes position in country.

'Howard' told him that he was the owner of a farm on Long Island and could use some help. The Budds were delighted and he stayed and talked with them for a while. A few days later, he returned and confirmed that Edward did indeed have the job. They asked him to stay for lunch and over the meal Fish made friends with Grace, allowing her to sit on his lap at the table. As he was leaving, he mentioned to them that his next stop was a children's birthday party that his sister was throwing for one of her kids and wondered whether perhaps Grace would like to go. Mrs Budd was initially unsure, but the man seemed so charming and correct and her husband said that it would be fun for the girl. They told Grace to go and get dressed before waving goodbye to her at the door. She was wearing a white confirmation dress, and holding the hand of one of the worst child killers the world has ever known. Needless to say, they never saw their daughter again.

As the day wore on and she failed to return, the Budds became anxious. When they reported the incident to the police they were horrified to discover that there was no farmer on Long Island by the name of Frank Howard and the address they had been given for the party was fictitious. In spite of extensive publicity in the press and hundreds of tip-offs from people who thought they had seen something, no progress was made in the investigation into Grace's abduction. Detective Will King of the New York Police Department Missing Persons Bureau threw himself wholeheartedly into the case, but despite travelling thousands of miles, found not a trace of Frank Howard.

Six years after Grace's disappearance, in 1934, the

Budds received a chilling letter. Although unsigned, it was undoubtedly from their daughter's abductor. In graphic detail, it described Grace's murder.

He reminded them how he had had lunch with them and how Grace had sat on his lap and kissed him. At that point, he wrote chillingly, 'I made up my mind to eat her'. After they had left the Budd basement, he had taken Grace to an empty house in Westchester and left her outside picking wild flowers. He went upstairs and undressed so that he would not get any blood on his clothes. He then called to her from the window and hid in a closet. When he leapt out naked, she burst into tears and turned, trying to run downstairs again, but he grabbed hold of her. She struggled, biting and scratching and screaming that she was going to 'tell Mama' but he was too strong for the little girl. He put his hands around her tiny neck and choked her until she was dead. He then wrote that he had cut her body into small pieces that he could carry to his rooms. There he cooked these pieces of flesh and ate them. 'How sweet and tender her little ass was roasted in the oven,' the letter continued. 'It took me nine days to eat her entire body. I did not fuck her tho I could of had I wished. She died a virgin.'

Fish would confess to his lawyer when he was later in custody that this last part was untrue and that he had in fact raped Grace after killing her.

Amazingly, the diligent Detective Will King succeeded in tracing the author of the letter. Fish had made a very bad mistake by using headed notepaper that had been left behind in his rooms by the previous tenant. The logo at the top of the paper belonged to the New York Private Chauffeurs' Benevolent Association, an employee of which admitted that he had taken home some paper when he had been renting accommodation on East 52nd Street. On investigation, it transpired that these rooms were now rented by A. H. Fish. When King examined the handwriting in the boarding house's register, he found it to be identical to that of the writer of the letter to the Budds.

Fish was away, however, and Will King waited for three weeks until he showed up. When confronted, Fish agreed without hesitation to accompany the detective to the police station to answer questions. However, as they left the building, Fish suddenly lunged at King with a razor. King dodged his hand, however, and quickly disarmed the weaker man, slamming handcuffs on his wrist.

At police headquarters Fish immediately confessed to killing Grace Budd. Questioned further, he claimed to have killed a staggering four hundred children since 1910, roaming through twenty-three states, from New York to Montana. His victims were mainly from the poorer classes – African-American children in the main – chosen because, as he was well aware, the authorities paid less attention when one of them went missing.

One such was seven-year-old Staten Island boy, Francis McDonnell, killed by Fish four years before he abducted Grace Budd. Francis was playing with some friends close to his home when his mother saw a man who she thought was behaving strangely, walking up and down the street, wringing his hands and muttering to himself. But she had things to do and went indoors, thinking no more about him. Later that day, the man, Fish, of course, lured her son into some woods where he sexually molested, mutilated and strangled him. They found Francis's body the following day, but it would be ten years before they learned the name of his killer.

The previous year, Fish had abducted, tortured and killed another boy, Billy Gaffney. In his confession, he said:

I brought him to the Riker Avenue dumps. There is a house that stands alone, not far from where I took him. I took the boy there. Stripped him naked and tied his hands and feet and gagged him with a piece of dirty rag I picked out of the dump. Then

I burned his clothes. Threw his shoes in the dump. Then I walked back and took the trolley to 59 Street at 2.00 a.m. and walked from there home. Next day about 2.00 p.m., I took tools, a good heavy cat-o-nine tails. Home made. Short handle. Cut one of my belts in half, slit these halves in six strips about 8 inches long. I whipped his bare behind till the blood ran from his legs. I cut off his ears, nose, slit his mouth from ear to ear. Gouged out his eyes. He was dead then. I stuck the knife in his belly and held my mouth to his body and drank his blood. I picked up four old potato sacks and gathered a pile of stones. Then I cut him up. I had a grip with me. I put his nose, ears and a few slices of his belly in the grip. Then I cut him through the middle of his body. Just below the belly button. Then through his legs about two inches below his behind. I put this in my grip with a lot of paper. I cut off the head, feet, arms, hands and the legs below the knee. This I put in sacks weighed with stones, tied the ends and threw them into the pools of slimy water you will see all along the road going to North Beach. I came home with my meat.

It became apparent to police that Fish was the so-called 'Vampire Killer' who had abducted and murdered four girls in 1933 and 1934, luring them to a basement before flogging them and garrotting them with a rope. He was also responsible for the 1932 murder of a sixteen-year-old girl on Massapequa, Long Island. He had been painting a building there at the time of her disappearance.

Albert Fish's life could only be described as harsh and brutal. Born Hamilton Fish in 1870, he developed into a sickly, introverted child who suffered from headaches, blackouts and a bad stutter after falling from a cherry tree. When his father died in 1875, his mother placed him in an orphanage where he changed his name to Albert to avoid the nickname 'Ham and Eggs' with which the other orphans had labelled him.

It was a tough regime. Beatings and whippings were frequent, but pain was never something Albert shied away from – on the contrary, he began to enjoy it, to the extent that he would experience erections, something else for the other kids to mock him with. Back with his mother by the age of twelve, he entered into a homosexual relationship with a telegraph boy who introduced him to the world of perverted sex. Coprophagia and the drinking of urine became regular features of their relationship, while young Albert liked nothing better than to spend his weekends watching boys undress at the public baths.

By 1890, aged twenty, he was working as a male prostitute in New York, but his spare time was spent stalking and raping young boys. Then, in 1898, he surprisingly tried to change his ways by getting married. He took a job as a house painter but old habits die hard and his molestation of children – mostly boys under the age of six – continued unabated. Having become interested in castration around this time, he was about to try it out on a man he had met but the man fled before Fish was able to carry it out.

He was sent to New York's notorious Sing Sing prison in 1903 for embezzlement. For a man like Fish, however, it was really no hardship. Sex was easier to come by in a prison crammed with desperate, frustrated inmates.

Throughout, he remained married, but in 1917, his wife left him for another man and Fish's behaviour seems to have become odder than ever. He said he began to hear voices and on one occasion wrapped himself in a carpet, claiming that he had been ordered to do so by St John. His children witnessed him beating his own naked body with a piece of wood studded with nails until blood poured from his wounds. On another occasion, they watched as he stood at the top of a hill, his hands raised skywards, exclaiming 'I am Christ!'

Horrifically, he also inserted needles into his groin. Following his arrest, an X-ray uncovered twenty-nine of them. He was also partial to inserting into his anus an alcohol-soaked ball of cotton wool which he would then ignite. It was a way, he believed, of cleansing himself of his sins. It would take more than that, however.

Albert Fish was delighted to hear that he had been found guilty and sentenced to death, noting that being electrocuted would represent 'the supreme thrill of my life'.

He was strapped into Sing Sing's electric chair, 'Old Sparky', at 11.06 on 16 January 1936 and three minutes later was dead, having muttered the words 'I don't know why I'm here!' just before the switch was thrown.

THE LONELY HEARTS KILLERS

Martha Jule Seabrook was a big girl. Born in Milton, Florida in 1919, she was obese by the age of ten, but, due to a glandular condition, was also physically mature. Inevitably, something of an oddity at school, she was ridiculed and bullied. It wasn't much better at home, where her mother was constantly on her case and, as she would later claim, she was the victim of sexual abuse from her brother. By the time she was a teenager, she had retreated inside herself and lived a lonely existence with no friends to speak of.

Life got better, however. She enrolled in a nursing school in Pensacola and graduated at the top of her class in 1942, aged twenty-two. She remained obese, however, and this made finding nursing work difficult. Instead, she took a job in a funeral parlour preparing female bodies for burial. Soon, however, she tired of hanging out with dead people, although at least they could not make fun of her weight. She moved to California where she at last found a job as a nurse in a US Army hospital. She began to date soldiers she met in the town's bars and was soon pregnant. Her lover was horrified, however, and attempted suicide. She fled back home to Milton, ashamed and alone.

In Milton she put on a wedding ring she had bought, telling everyone that she had married a naval officer in California who was now at sea but would be coming home soon. Realising, of course, that she would not be able to keep up this pretence forever, she composed a telegram to herself saying that her 'husband' had been killed in action, feigning hysterics when she received the news. Her sad story even ended up in the local newspaper. A few months later, in spring 1944, she gave birth to a daughter.

She fell pregnant again later that year, but this time the man, Alfred Beck, did the decent thing and the couple married. It was short-lived, however, and just six months later they were divorced.

Martha hit a new low, retreating into a fantasy world of romance and unreality. But her professional life picked up when in 1946 she landed a position at a children's hospital in Pensacola, eventually being promoted to nurse superintendent of the institution. She was still very lonely, however, and dreamed of finding a soul-mate, someone with whom she could share her life. Desperate, she placed an advert in *Mother Dinene's Family Club for Lonely Hearts*, carefully omitting to mention that she weighed around seventeen stone.

Her Prince Charming turned out to be a Hawaiian of Spanish descent who had been brought up in Connecticut. Raymond Martinez Fernandez had been a sickly child, but by the age of twenty when he had travelled to Spain to work on his uncle's farm, he was a darkly handsome, well-built young man. In Spain he fell in love with and married a local woman, Encarnacion Robles.

At the outbreak of the Second World War, Raymond was serving in the Spanish merchant marine but is said to have been engaged by the British secret service as a spy. Little is known about his work during this time, but the British spoke well of his efforts on their behalf. The war over, he decided to return to the United States and once established there, planned to send for his wife and their new son, their second child. On board a freighter bound for Curacao in the Dutch West Indies, however, he suffered an accident that changed his life completely. As he climbed a flight of stairs leading to the ship's deck, a steel hatch crashed down onto his head, fracturing his skull. He was stretchered off the vessel in December 1945 and remained in hospital for the next four months. When he emerged, he was a different person. The warm and sociable young man he had been was replaced by a surly, cold person, liable to erupt into anger at any moment.

He boarded a ship bound for Alabama, but was found at customs to be in possession of a large quantity of clothing and other items that he had stolen from the ship's storeroom. He spent the next year in the federal penitentiary at Tallahassee. Sharing a cell with a Haitian man, he was introduced to the mysteries of the ancient West African religion, Vodun, and the rituals of voodoo.

Fernandez began to believe that he could gain a mysterious power over women using voodoo. He could make love with them over great distances by sending them envelopes that contained magical voodoo powder. A lock of his target's hair or a personal item could also heighten the control he wielded over them.

Released from prison in 1946, he moved in with his sister in Brooklyn and started to write to gullible women who had placed ads with lonely hearts clubs. He made contact, met the women and seduced them before fleecing them for as much as he could get. The women, embarrassed and humiliated, rarely reported the incidents to the police and Fernandez would just move on to his next victim.

He travelled back to Spain in October 1947, but in the company of one of his victims, Jane

Lucilla Thompson, a woman he had wooed by correspondence before persuading her to buy them both cruise tickets. Astonishingly, he took her with him when he went to visit his wife Encarnacion and his children. The two women seemed to get on and the three of them were seen dining out together. One night, however, there seems to have been some kind of disagreement and Fernandez was reported to have run from the hotel room he shared with Jane. Next morning she was found dead and quickly buried without a post-mortem or an investigation. He hurriedly left town and sailed back to the United States where he moved into Jane's apartment in New York. The fact that her elderly mother still lived there did not seem to bother him.

Meanwhile, he continued his philandering with lonely women across America. One of the women he contacted and began a relationship with by correspondence was Martha Seabrook Beck. His was the first and only letter she received from her ad with Mother Dinene's club and he described himself as a wealthy businessman living in New York City. His words seemed to the desperate Martha to be sincere and courteous. She wrote back and in the next two weeks exchanged a dozen letters with him. She worried about sending photographs, fearing that her size would put him off. So, she sent pictures in which her full bulk was hidden. Of course, it mattered not a jot to Raymond Fernandez what size she was. The only size that mattered to him was that of her bank account.

He followed his standard procedure, asking for a lock of her hair and performing the voodoo ritual that he believed put her under his spell. They arranged to meet and on 28 December, he climbed off a train in Pensacola. Of course, he made no outward sign of being surprised at the seriously overweight woman waiting to greet him, but Martha was delighted by his Latin good looks. Soon, he was sharing her bed.

When Fernandez returned to New York, he told her he would soon be back or that he would send money so that she and her children could join him in New York. She took this as nothing short of a marriage proposal and told everyone. When he wrote to her explaining that she had misinterpreted him and that he would not be coming back, she threatened suicide. He agreed to let her visit him. She stayed for two wonderful weeks but when she returned to Pensacola, she discovered that she had been fired from her job because of her scandalous relationship. She upped sticks and got on a bus to New York with her children.

When she arrived on his doorstep in January 1948, he allowed her to stay but persuaded her to abandon her children outside a Salvation Army shelter. She would not see them again until the electric chair was staring her in the face just over two years later.

Fernandez was soon explaining to Martha how he made his money, the scams he pulled on widows, divorcees and spinsters, and Martha saw nothing wrong in helping him to continue in his line of work. She had now completely committed herself to him and he seemed to be happy to let her into his life. She would even lend more credibility to his scams.

They selected a victim.

In February, with Martha pretending to be his sister-in-law, they travelled to Pennsylvania where at the end of the month Fernandez married Esther Henne with whom he had been corresponding for some time. The happy couple returned to Fernandez's apartment in New York where he tried to persuade his new wife to sign over to him her insurance policies and pension. When she heard about his trip to Spain and how Jane Thompson had died during the trip, she became frightened and fled the apartment.

She was not his last wife, however. He married Myrtle Young in Arkansas in August 1948 but Martha made life so difficult for the woman that she began to become troublesome. Tiring of his new wife, Fernandez dosed her with drugs and put her on a bus back to Arkansas. Stretchered comatose from the bus in Little Rock, Myrtle died in hospital the following day.

Late in 1948, the couple settled on a victim they hoped would bring them a decent payout. Janet Fay was a sixty-six-year-old widow who lived in Albany, New York, a woman who was a regular churchgoer and who had that thing that Fernandez always looked for in his women – a fat bank account. Soon, Janet had accepted his proposal of marriage and in January 1949, she cleaned out her Albany bank accounts – a sum of $6,000 – and they moved into an apartment on Long Island with Martha, posing as Fernandez's sister.

They lasted one night in the apartment. Martha became insanely jealous when she caught sight of Raymond in bed with his new wife and claims to have suffered a blackout during which Janet was bludgeoned on the head with a hammer. She said she came to with the elderly woman lying there with blood pouring from her wound. Janet was then garrotted with a scarf.

Amazingly, the murderous couple tidied up the mess, dragged Janet's body into a closet and went to bed. Next day, they bundled her into a trunk which they left with his sister for eleven days before burying it in the cellar of a rented house and covering the grave with cement.

Meanwhile, they typed letters, signing them with Janet's name, and sent them to her family to reassure them. The family were immediately suspicious, especially as Janet had never learned to type or possessed a typewriter. They went to the police.

By this time, however, Martha and Fernandez had left town, making for Grand Rapids where a forty-one-year-old widow named Delphine Downing and her two-year-old daughter Rainelle became their next victims. They moved in with Delphine in January 1949 and all went well until one morning she happened upon Fernandez without his toupee in the bathroom. She had not known that he was bald. She went mad, accusing him of deceiving her but Martha persuaded her to take some pills to calm her down. Fernandez found a gun belonging to Delphine's late husband and, wrapping it in a towel to muffle the sound, placed it against her head while she slept. He pulled the trigger and killed her while her young daughter looked on. They buried the dead woman in the basement and once again used cement to conceal the grave.

They were left with the problem of Rainelle, however, who would not stop crying. As Fernandez searched the house for what valuables he could find, the constant crying began to irritate him and he ordered Martha to kill the girl. Initially she refused, no doubt remembering her own young children, but she soon relented, filling a metal bath with water and plunging the toddler's head into it until she was lifeless. They dug a smaller grave next to Delphine's and buried the dead baby.

Foolishly, they decided not to leave town immediately, going to see a movie instead. On their return they started to pack, but it was too late. A knock at the door signalled the arrival of the police and the end of the road for the Latin lothario and his large partner in crime.

There was no death penalty in Michigan, so the pair were extradited to New York where they would face death in the electric chair if found guilty.

In the boiling heat of the summer of 1949, the two became the stars of one of the most sensational trials New York had ever seen. Newspaper reporters fell over each other trying to get the lurid details of the relationship between Martha and Fernandez to their offices. Women waited in long queues trying to gain entrance to the courtroom where the explicit sexual details of the relationship were unfolding. The press focused on her size, humiliating her with nicknames such as 'Big Martha'. She explained the problems she had encountered as a child, the incestuous attacks and her suicide attempts, but there was only one verdict. On 18 August, after a trial lasting forty-four days, the jury spent just one night deliberating before pronouncing the couple guilty of first-degree murder. They were sentenced to die in the electric chair on 10 October at New York's notorious Sing Sing prison.

The circus continued for the next couple of months as Martha and Fernandez proclaimed undying love for each other one day and loathing the next. At the last minute she sent him a note telling him she loved him and he announced, 'Now I am ready to die! … tonight I'll die like a man'.

Raymond Fernandez, the great lover, was first into the execution chamber. His last words were, 'I want to shout it out. I love Martha! What do the public know about love?' But he was terrified and had to be carried struggling to the chair.

A few minutes later, Martha walked in, wedging her huge frame into the chair with difficulty. As they strapped her in, she mouthed the word, 'So long', but no sound emerged. By 11.24 she was dead.

ALBERT DESALVO
THE BOSTON STRANGLER

Between June 1962 and January 1964, the city of
Boston was gripped by a terrible panic. A series of
gruesome murders were terrorising the city's single
women, forcing them to hide behind their locked
doors and making them fearful of the slightest noise.
The killer sexually abused and strangled his victims,
leaving a trademark stocking tied in a neat bow
around their necks. The media gave him a number
of nicknames, but the one that stuck still brings a
shudder to those who lived through those years –
the Boston Strangler.

The first victim was fifty-five-year-old divorcee
Anna Slesers who had emigrated to the United
States from Latvia in 1952. She had been hit on the
head with a blunt instrument before being strangled
while she lay on the floor unconscious. The killer
had used the cord of her bathrobe and left it tied
in an elaborate bow. He had opened her bathrobe
and grotesquely spread her legs wide apart before
sexually assaulting her with an unknown object.

Before leaving, he had ransacked the apartment, scattering the contents of her handbag on the floor. Her gold watch and jewellery had not been taken, however.

Sixteen days later, on 30 June, he killed again. Sixty-eight-year-old Nina Nichols had been on the phone to a friend when her doorbell rang. She said she would call back and went to answer the door. When she failed to ring back, the friend called her, but getting no answer, she phoned the janitor, asking him to go and check. Nina Nichols was found in much the same position as Anna Slesers. She had been sexually assaulted with a wine bottle and around her neck was the trademark bow, formed out of the two nylon stockings he had used to strangle her. There was semen on her thighs but not in her vagina. The apartment had again been ransacked, but once again he left behind valuables.

The strangler was having a busy day because about three hours after he had killed Nina Nichols, he killed again.

Retired nurse, Helen Blake, a sixty-five-year-old divorcee, who lived in the Boston suburb of Lynn, was strangled between 8.00 and 10.00 am, but her body was not discovered for two days, after friends became worried that she had not been around and was not answering her phone. Police officers found her lying face down on her bed. She had been sexually assaulted, like the others, with an object. He had strangled her with her stockings and then tied her brassiere in a delicate bow around her bruised neck. This time he had bothered to remove a couple of diamond rings from her fingers and had made an unsuccessful attempt to break into a metal strongbox.

The city was, by now, fervent with anxiety and fear. Women were warned not to open their doors to strangers, warnings that had not stopped the last couple of victims letting the killer in, because there were no signs of forced entry at their apartments. All police leave was cancelled and all other cases were ignored as every detective in Boston was put onto the Strangler case. None of this seemed to make any difference, however, because he continued to kill at will. Seventy-five-year-old widow, Ida Irga, was found strangled on 21 August. She had been dead for two days when she was found. He had used his hands to strangle her this time, but had then tied a pillow case in a bow around her neck. She had been sexually assaulted with an object and bitten. This time her legs were spread apart, balanced on two chairs, exposing her private parts.

Just a day later, he killed another elderly woman. When she was found, sixty-seven-year-old Jane

Sullivan had been dead for ten days, kneeling in the bathtub, her face immersed in six inches of water. A large Irishwoman, she had struggled with her assailant, suggesting that he was a man of some strength. She had two stockings tied in a bow around her neck and had been assaulted sexually with a broom handle.

People began to relax when nothing happened for three months, but on 5 December, he was back. Twenty-one-year-old Sophie Clark, his only African-American victim, failed to answer the door to two friends. When they let themselves in, they made a horrific discovery. She had been raped – the first killing where rape could definitely be established – and there was a semen stain on a nearby rug, indicating that the Strangler had also masturbated over her dead body.

One of Sophie Clark's neighbours gave police their first description of a man they believed could be the killer. She had let a man into her apartment who claimed that he had been sent to repair her bathroom ceiling. When he had started to make comments about her figure, she became concerned. She frightened him off by saying that her husband was asleep in the bedroom. He mumbled that he had the wrong apartment and fled. He was between twenty-five and thirty years old, she said, of average height and with honey-coloured hair. When they checked, they discovered that the building supervisor had not sent anyone to do repairs that day. She had met the Boston Strangler.

On the last day of 1962, twenty-three-year-old Patricia Bisquette's boss became concerned when she failed to show up for work. He called the building's janitor who gained entry through a window. She lay dead in bed with the covers pulled up to her chin. When they uncovered her, the trademark bow had been tied around her neck with her stockings and one of her blouses.

On 13 February 1963, a German girl, Gertrude Gruen, fought off an attack by the Strangler. He knocked on the door saying he had been sent to do some work. She did not want to let him in, but after an argument, she relented. When she had her back to him, he grabbed her, wrapping a powerful arm around her neck. She grabbed his hand and sank her teeth into it, to the bone. He pushed her away and she began to scream for help. He fled.

Unfortunately, she was unable to give a description of his face, but told them he had a beaky nose and was about 5 foot 8 inches in height.

His next victim was not so lucky. Sixty-nine-year-old Mary Brown was killed on 9 March in Lawrence, an industrial town twenty-five miles from Boston.

Her skull had been smashed with a piece of lead piping and she was not considered as a victim of the 'Phantom' as the press were calling the killer. Her breasts had been exposed and a fork stuck into one of them. He had strangled her with his hands.

He also deviated from his normal modus operandi with his next victim, twenty-three-year-old student, Beverley Sams. Although her position and the bow around her neck were as usual, she had been killed by four stab wounds to the throat and there were a further eighteen stab wounds around her left breast.

There were no further incidents throughout the summer of 1963, but there was no relaxation of the pressure on the police to make an arrest. They even recruited clairvoyants and seers to try to solve the case but to no avail.

It started up again on 8 September when Evelyn Corbin, a fifty-eight-year-old divorcee, was found strangled with her stockings. There was semen in her mouth as well as in her vagina.

The 23 November 1963, the day that Lee Harvey Oswald assassinated President John F. Kennedy, was also the last day of Lawrence Sunday school teacher Joanne Graff, who was strangled and raped. Earlier that day, a couple had heard someone in the corridor outside their apartment. They opened the door to find a man knocking at the door of the apartment opposite. When he asked if Joanne Graff lived there, they told him that she lived on the floor below. He went downstairs and they heard the door below open and close. Concerned, they telephoned Joanne ten minutes later but there was no reply.

He killed for the last time on 4 January 1964. Nineteen-year-old Mary Sullivan was found seated on her bed. Her legs had been parted and she had a broom handle inserted into her vagina. There was semen in her mouth. Propped against her foot was a greetings card wishing its finders a 'Happy New Year'.

The murders had ended but there was a new threat, a rapist known as 'The Green Man' because of the green clothing he wore. His area of operation was wide – he covered Massachusetts, Connecticut, New Hampshire and Rhode Island and he was busy, raping four women in one day. He would gain entrance to an apartment, sometimes by forcing the lock, and threatened his victims with a knife. He was never physically violent and sometimes apologised as he left his victim.

In November 1964, Albert DeSalvo, a small-time crook, was arrested after being identified as a man who had assaulted a woman who woke to find him in her bedroom. He was dressed entirely in green and even wore green sunglasses. He tied her to the bed, tore off her nightclothes, kissed her and bit her from head to foot before finally ejaculating on her stomach. He abused her sexually for some time and then apologised and left.

She gave police such a good description that, on looking at the sketch produced by an artist, one of them said that he looked like the 'Measuring Man'.

The 'Measuring Man' had been the perpetrator of a series of bizarre sexual offences in the Cambridge area in the early 1960s. A man in his late twenties would knock on an apartment door and if it was opened by a young, attractive woman, he would introduce himself as an employee of a modelling agency that was on the lookout for prospective models. He told her she could earn $40 an hour, reassuring her that it was all above board and would not involve nudity. All he needed to do, he said, was take their measurements. He would take out a tape measure and take down their vital statistics. He then told them that someone from the agency would call them if they were suitable, before taking his leave of them. In March 1961, Albert DeSalvo was arrested as he tried to break into a house. He was the 'Measuring Man'.

Albert DeSalvo was twenty-nine years old, a construction worker who had been arrested frequently for burglary. Born in Chelsea, Massachusetts in 1931, he had a troubled upbringing, being beaten often by his abusive father. At an early age, he was well known to the police. He enlisted in the US Army in 1948 and met his wife Imgard during a posting to Germany. He received an honourable discharge in 1956.

When his daughter was born with a physical handicap, Imgard became worried that if she had another child, it too would have problems. She stopped having sex with Albert, a problem for a man of his voracious sexual appetite.

Meanwhile, he was still getting into trouble with the law, usually for house-breaking, but he still managed to hold down a job. He was viewed by others as a hard-working and a devoted family man.

After his arrest in 1960, DeSalvo confessed to being the 'Measuring Man', admitting to assaulting three hundred women and breaking into four hundred apartments. He received an eighteen-month prison sentence and was released in April 1962, just two months before the Boston Strangler killed his first victim.

Now, while being held awaiting trial on the Green Man rapes, in Bridgewater State Hospital, he confessed to another inmate, George Nassar, that he was the Boston Strangler. Nassar passed it on to his lawyer and the police were informed. Some speculated that DeSalvo, with his photo-graphic memory, could have soaked up all the information he seemed to have about the Strangler murders from newspaper accounts. DeSalvo, people said, had nothing to lose. He was going to be in prison for the rest of his life, anyway. This was just a way of earning money from book and movie deals for his wife and their handicapped daughter.

There was a great deal of debate over his sanity when the Green Man case came to court. His lawyer, F. Lee Bailey, tried to prove that he was not mentally competent to stand trial, using his confession to the thirteen murders to confirm this. Experts also testified that he was a paranoid schizophrenic, but the jury did not agree. After only four hours' deliberation, they pronounced him guilty of all charges and he was sentenced to life in prison.

In November 1973, Albert DeSalvo was stabbed to death at Walpole State Prison. Some suggested that he had been killed because he was about to reveal the true identity of the Boston Strangler.

He was never charged for the Boston Strangler killings and neither was anyone else.

CHARLES MANSON

It was 1967 and the Summer of Love was in full swing in San Francisco. The streets of the city's Haight-Ashbury area were a mecca for gaudily clad hippies and dropouts, and drugs and sex were in plentiful supply. It was into this world that thirty-two-year-old Charles Mille Manson arrived, newly released from a ten-year stretch in prison for violation of the Mann Act which prevented the transportation of women across a state line for immoral purposes.

San Francisco was a revelation for Charlie. He had, after all, spent more than half his life in institutions of one kind or another. Life had never been kind to him.

He was born in 1934 to sixteen-year-old Ada Kathleen Maddox in Cincinnati. His father was unknown and in fact, due to his mother's promiscuity, could have been any one of a number of men, although a Colonel Scott from Ashland, Kentucky, is often cited. His mother gave him the name Manson, from a man to whom she had been married briefly. She was a poor role model to her young son, a heavy drinker and possibly even a prostitute, and when Charlie was just five years old, she was sent to prison for the armed robbery of a petrol station with her brother. Her son was sent to West Virginia where he stayed with an aunt and uncle, returning to his mother when she was paroled in 1942. Life consisted of a series of cheap, run-down hotel rooms and his mother's men.

She tried to have the boy fostered, but was unsuccessful. Instead, a court sent him to Gibault School for Boys in Terre Haute, Indiana, a well-known residential facility for delinquent and pre-delinquent young boys. It was supposed to make Charlie a better person, but he hated its strict discipline and ran back to his mother after just ten months. It was the last thing Ada wanted and she informed him that from now on he was on his own. Charlie responded by robbing a grocery store to get enough cash to rent a room.

The only way he could survive was by burglary and theft, but he was soon in trouble and was sent to a juvenile centre in Indianapolis. He ran again, but was recaptured and sent to another institution from which he also escaped in the company of another boy. They tried to get to the other boy's uncle, carrying out a couple of armed robberies en route, but were captured and Manson was sent to the Indiana

School for Boys. In 1951, he and another couple of boys escaped. They were picked up in Utah, driving a stolen car and leaving a string of robberies in their wake. This time it was more serious, however. They had driven a stolen vehicle across the state line, making their offence a federal one. Manson was sent to the National Training School for Boys, a federal government juvenile correctional institution at Fort Lincoln in Washington DC, where he was found to be illiterate and dangerously anti-social. He was also described by a psychiatrist as 'slick' but 'extremely sensitive'. It would later prove a lethal mixture of character traits.

In 1952, he committed his first crime of real violence and the last violent one until 1969. It was just a month before he was due to appear before a parole board when he grabbed another inmate and held a knife to his throat before sodomising him. His status upgraded to 'dangerous', he was transferred to the Federal Reformatory at Petersburg, Virginia, later being moved to a more secure facility at Chillicothe, Ohio. He was sensible for once in his life, remaining a model prisoner until his release in 1955.

Marriage to a Wheeling waitress, Rosalie Willis, produced a child, Charles Manson Jr. Manson worked as a car park attendant and busboy to make ends meet, but he also stole cars to supplement his meagre income. In October 1955, he was arrested for car theft and sentenced to five years' probation, but he violated the conditions of that probation and in March 1956 was sent to prison for three years at Terminal Island in San Pedro. Shortly before a parole hearing, he tried to escape and five years' probation was added to his sentence.

Manson was finally released in 1958, but Rosalie and his son were long gone; she had divorced him while he was incarcerated. He became a pimp to a sixteen-year-old prostitute, but not for long. In 1959, he was in court again for forging a treasury cheque. He received a ten-year suspended sentence.

He married again in January 1960 but, indicted on Mann Act charges, his ten-year sentence was invoked and he was sent to McNeil Island penitentiary in Washington. He was described by prison psychiatrists as a man with 'deep-seated personality problems'.

In prison, Manson watched as English pop combo the Beatles stormed America and, like many young Americans, became obsessed with their music and their style. He learned to play guitar – taught by Alvin Karpis of the Ma Baker Gang who had been in prison since 1936 – and became an aspiring songwriter, spending much of his time in his cell composing songs.

In San Francisco, following his eventual release, Manson could be found busking on street corners but it was not long before he hooked up with a girl, Mary Brunner, a librarian at the University of California at Berkeley. After he moved in with her, however, he began to demonstrate his manipulative and controlling personality by persuading her to allow girls that he met on the streets to also move in. Before long, there were eighteen women living in the apartment, mostly emotionally troubled run-aways – girls who had found that their parents no longer understood them and that society seemed to be against them.

Gradually, Manson became like a guru to these young women, listening to their problems and giving them advice. He also began to explain to them his philosophy, a heady mixture of scientology and religion that was swallowed hook, line and sinker by these impressionable young women. The ready supply of drugs – amphetamines, marijuana and LSD – made manipulation of their thoughts and beliefs even easier. Before long they would have followed Charlie anywhere.

Apeing the Merry Pranksters, the group of writers and artists led by Ken Kesey who were amongst the precursors of the hippie movement, Manson bought an old school bus and turned it into a mobile commune. With his girls – the group now calling itself 'The Family' – he drove to Washington State and then down the coast through Los Angeles to Mexico. When they finally arrived back in the San Francisco area, they settled in Topanga Canyon.

Manson had still not given up on his dreams of becoming a pop star and one day he got a lucky break. A couple of the girls were out hitch-hiking when they were picked up by rock star Dennis Wilson, a member of the hugely successful Beach Boys. The girls went back with him to his house and other members of the Family started to visit. Before long, to Wilson's distress, they had all moved in. He spent a fortune on them in the next few months, even paying for studio time for Manson to record his songs. Manson gained introductions to industry luminaries through Wilson, one of them the successful record producer Terry Melcher, son of Doris Day. The Beach Boys even recorded one of his songs, a number titled *Cease to Exist*; they changed the words to 'cease to resist' and re-titled it *Never Learn Not to Love*. It was released as the B-side to their single *Bluebirds Over the Mountain* and was included on the album *20/20*.

His musical career foundered, however, and before long Wilson had thrown them out of his house. They moved to an old ranch, Spahn's Movie

Ranch, which had been used to film a number of westerns, before upping sticks again, settling at a couple of ranches closer to Death Valley.

Manson had continued to evolve his increasingly crazy and violent philosophy. The catalyst arrived in 1969 with the release of the Beatles' album that has come to be known as *The White Album*. Still obsessing about the group, Manson read all kinds of things into the album, believing that it had been recorded only for him and finding secret messages in its songs. It confirmed his belief that African-Americans in US cities would shortly rise up and slaughter the white population. To him, the Beatles represented 'the soul' and he described them as 'part of the hole in the infinite'. *The White Album* contained predictions of the social upheaval about to be unleashed, in messages that were directed solely at the Family.

The track on the album about which he obsessed most was *Helter Skelter* which he thought was a call to action and a description of the mayhem about to erupt. Living back in Topanga Canyon, in a building painted bright yellow that Manson dubbed the Yellow Submarine, he told his followers that they would be safe, hidden in a bottomless pit beneath Death Valley. When finally the black race failed in its bid to rule the world, the Family – enlarged to 144,000 members by that time – would emerge to seize control. He would be the fifth angel, he claimed, the other four angels being none other, of course, than John, Paul, George and Ringo.

They wrote a batch of songs that would contain coded messages intended to trigger the violence and invited Terry Melcher out to the ranch to hear them. When Melcher, understandably, failed to show up, Charlie was incandescent with rage and decided to take revenge. He also thought that perhaps if the Family provided an example to the blacks, it would hurry along their uprising.

Manson targeted a house at 10050 Cielo Drive in Benedict Canyon, Los Angeles, thinking initially that Terry Melcher lived there. The property was now being rented, however, by film director Roman Polanski and his twenty-six-year-old pregnant wife, Sharon Tate.

On 9 August 1969, Charlie unleashed Helter Skelter, ordering Family acolytes Charles 'Tex' Watson, Patricia Krenwinkel, Susan Atkins and Linda Kasabian to go to the house and 'totally destroy everyone in it as gruesome as you can'. They did not let him down.

The first to die was eighteen-year-old Stephen Parent who was driving out of the grounds of the house after visiting caretaker William Garretson who lived in a guest house on the property. Tex Watson shot him dead as he drove slowly through the darkness. He then cut a hole in a screen behind which was an open window. Leaving Kasabian to keep watch at the gate, they clambered through the window and into the house.

They found Polanski's friend Wojciech Frykowski on the couch in the living room. As he roused himself from sleep, he heard the chilling words from Watson, 'I'm the devil and I'm here to do the devil's business'. The girls, meanwhile, rounded up the other occupants – Sharon Tate, thirty-five-year-old Jay Sebring, one of America's top men's hair stylists, and twenty-five-year-old coffee heiress, Abigail Folger. Tate and Sebring were tied together by the neck and the rope was thrown over a roof beam, meaning that they would choke if they made any effort to escape. Watson emptied Folger's purse and then lunged at her with his knife, time and time again. Frykowski, meanwhile, had loosened the towel with which they had tied him up and tried to get away. As he did so, however, Watson bludgeoned him on the head with his gun before firing two bullets into him. At that moment, Linda Kasabian appeared at the door, saying that someone was coming, in an effort to bring the grisly proceedings to an end. Her effort was in vain, however.

Abigail Folger, meanwhile, had run to the pool area of the house, but Watson and Krenwinkel cornered her and stabbed her repeatedly. She was later found to have been stabbed fifty-one times. In the house, Sharon Tate was pleading for her and her unborn baby's life. Coldly, Susan Atkins informed her that she did not care about her or her baby. She and Watson stabbed her sixteen times.

Before they left 10050 Cielo Drive they complied with Manson's wish that they leave a sign of some kind, 'something witchy', he had said. Atkins picked up a towel soaked in Sharon Tate's blood and used it to write the word 'pig' on the wall.

Manson's blood was up. The following night he ordered Watson, Krenwinkel and Leslie van Houten to kill a retired supermarket executive Leno LaBianca and his wife Rosemary at their home in Waverly Drive. The couple had already been victims of what the Family called 'creepy crawls'. They would come back home to find items missing from inside the house and their dogs outside when they knew for certain they had left them inside.

This time Manson came along with them, having criticised them for doing a 'messy job' the previous night. He left before the killing began, however. The couple were stabbed to death, the word 'war' being carved horrifically on Leno's stomach. Rosemary

LaBianca was stabbed a total of forty-one times. On the way out, using the LaBiancas' blood, Krenwinkel wrote 'Rise' and 'Death to pigs' on the walls and a misspelt 'Healther Skelter' on the fridge door.

The LAPD failed to make any connection between the deaths of the movie star and her celebrity friends and the retired couple. It was surmised that the Cielo Drive killings were probably the result of a drugs deal gone wrong. They also failed initially to make the link to the murder a few weeks previously of Gary Hinman, killed by Family members Bobby Beausoleil, Mary Brunner and Susan Atkins because he refused to hand over to the Family, money that Manson thought he had inherited. When the investigating officers learned the words 'political piggy' had been scrawled on the wall at the scene of the crime in Hinman's blood, however, they realised that there was a connection. Their investigations led straight back to the Family and Charles Manson.

Police raided the Family's desert ranches in October and more than twenty Family members were rounded up, including Manson. But the case was blown wide open when Susan Atkins stupidly boasted to cellmates about the killings.

Watson, Krenwinkel and Kasabian were indicted in connection with the Cielo Drive murders and were treated as suspects in the LaBianca case. Kasabian had not been picked up at the ranches but when she gave herself up, everyone involved was now in custody.

When the case came to court, Linda Kasabian had been granted immunity in exchange for testifying against the others. It was a strange trial and the girls remained loyal to the bitter end, making it seem with their testimonies that they had dreamed it all up themselves and that Charlie was innocent. It was to no avail and on 25 January 1971, Manson, along with Krenwinkel and Atkins, was found guilty on all seven counts of murder, Leslie van Houten being found guilty on two counts. Later that year, Tex Watson was also found guilty on seven counts. They were all sentenced to death but when the US Supreme Court declared execution unconstitutional in 1972, their sentences were commuted to life imprisonment.

At the age of fifty-five, Tex Watson became a born-again Christian and runs the Abounding Love Ministeries website from his prison cell; Susan Atkins remained in prison until her death, aged sixty-one, in August 2009; sixty-two-year-old Patricia Krenwinkel is, following the death of Susan Atkins, the longest-incarcerated female inmate in the California penal system; Linda Kasabian retreated into anonymity, refusing interviews and media coverage over the forty years since the killings.

Charles Manson, now seventy-four, languishes in San Quentin State Prison, the swastika he carved into his forehead after his trial still faintly visible.

ED KEMPER

He was a man-mountain, six feet nine inches tall and three hundred pounds in weight when in 1969, aged twenty-one, he was released into the care of his mother, Clarnell, from the Atascadero State Mental Hospital for the criminally insane. He had killed his grandparents when he was fifteen, shooting them following an argument. His grandmother had told him not to shoot any birds when he picked up a gun to go out into the fields around their remote farmhouse at North Fork, high in the Sierra Mountains. He didn't; he shot her instead. Then when his grandfather came home for lunch, he shot him too, as he climbed out of his truck.

Ed had always been a bit strange. At the age of nine, for instance, he buried the family cat alive in the back garden of the family home in Burbank, California. He then dug it up, cut off its head and put it on the end of a stick. He practised murdering people by mutilating his sisters' dolls and engaged in strange sex games with them. Inappropriate behaviour towards his sisters once persuaded his mother to lock him in the basement every night for eight months to prevent him from molesting them.

Before his release, doctors had warned him not to move back in with his mother as they believed that she was at the root of all his problems. Needless to say, after he did, the two fought like cat and dog and she blamed him for the fact that she could not get any dates. Eventually, he could stand it no longer and moved in with a friend in a rented flat at Alameda, near San Francisco.

He worked at a Green Giant canning factory but failed to find a girlfriend, instead playing out in his imagination violent fantasies fuelled by pornography and detective magazines. His job came to an end in 1971 when he was involved in a motorbike accident. He received compensation of $15,000 but was no longer fit to work.

His first murders followed a tempestuous argument with his mother in spring 1972. He left her house in a rage and decided to take it out on someone, preferably a female. Cruising along a highway, he picked up two eighteen-year-old girls, Mary Anne Pesce and Anita Luchessa, hitchhiking to Stanford University where they were both students. As he drove with the girls seated in the car, he pulled a gun and calmly announced that he was going to rape them.

He pulled off the highway onto a side road where he stopped. He forced one of the girls at gunpoint to climb into the boot of his car and then handcuffed the other before stabbing and strangling her. He opened the boot and stabbed the other, terrified girl. He drove the bodies back to his apartment – he had his own place by this time – where he cut off their heads and hands.

Later that night, he had sex with the bodies after removing all their clothes, and the following day he buried the heads and bodies in different places in order to make identification as difficult as possible if they were ever found. He was right. When one of the heads was discovered the following August, it was impossible to tell, without the remainder of the body, how she had died.

The following September, he was out cruising again when he picked up another young hitchhiker, fifteen-year-old ballet student, Aiko Koo. When he announced to her that she was being kidnapped, she became hysterical and he calmed her down by pulling out his gun and threatening her with it. He smothered her into unconsciousness somewhere to the north of Santa Cruz, before strangling her and having sex with her dead body. With her body in the boot of his car, he drove to his mother's house where he spent the evening before taking the body back to his apartment where he once again had sex with her. Next morning, he drove her out into the country and again buried the various parts of her body in different places. He held on to the head, however. It was in the boot later that day when he paid a visit to his psychiatrist. The shrink would have had a field day had he known.

In November 1972, Ed Kemper's records were sealed, meaning that there would be no record available of the 1969 murders of his grandparents. His mother had been fighting for it and his progress had been noted by two psychiatrists.

Ed, however, had not changed.

On the afternoon of 7 January 1973, driving around the Cabrillo College campus, he picked up nineteen-year-old Cindy Schall and dispatched her in a secluded wooded area with a single shot to the head from a gun he had recently purchased. That was one of the benefits of having his records sealed – he was able to own a gun.

He drove the girl's body back to his mother's house where he was living once again and hid her in the closet in his bedroom. Next morning, after his mother had left for work, he dismembered the body, remembering to remove the bullet to prevent anyone finding the body or tracing the bullet back to his gun. He threw the body parts into the sea from a cliff. Some would be found within a few days. He buried her head beneath his mother's bedroom window. 'She always wanted people to look up to her,' he later quipped.

It was obvious that a serial killer was on the loose and the newspapers dubbed him the 'Co-ed Killer' because of the type of girls who were disappearing. Female students were warned against hitchhiking or accepting lifts from strangers, but he still succeeded in picking up a couple of girls on the University of California Santa Cruz campus less than a month later, on 5 February. He had once again had a row with Clarnell and was angry and vengeful. Rosalind Thorpe and Allison Liu became the targets of his vengeance.

Not far from the university, he shot and killed the girls before wrapping them in blankets and putting them in the back seat of his car. He drove back to his mother's house and while his mother was out in the backyard, he decapitated them and had sex with them. It gave him even more of a thrill to know that his mother was nearby as he did this. As before, their dismembered bodies were thrown into the sea.

Several months later, Kemper bought another gun, a .44, but a diligent sheriff, noticing the name, decided he would pay him a visit. He told Kemper that he would take the gun away and that it would be retained by the police until it could be decided by a court whether he could legally own it. Kemper fetched the gun from the boot of his car but he was very shaken after the sheriff drove off. His car had a bullet hole in it and had been carrying blood-soaked bodies very recently. He realised that before long he would be found out.

It was time to end it and he would do that by killing his mother and then giving himself up.

On 20 April 1973 – Good Friday – Ed Kemper and his mother had a raging argument in which she, as usual, humiliated him. The following morning, just before dawn, he went into her bedroom and, as she slept, viciously smashed her skull with a claw-hammer before slitting her throat. He then raped her dead body and cut her head off, taking it through to the living room and placing it carefully on the mantelpiece like a holiday souvenir. He then proceeded to play darts, using the head as a dartboard.

He called a friend of his mother, Sally Hallett, and invited her over to the house for a surprise dinner. As soon as she walked in the door, he clubbed her and then strangled her. As usual, he cut off her head before climbing into his mother's bed and going to sleep. When he woke, he got into his car and drove for miles, through a number of states. In Colorado he pulled over, called the police and told them to come and get him. It was over.

Waiving his right to an attorney, he confessed to everything. He told them about the trophies he had kept from his victims – hair, teeth and skin. He described how he had sliced off the flesh of two of the girls' legs and cooked it in a macaroni casserole. They asked him what would be a fitting punishment for his crimes and he replied calmly, 'Death by torture'.

Declared by psychiatrists to have been sane when committing the murders, Ed Kemper was found guilty of eight counts of first-degree murder and sentenced to life in prison where he has turned out to be a model inmate, quiet and well behaved.

His mother would have been proud.

TED BUNDY

He was a charmer who had little trouble getting women to go with him or to help him. However, his uncontrollable sexual impulses turned him into a killer of at least thirty-five young women between 1973 and 1978. Some estimates put his tally at anywhere up to one hundred. He became desensitised to the dreadful acts of which he was guilty, claiming that the murders were carried out simply to prevent his victims identifying him after he had raped them.

His beginnings had been inauspicious. He was born in a home for unmarried mothers in 1946, probably the result of a liaison between his young mother and her violent and abusive father. His grandparents took him in and pretended that he was their child, trying to avoid the social stigma that surrounded unmarried mothers in those days. So, Bundy grew up believing his mother was his sister. When he finally learned the truth years later when he was at university, he was, understandably, devastated.

He was always a loner, unable to form relationships, a compulsive masturbator who was also a peeping tom. He retreated into himself, his only real interest being the violent pornography that he devoured. He became a thief and was twice arrested for theft as a teenager.

In 1951, his mother married a man called Johnny Bundy and her new husband adopted Ted as his son, giving him his name. Ted, meanwhile, still believed his mother was his sister.

Although he was socially inept, Bundy was, nonetheless, a good student, winning a scholarship to the University of Puget Sound to study psychology and oriental studies. Two semesters later, he transferred to the University of Washington in Seattle where he started seeing a woman. She dumped him when she graduated in 1968, citing his immaturity as the reason.

A strange change came over Bundy around this time. When he was told the truth about his mother, he underwent a personality change, becoming a more focused individual and a great deal less introverted and retiring. In fact, he became so outgoing that he landed the job of managing the Seattle office of Nelson Rockefeller's 1968 presidential campaign. He also found another girlfriend in Elizabeth Kloepfer, a divorcee with a young daughter. Bundy and Elizabeth would remain together until his 1976 arrest for kidnapping.

It is not certain when Ted Bundy killed for the first time. Some suggest that he had been killing when he was a teenager, but the first definite murder that can be attributed to him was in 1974 when he was twenty-seven years old. Around this time, he dropped out of university and, coincidentally, young women started to disappear in the American Northwest.

When not breaking into buildings and attacking women, he had a cunning modus operandi. He would wear a cast on an arm or use crutches or a stick to give the appearance of being, in some way, incapacitated. Then he would ask a girl if she would carry something, books or a box, for instance, to his car. When they reached the vehicle he would pull out a crowbar and smash it down on his victim's head. He would then bundle her into the car and speed off. He was almost caught on a number of occasions. Once, at the Lake Sammanish Resort in Washington State, a number of young women told police how they were approached by a young man saying his name was Ted. He asked them to help him unload his sailing boat from the back of his car. The women had refused and then noticed that he did not have a boat attached to the car.

One girl did help him, however. Twenty-three-year-old Janice Ott was never seen again and a few hours later, nineteen-year-old Denise Naslund also vanished. Witnesses described her as having been in the company of a good-looking, dark-haired young man. The description fitted Bundy.

Other girls had been disappearing in the American Northwest – in all, six would vanish in seven months.

On 12 March 1974, he kidnapped nineteen-year-old Donna Gail Mason as she walked to a jazz concert on the Evergreen State College campus in Olympia and murdered her. A month later, eighteen-year-old Susan Rancourt disappeared as she walked across Ellensburg's Central Washington State College campus in the dark. At the beginning of May, twenty-two-year-old Kathy Parks was abducted at Oregon State University in Corvallis as she walked to another dormitory where she was going to enjoy coffee with friends. On 1 June, twenty-two-year-old Brenda Ball disappeared after leaving the Flame Tavern in Burien, Washington. Ten days later, eighteen-year-old Georgeanna Hawkins disappeared from behind her sorority house at the University of Washington.

In almost every one of these cases, witnesses reported a man calling himself 'Ted', with his arm or a leg in a cast, asking for help to carry something to his car which was reported to be a Volkswagen Beetle. Bodies began to turn up – Janice Ott, Denise

Naslund and an unidentified young woman were found on a patch of wasteland, their bodies having been eaten and scattered by animals.

A huge manhunt was launched and, amazingly, although several people told police that the description of the wanted man closely resembled Ted Bundy, they swiftly eliminated the clean-cut young man from their enquiries.

Bundy decided to study law, enrolling at the University of Utah Law School where he relaunched his career as a murderer in October 1974. This time he spread his net a little wider, travelling to Salt Lake City to kill sixteen-year-old Nancy Wilcox when she left an all-night party on 2 October. Sixteen days later, seventeen-year-old Melissa Smith, daughter of the Midvale police chief, was raped and strangled after leaving a pizza restaurant. Her remains would later be found in the Wasatch Mountains. October was a busy month; on the 18th, he abducted Laura Aimee from a Halloween party in Lehi in Utah. Her body would be discovered by hikers the following month at the bottom of American Fork Canyon.

His next attempt failed. Carol DaRonch was at a shopping mall in Murray, Utah, when Bundy approached her and, telling her he was a police officer, said that someone had been seen trying to break into her car. She went with him to the vehicle, where he told her she had to accompany him to the police station. As they drove off, he suddenly tried to put handcuffs on her, but she struggled, only just preventing him from bringing his crowbar crashing down on her head. She managed to clamber out of the vehicle and survived. Seventeen-year-old Debbie Kent did not. He killed her at a nearby high school just an hour after leaving Carol DaRonch. Later, police officers would find a small key in the car park outside the school. It unlocked the handcuffs that Carol DaRonch had taken from his car.

He moved his killings to the neighbouring state of Colorado, although still attending university in Utah. On 12 January 1975, twenty-three-year-old Caryn Campbell disappeared in the short space between the elevator and her room at the Wildwood Inn at Snowmass where she was on holiday with her fiancé and his children. Her remains would be found the following month. Her skull had been crushed and she had been raped.

Twenty-six-year-old Vail ski instructor, Julie Cunningham, disappeared on 15 March and twenty-five-year-old Denise Oliverson on 6 April, abducted while cycling to her parents' house in Grand Junction. Thirteen-year-old Lynette Culver was snatched from a school playground in Pocatello, Idaho on 6 May, and after 28 June, fifteen-year-old

Susan Curtis was never seen again after walking to her dormitory during a youth conference at Brigham Young University in Provo in Utah.

Bundy was finally arrested by a diligent patrolman in Grainger, Utah on 16 August 1975. When he noticed Bundy driving slowly in an area where some of the abductions had taken place, he indicated to him to pull over. Instead, Bundy sped off and the officer gave chase and caught up with him. In the car was found a ski mask and all the tools of his trade – a crowbar, rubbish bags and an icepick. When he was identified by Carol DaRonch they knew they finally had their man. He was extradited to Colorado where he was also wanted for murder and was held at the jailhouse at Pitkin County Court in Aspen.

Bundy managed to escape on 7 June 1977, leaping from a courthouse window during a recess and vanishing into the holiday crowds. He was free for six days, eventually arrested by a couple of alert deputies as he drove suspiciously at a roadblock.

Sensationally, however, he escaped again on 30 December, through a roof space above his cell, taking with him $500 that he had managed to save while incarcerated awaiting his trial which had been set for 9 January 1978. He stole an MG in town but when its engine gave out in a blizzard in the mountains, he hitchhiked to Vail and travelled by bus, train and plane to Tallahassee in Florida, renting a room under the name Chris Hagen in a boarding house.

Ever resourceful, Bundy established a whole new identity for himself, even obtaining a false birth certificate and social security card in his new name. Shoplifting and stealing purses and credit cards kept him in funds.

The boarding house in which he had a room was close to the sorority houses of Florida State University and it was not long before he began to have familiar urges.

On the evening of 15 January 1978, a student, returning to her sorority house, spotted a man lurking in front of the building. As she was about to telephone the police, a fellow student, Karen Chandler, staggered out of her room with blood pouring from a serious head wound. She shouted hysterically that she and her roommate Kathy Kleiner had been attacked by a madman. Karen and Kathy lived, but two other students, twenty-year-old Lisa Levy and twenty-one-year-old Margaret Bowman were not so lucky. Bundy had battered Lisa Levy with a piece of wood and then strangled her. He had bitten her on the buttocks and nipples and had sexually assaulted her with a bottle of hairspray.

He had not finished for that night, however. A few blocks away he broke into a house in which student Cheryl Thomas was sleeping. He beat her savagely, but she survived. At the foot of her bed police found a ski mask. The evidence was there, but forensic science was not as advanced as it is today and Bundy was, of course, completely unknown to the Florida authorities.

On 9 February, Bundy travelled to Lake City in Florida where he abducted, raped and murdered a twelve-year-old girl, Kimberly Leach. Three days later, he stole another VW Beetle and drove west across the Florida panhandle. On 15 February, he was stopped by a Pensacola police officer who called in a check on Bundy's car registration. When he was told the car was stolen, there was a scuffle but Bundy was subdued. As the officer took him to the police station, Bundy growled, 'I wish you had killed me'.

He once again skilfully conducted his own defence at his trial, charming the jury with his winning personality and using the law to make the case last as long as possible. Graphic details emerged, such as the horrific fact that he often returned to the bodies of the victims he had dumped in remote places, grotesquely applying make-up to them, lying beside them and even having sex with them until putrefaction made it too disgusting, even for him. He kept photographs of them and even took clothing home with him. It came as little surprise when he was found guilty and sentenced to die in the electric chair.

Awaiting execution, Ted Bundy tried to blame pornography for his depraved crimes. He told how he had decapitated at least twelve of his victims with a hacksaw and kept the heads for some time in his apartment before getting rid of them.

He was executed on 24 January 1989. The crowds waiting outside the prison that morning cheered as two thousand volts coursed through his body.

DAVID BERKOWITZ
'SON OF SAM'

It was 17 April 1977 and the murderer known as the '.44 Caliber Killer' had struck again. Not only that, he had left a letter at the scene of the latest crime addressed to one of the police officers involved in the investigation. It read, complete with misspellings galore:

Dear Captain Joseph Borrelli,
I am deeply hurt by your calling me a weman hater.
I am not. But I am a monster. I am the 'Son of Sam'.
I am a little brat. When father Sam gets drunk he
gets mean. He beats his family. Sometimes he ties
me up to the back of the house. Other times he locks
me in the garage. Sam loves to drink blood. 'Go out
and kill,' commands father Sam. Behind our house
some rest. Mostly young – raped and slaughtered
– their blood drained – just bones now. Papa Sam
keeps me locked in the attic too. I can' t get out but
I look out the attic window and watch the world
go by. I feel like an outsider. I am on a different

wavelength then everybody else – programmed too kill. However, to stop me you must kill me. Attention all police: Shoot me first -- shoot to kill or else keep out of my way or you will die! Papa Sam is old now. He needs some blood to preserve his youth. He has had too many heart attacks. Ugh, me hoot, it hurts, sonny boy. 'I miss my pretty princess most of all. She's resting in our ladies house. But I'll see her soon. I am the 'Monster' – 'Beelzebub' – the chubby behemouth. I love to hunt. Prowling the streets looking for fair game – tasty meat. The weman of Queens are prettyist of all. It must be the water they drink. I live for the hunt – my life. Blood for papa. Mr Borrelli, sir, I don't want to kill anymore. No sur, no more but I must, 'honour thy father.' I want to make love to the world. I love people. I don't belong on earth. Return me to yahoos. To the people of Queens, I love you. And I want to wish all of you a happy Easter. May God bless you in this life and in the next.

The letter was released to the public and 'Son of Sam' was born.

On 29 July 1976, two young women, eighteen-year-old Donna Lauria and her nineteen-year-old friend, Jody Valenti, were talking in Jody's car outside the apartment building where Donna lived with her parents in the Bronx. It was getting late, around one in the morning and Donna's parents had already come to the car to tell the girls to call it a night.

After Mr and Mrs Lauria had gone upstairs, the girls talked a little longer before Donna suddenly noticed a man standing beside the car's passenger door. As she wondered out loud to Jody what the man wanted, he suddenly pulled out a Charter Arms .44 Bulldog handgun from a paper bag he was carrying, knelt down and fired five bullets in quick succession into the car, one of the bullets hitting Donna in the neck, killing her instantly. Another ripped into Jody's thigh but she slammed her fist on the car's horn as the shooter ran off. She scrambled from the car just as Donna's father ran down the stairs. They rushed to the hospital, but it was too late for his daughter.

It was a bizarre attack and one with no obvious motive. Police were puzzled, wondering if it might have been a mob hit gone wrong or just a lone psychopath.

Three months later, on 23 October, a twenty-three-year-old was celebrating his last few days as a civilian at a bar in Queens. In four days, Carl Denaro would be enlisting in the US Air Force and he wanted to have a few beers with his friends before leaving.

When the party ended at around 2.30 am, Carl offered to drive home a college friend, Rosemary Keegan. Near her house, he parked his Volkswagen Beetle and they talked. Without warning, the side window of the car seemed to explode and bullets flew into the interior of the car. Carl was wounded in the head but, though terrified, Rosemary was quick-thinking, turning the ignition key and driving the car as fast as she could back to the bar they had left just a short while ago. She saved Carl's life, although a piece of his shattered skull had to be replaced by a metal plate.

Just over a month later, on 26 November, sixteen-year-old Donna DeMasi and her eighteen-year-old friend Joanne Lomino were returning home on the bus from a night at the movies. After the bus had dropped them close to Joanne's house, she noticed a man standing nearby. She whispered to Donna to walk faster. The man was following them.

Coming up close behind them, he began to ask a question – 'Do you know where...? – but halfway through the sentence he drew a gun out from underneath his jacket and shot them. He then emptied the gun by firing at a nearby house.

The girls' screams brought people, including Joanne's family, running from the surrounding houses. The girls were rushed to hospital where

Donna was found to have been extremely lucky. The bullet that had struck her had missed her spine by centimetres and exited her body. Joanne was less fortunate. Her spine had been hit and although she would live, she would be paraplegic.

For two months all went quiet, but he struck again on 30 January 1977. Twenty-six-year-old Christine Freund and her fiancé John Diel had left a wine bar in Queens at around ten minutes past midnight and as they walked to their car they failed to notice a man watching them from the shadows. They had just got into the vehicle when two gunshots smashed the windscreen into a thousand pieces. Christine lifted her hands to her head. She had been hit by both bullets and blood was pouring from the wounds. She died in hospital a few hours later.

Two officers, Detective Sergeant Joe Coffey and Captain Joe Borelli, looked into the backgrounds of Christine Freud, Donna Lauria, Donna DeMasi and Joanne Lomino but could find nothing to connect them and any suspect. They concluded that their perpetrator was a lone psycho stalking attractive young women. A task force was formed to find him.

The killer, meanwhile, kept busy. On 8 March, Virginia Voskerichian, a student at Barnard College, was walking home from classes in the wealthy Forest Hills Gardens area when a man appeared walking towards her. As he approached, he drew a pistol from under his coat and pulled the trigger, hitting her in the face at close range with a single shot. She died on the spot. Running away, the killer passed a man who had witnessed the incident. 'Hi, mister,' the shooter said as he ran past, as if nothing had happened.

The bullet came from the same gun as the one that had killed Donna Lauria the previous July, but police were at a loss as to how they could prevent such random shootings. All they could do was issue an incomplete description of the killer. He was a white male, twenty-five to thirty-six years old, six feet tall, of medium build and with dark hair. It wasn't much to go on but Deputy Inspector Timothy O'Dowd, who was in charge of the Operation Omega task force assembled to find the killer, was determined to give it his best shot.

The killer's next victims were a couple of young lovers kissing in their car near the Hutchinson River Parkway on 17 April. A car pulled up alongside their vehicle at around three in the morning, and eighteen-year-old Valentina Suriani and her twenty-year-old boyfriend Alexander Esau were both shot dead, Valentina dying at the scene and Alexander later in hospital.

This time it was a little different. He left a letter

for Borelli and at least had given himself a name.

A psychological profile of the man they were looking for described him as a paranoid schizophrenic who might have thought that he was in possession of some kind of power, perhaps demonic. He was, inevitably, a loner who had problems in making relationships, especially with women.

Of course, the task force was inundated with calls about suspicious men who were more often than not just a little odd or, at least, different to the people who were calling in. The checking of all these calls provided a mountain of work.

Sam, meanwhile, took it upon himself to put pen to paper again, writing to the well-known *Daily News* reporter, Jimmy Breslin.

Hello from the cracks in the sidewalks of NYC and from the ants that dwell in these cracks and feed in the dried blood of the dead that has settled into the cracks. Hello from the gutters of NYC, which is filled with dog manure, vomit, stale wine, urine, and blood. Hello from the sewers of NYC which swallow up these delicacies when they are washed away by the sweeper trucks. Don't think because you haven't heard [from me] for a while that I went to sleep. No, rather, I am still here. Like a spirit roaming the night. Thirsty, hungry, seldom stopping to rest; anxious to please Sam. Sam's a thirsty lad. He won't let me stop killing until he gets his fill of blood. Tell me, Jim, what will you have for July 29? You can forget about me if you like because I don't care for publicity. However, you must not forget Donna Lauria and you cannot let the people forget her either. She was a very sweet girl. Not knowing what the future holds, I shall say farewell and I will see you at the next job? Or should I say you will see my handiwork at the next job? Remember Ms. Lauria. Thank you. In their blood and from the gutter – 'Sam's creation' .44.

On 10 June, Jack Cassara received a bizarre get-well note in his mailbox, from someone called Carr. It wished him well following his fall from the roof of his house and was signed 'Sam and Francis'. What was strange about it was that Cassara had not fallen from his roof. He called Sam and Francis Carr, whom he had never met, and arranged to meet. They told him that they too had been receiving odd notes, about their dog Harvey and how he had been shot. Harvey had not been shot. They called in the police to investigate.

Later, Cassara's nineteen-year-old son Stephen remembered that a man called David Berkowitz had rented a room from them for a short time in

1976 and he had failed to return for his $200 deposit when he left. He recalled that Berkowitz was always bothered by their dog.

Jack Cassara's wife Nann passed the information on to the Carrs, whose daughter Wheat was a dispatcher for the Yonkers police. She became convinced that Berkowitz was Son of Sam.

It transpired that Craig Glassman, a deputy sheriff who was a neighbour of Berkowitz, had received an anonymous letter that claimed that he, the Cassaras and the Carrs were part of a demon group. Glassman was certain it came from Berkowitz but he told the Carrs that it in no way suggested that Berkowitz was the killer.

In the early hours of the morning of 26 June the windows of Sal Lupo's car, parked outside the Elephas disco in Queens, exploded. As the sound of gunfire deafened him and his passenger, Judy Placido, she glanced in the mirror and saw that she was covered in blood. She had been shot three times and Sal took a bullet in the arm, but they were lucky – they lived.

Son of Sam's last victims were shot a couple of days after the anniversary of his first murder, in the early hours of Sunday 31 July. Attractive blonde Stacy Moskowitz and her boyfriend Bobby Violante were walking in a park when Stacy spotted someone lurking in the shadows. As the couple hurried back to the car, the man disappeared. They kissed before getting into the vehicle and that was when Berkowitz pounced, pumping bullets into them. Stacy fell out of Bobby's arms like a sack of potatoes. Bobby had also been hit, twice in the face. He fumbled the car door open and slammed his fist on the horn.

Stacy died thirty-eight hours later in hospital. Bobby lost an eye and for the remainder of his life would have only partial sight in the other.

Meanwhile, the letters to the Carrs and the Cassaras were passed to the Omega task force. They also finally had a good description of Son of Sam from a woman who had seen a man she was certain had been concealing a gun on the night Stacy Moskowitz was killed. She had seen him screw up a parking ticket that had been put on his car. It was that parking ticket that finally brought Son of Sam's reign of terror to an end.

On 10 August, Berkowitz's apartment house at 35 Pine Street was put under surveillance. The officers waited until a man walked out of the building, a paper bag in his hand. He walked slowly towards the Ford Galaxy that the watching officers knew belonged to Berkowitz. Climbing in and placing the bag on the passenger seat, he was about to turn the key in the ignition, when a police officer approached from the rear of the car. He yelled 'Freeze!' and pointed a gun at the man's head, just as Berkowitz had done to his victims.

The man in the car turned slowly, a stupid smile on his face. He was ordered to get out of the vehicle and to put his hands on the roof.

'Now that I've got you,' said the officer, 'who have I got?'

'You know,' the man replied in a soft voice.

'No, I don't. You tell me,' said the officer.

He paused and, the smile still on his face, said, 'I'm Sam. David Berkowitz'.

His life had been a sad and lonely one. Put up for adoption even before he was born, he was always big for his age and was uncomfortable with other people. He became a bully and developed a nasty streak that made neighbours wary of him. He fell apart after the death of his adoptive mother and became even more introverted and reclusive. Abandoned by his adoptive father who had remarried and moved to Florida, his life became meaningless and he drifted into a fantasy world, never to return.

Before the murders, Berkowitz had been an arsonist, setting 1,488 fires in New York and keeping a diary of them all. He was acting out a control fantasy, according to psychiatrists. Gradually, he sank into paranoia, believing people were out to kill him. He locked himself away in his apartment for a month, scrawling crazy messages on the walls.

He claimed the demons in his head ordered him to kill and he had begun by stabbing a couple of women just before Christmas in 1975. He developed a fantasy in which the Cassaras, whom he rented from, were demons and he believed Jack Cassara to be the head of devil dogs that roamed the streets of New York. Sam Carr was the host of a powerful demon named Sam. It was from this strange fantasy that he took the name Son of Sam. Sam was the devil.

Berkowitz pleaded guilty and was sentenced to 365 years in prison. New Yorkers began to go out at night again.

THE HILLSIDE STRANGLERS

As Detective Bill Geddes approached the green Mercury Bobcat parked in a cul-de-sac near the small town of Bellingham in Washington State, he feared the worst. And that was what he saw when he looked through the rear window of the vehicle. Huddled together on the back seat of the car were the crumpled bodies of two girls who had gone missing the previous evening. They were both fully clothed and had both been viciously strangled before being sexually assaulted.

Murder had come to the Northwest in the form of a couple of America's most vicious serial killers – the Hillside Stranglers.

There was not a lot of crime in Bellingham and police chief Terry Mangan was not initially worried about the report of two girls, Karen Mandic and Diane Wilder, being missing. However, when Karen's boyfriend insisted that she would never go away without telling him and he discovered that she had left her cat unfed, Mangan began to worry.

The night before the report was filed, 11 January 1979, Karen had told her boyfriend that she and Diane had a house-sitting job at the home of a couple who were away on holiday. She had been offered the job by a security supervisor named Kenneth Bianchi, who asked them to stay in the house for a couple of hours while the house's alarm system, which had failed, was taken away and repaired. At $100 for a couple of hours watching TV, it was a lucrative offer.

Mangan checked with the security company to be told that Bianchi was a conscientious young man who could not conceivably have had anything to do with the girls' disappearance. He was a devoted father and, anyway, he did not have the authority to offer the girls such a job. Questioned by Mangan, Bianchi vehemently denied offering the girls the job or even having heard of Karen Mandic.

The chief was now very worried and was sure this was going to end badly, namely with the discovery of the girls' bodies.

Meanwhile, more emerged about the house-sitting job. Karen had said to her boyfriend that she had been told to tell no one about it. Furthermore, the woman living next door to the house, who watered the plants while the owners were away, was asked by the same man who had spoken to Karen to stay away as there would be armed guards patrolling while the alarm system was out of operation. Mangan realised with horror that the girls had been set up. Someone had lured them to the house.

When police officers opened the door of the house they dreaded what they might discover inside, but all was normal apart from a man's wet footprint on the kitchen floor. Still wet, it would have been made at the most within the last twelve hours.

Shortly after, however, a woman responded to a radio appeal, telling police that she had spotted the green Mercury.

The prime suspect was Bianchi who at that point was out driving his security truck. His boss called him and asked him to go to a guard shack to await instructions. The police arrived and arrested the young man, who seemed very surprised, and at the station he continued to deny having spoken to Karen Mandic, maintaining it must have been someone using his name. When his house was searched, however, police found expensive new phones and a new chainsaw hidden in his basement. They had been stolen from places where he worked as a security guard. At least they could arrest him for theft.

The girls were found to have been strangled from behind and it seemed as if the killer had been above them, as if they had been going downstairs in front of him. On the stairs of the house they had been asked to look after, a pubic hair was found. Two more fell from Diane Wilder's body when she was examined. Semen stains were found on both girls' underwear and menstrual blood was found on Bianchi's underpants. Diane Wilder had been menstruating at the time of her murder. There was little doubt; Kenneth Bianchi was guilty.

That night, he had been waiting for them at the house. Karen had driven up first and he had accompanied her inside. By the time Diane turned up a few minutes later, her friend was probably already dead. They had not been raped and he had merely ejaculated on the underwear.

When the police started checking on Bianchi, they called a police officer at Glendale, eight miles north of Los Angeles, where Bianchi used to live. When it was explained to him why they were checking, the officer was speechless. There had been a dozen similar murders in Los Angeles in the past fourteen months. They were carried out by a sex killer the papers were dubbing the 'Hillside Strangler'. Coincidentally, there had been none in the LA area since Bianchi had left town.

Kenneth Bianchi had been born in 1951 to a seventeen-year-old alcoholic prostitute in Rochester,

New York. Put up for adoption, he found a home with Frances Bianchi and her husband, a factory worker. He was a difficult child and by the age of eleven was being treated at the DePaul Psychiatric Center for a variety of problems including 'involuntary urination, tics, absenteeism, and behaviour problems'. His mother dealt with his bladder problems by making him wear sanitary towels. At school, he was lazy, inattentive and disruptive, although he was not lacking in intelligence.

He made it through high school without incident and seemed, in fact, to have turned into a well-groomed, clean-cut kid. But he was odd, a fact confirmed by his claim in a letter to his girlfriend to be the Alphabet Killer, a serial killer operating locally. She just thought it was another example of his strange behaviour.

In 1971, he married Brenda Beck but the marriage lasted only eight months. Bianchi had never let marriage get in the way of his relationships with other women and Brenda walked out as a result. His women were very special to him and he imposed high standards on them. No V-neck sweaters or tight jeans and they had to be totally devoted and faithful to him. His utter lack of faithfulness in return was, of course, irrelevant.

Having tried and failed to become a police officer,

he got a job as a security guard, but merely used the position to steal things for his girlfriends.

In 1975, aged twenty-six, he moved to Los Angeles, moving in with his cousin, Angelo Buono, a nasty piece of work who was an upholsterer and pimp, had been married several times and who abused his children both sexually and physically. He initiated Kenneth Bianchi into his deviant world of perverted and sadistic sex.

Bianchi got a job and moved into an apartment of his own in Glendale, buying a 1972 Cadillac sedan for which he struggled to make the payments. Soon he met a woman named Kelli Boyd and in May 1977 she announced that she was having his baby. He wanted to marry her, but she was reluctant to take that ultimate step, wary of his jealousy, immaturity and compulsive lying. She was even more reluctant when he obtained a fraudulent degree and credentials, rented an office and set himself up as a psychologist. Fortunately, he failed to win many clients.

In 1977, as the Hillside Strangler began to hog the front pages of the newspapers, Bianchi started to pretend he had lung cancer that would require chemotherapy and radiation treatment. He took time off work, even, at one point when he was home, being questioned by detectives investigating the Strangler case; one of the murders may have taken place in the apartment building in which he and Kelli lived. They were only routine enquiries, however, and he was never a suspect.

After the birth of their son, Kelli decided she had had enough and moved back home to live with her parents. Shortly after, however, she agreed to give him another chance. He moved in with her in the small north-western town of Bellingham.

He left behind a trail of bodies.

It had started a few months earlier in October 1977. Two girls that Bianchi and Buono wanted to pimp gave them a fake list of potential clients. They were furious and the first to feel their anger was eighteen-year-old Yolanda Washington, who was strangled with a cloth and left on a hillside. As she had been a prostitute, police did not consider it significant that she had had sex with two men shortly before she died.

A few weeks later, on 1 November, sixteen-year-old Judy Miller was found raped and strangled, with ligature marks on her ankles, wrists and neck, and five days after, twenty-one-year-old waitress Linda Kastin's naked body was found near Glendale Country Club. She had been sodomised and bore identical ligature marks to Judy Miller.

The women who had been killed so far lived lives on the fringes of society and police only became interested when a couple of younger girls from safe, middle-class backgrounds were found dead. Twelve-year-old Dolores Capeda and Sonja Johnson had last been seen standing by a two-tone sedan after getting off the school bus. Their bodies, bearing the Hillside Strangler's characteristic marks, were found by a nine-year-old boy.

In custody, Kenneth Bianchi provided a detailed account of how their next victim, Kristine Weckler, died. 'She was brought into the kitchen,' he said, 'and put on the floor and her head was covered with a bag and the pipe from the gas stove was disconnected, put into the bag and then turned on. There may have been marks on her neck because there was a cord put around her neck to make a more complete sealing.' Kristine took ninety minutes to die.

The bodies were turning up in quick succession. Twenty-eight-year-old Jane King was found on 23 November beside a slip road on the Golden State Freeway, and on 29 November Laura Wagner was found dead.

Police worked out that more than one person was involved, as it would have required two people to have carried the bodies to some of the locations.

However, Bianchi and Buono decided to have a break and let things cool down a little. Nothing happened for a couple of weeks, but on 13 December, seventeen-year-old Kimberly Diane Martin became their ninth victim. A helicopter spotted the tenth on 16 February 1978, in the boot of a car that had been pushed over a cliff.

By this time, Bianchi had moved to Bellingham to be with Kelli and his son. He had decided to go solo and call Karen Mandic.

Under arrest for murder, Bianchi began to claim that he had been forced to kill by one of his multiple personalities, an evil character he called 'Steve Walker'. Under hypnosis, 'Steve' introduced himself. He was eventually proved to be faking it, however, and confronted by the truth, agreed to testify against Buono in return for being spared the death penalty.

He explained how he and his cousin operated. They would pretend to be police officers and would tell prostitutes that they were being taken to the station to be booked. Sometimes they would simply ask for directions and while engaged in conversation, grab their victim and bundle her into the car.

Before his trial, Bianchi dreamed up a bizarre plan with Veronica Compton, a woman with whom he had been corresponding. She was to kill a woman and place Bianchi's semen at the scene, proving that the Hillside Strangler was still out there and throwing the police investigation into turmoil. He smuggled some semen out in a rubber glove hidden inside a book but the woman she tried to kill fought back and Compton was arrested.

Bianchi was given two life sentences in the state of Washington. Transferred then to California, he was given additional life sentences for the other murders. He remains in prison, aged fifty-nine.

Angelo Buono was found guilty of nine murders in 1982. He died in prison in 2002, aged sixty-seven.

CLIFFORD OLSON

The people of Lower Mainland and Fraser Valley in the region of British Columbia had good reason to be scared. In just a few months between November 1980 and July 1981, several children had gone missing. Many of the parents complained that the police were not taking their reports seriously enough; that was until the bodies started turning up.

It was easy to see how these children were lured into the trap. A man, of quite small stature at only 5 feet 7 inches and weighing just 12 stone, was posing as a construction worker. When he approached the youths with the promise of well-paid work, many of them jumped at the offer. The work was genuine, but what the youths did not know was that it involved after-curriculum activities! The words 'Do you fancy a beer after work?' became his catchphrase; the way to lure a youngster into a secluded location, to talk them into going to a motel room with him so that he could carry out his fantasies.

Clifford Robert Olson was born on 1 January 1940 in Vancouver, British Columbia. He was a strange child, a little withdrawn and yet at times deliberately misbehaving to attract attention. He found it hard to make friends and started skipping classes by the time he was just ten years old. His truancy cost him his grades, and from the age of fifteen he was constantly in trouble. He was frequently being picked up by the local police for misdemeanours which ranged from bullying to selling fake lottery tickets, and neighbours frequently complained about the boy who tormented dogs and cats in the vicinity.

When he finally left school, Olson's first job was at a racetrack and by the time he was seventeen, his criminal activities had moved up a gear. He was arrested for just about everything – possession of firearms, fraud, car theft, breaking and entering, armed robbery and parole violations, to name but a few. It is not surprising, therefore, that in July 1957 he was sentenced to a term in the New Haven Borstal Correctional Center. He spent his every waking hour trying to escape, and on one occasion he succeeded just long enough to steal a power boat. By the time Olson was forty-one years old he had spent only four years of his adult life as a free man.

It was hard to understand why Olson was the way he was, since his siblings had grown into normal, law-abiding citizens. His childhood had not been traumatic but his parents had long-since ceased to bail out their son. Eventually they turned their backs on him, for fear that his reputation would tarnish that of the remainder of the family.

It was a grey, cold November afternoon in 1980 when Olson took his first victim. Twelve-year-old Christine Weller was riding her bicycle home towards the Bonanza Motel. She had met up with some friends in the local shopping mall and, realising that she was going to be late home for tea, borrowed a friend's bicycle to make the three-minute ride back to the motel where she lived with her parents.

When Christine didn't arrive at five o'clock, her parents' immediate reaction was that she was staying at a friend's house. She was a popular child, who loved to play outside, and it wasn't unusual for her to have sleepovers. After several days, Christine went on the missing person's list and the police and her parents believed that she had simply run away. It wasn't until they found the bicycle behind an animal hospital just off the highway close to the motel, that the police knew something more sinister had taken place.

On Christmas morning a man walking a dog reported that he had found a decomposed body lying at the back of a rubbish dump. It was the body of Christine Weller. She had multiple stab wounds in

HENRI LANDRU
Was it the constant smell of death during World War
One, the years spent in harsh French prisons, or perhaps
something more sinister that turned Henri-Desire Landru
into a deranged serial killer?

DR MARCEL PETIOT

The arrival of a new, young doctor in Paris caused a stir of excitement. His patients trusted him with their innermost secrets, little did they know that underneath the physician's facade lay a murderer of what he described as 'enemies of the state'.

PETER MANUEL
Scotland's first serial killer, Peter Manuel, was a deviant who could not be satisfied by normal sexual activity. His brutal crimes shocked the nation in the late 1950s, and no one would rest until the man they regarded as the 'sex beast' was hanged.

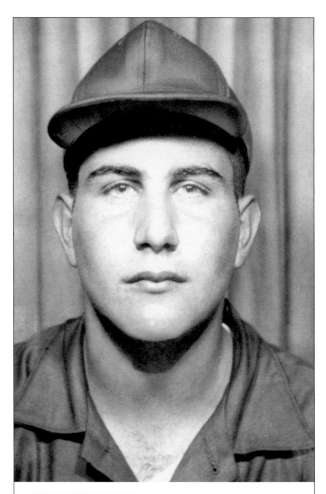

DAVID BERKOWITZ
David Berkowitz was better known as the 'Son of Sam'. His crimes in New York City during the 1970s became legendary because of the bizarre content of letters he wrote to the police and media giving his reasons for killing – a demon dog.

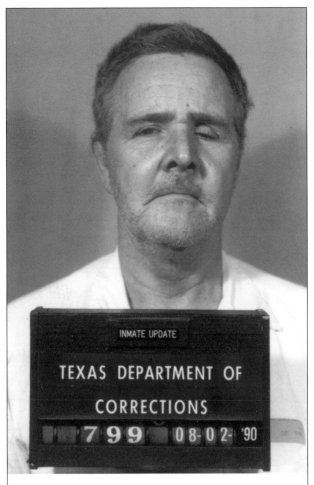

HENRY LEE LUCAS
Henry Lee Lucas confessed to over 500 murders after experiencing a 'religious conversion' while behind bars. Whether a prolific killer or an impulsive liar, Lucas definitely had a twisted list of crimes including rape, necrophilia, bestiality, molestation and, of course, murder.

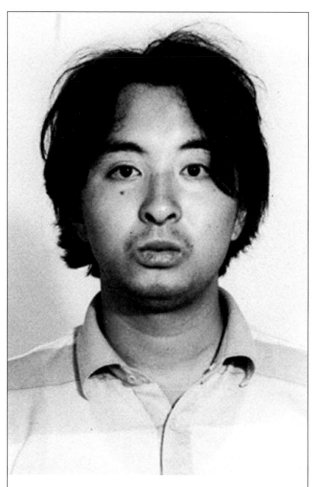

TSUTOMU MIYAZAKI
Tsutomu Miyazaki was Japan's most reviled serial killer. Although his crimes took place more than two decades ago, the mention of his name still sickens many Japanese. He was a voracious sexual predator who kidnapped young girls, ate their body parts and even slept next to their corpses.

ALBERT FISH
Albert Fish is one of the most deranged criminals to have
ever lived in the United States. By his own admission he
molested over four hundred children and murdered sixteen
over a period of twenty years. He was eventually caught for
the murder of Grace Budd and executed for that crime.

CHARLES MANSON
Charles Manson had a powerful ability to control his followers in his quest to 'take over the United States'. He was responsible for the deaths of nine people during a killing rampage in 1969.

her chest and abdomen and she had been strangled with a leather belt.

Christine's death was just the first of many to take place in the greater Vancouver area. Youths of both sexes, between the ages of nine and eighteen, gradually began to disappear, but it took the police a long time before they were aware that they had a serial killer on their hands.

The police were still looking into the murder of Christine, when thirteen-year-old Colleen Daignault went missing on Thursday 16 April 1981. Colleen was a shy girl who lived with her grandmother. She had spent the night with a friend, but told her grandmother she would be back home by four o'clock the following afternoon. Colleen had been standing at the bus stop waiting for the bus to take her home, when a car pulled up and a man leaned out of the window and caught her attention. Colleen became another statistic on the missing persons' list, and the police simply treated her case as a runaway. Her remains were not discovered until 17 September later that year.

Five days after Colleen disappeared, a sixteen-year-old boy went missing. Daryn Johnsrude had only been in Vancouver for two days when he went missing. The trip had been a birthday treat from his father, so that Daryn could visit his mother and his younger brother and sister. He quickly befriended some children of similar age who frequently met up at the local shopping mall. Many of these children lived in a complex owned by Olson, and Olson himself could often be seen hanging around the mall. He seemed to have an inordinate need to be with young people and, with his smiling face and pleasant manner, he became part of the gang. Mind you, behind his back some of the kids called him the 'creepy bogey man', but none of them suspected the sinister side to his nature.

Daryn's battered body was found lying in a dyke on the bank of the Fraser River on 2 May 1981. He had been killed by repeated blows to the head with a heavy object.

Daryn's murder was not initially linked to that of the two girls, as police believed that the stereotyped serial killer only went for victims of the same sex and of similar age. Had they broadened their horizons, Olson may not have been free to kill again and again.

Joan Hale caught the attention of Olson in the local village pub, which locals referred to as 'The Caribou'. When he made advances by offering her a drink, Joan succumbed to his charm and smiling brown eyes. Within days the couple were living together and making plans to get married. Just three months before the wedding booked for 15 May 1981, Joan gave birth to their son, Clifford Olson III, totally unaware that her future husband had already killed three children. Despite suffering abuse at the hands of her would-be husband, the wedding went ahead, Joan all the time believing that he would become a reformed character.

Later in May, Olson was picked up by the police for driving under the influence of alcohol, after crashing his car into a tree. His passenger was a sixteen-year-old girl, who he had picked up from a small farming district outside Vancouver. When the girl was questioned by police she claimed that Olson had been very kind to her by offering her a job. She held open her hand and showed the police a small blue pill that Olson had given her, which was later identified as chloral hydrate, a well-known knock-out drug. This time the girl had had a lucky escape.

The Olsons were regular attenders at a fundamentalist church, that was until rumours went around that Olson had sexually abused several of the children in the congregation. Olson had actually been caught in the act of sodomising a young boy in a sauna, and yet the parents never filed an official complaint. The easiest way out – the Olsons decided to attend a different church some miles away.

Olson had only been married for four days

when his sadistic urges overwhelmed him again. He picked up sixteen-year-old Sandra Wolfsteiner while she was hitchhiking outside her boyfriend's house. In fact her boyfriend's mother watched as she was picked up by a man in a silver car, not even giving it a second thought. It is believed that Olson offered Sandra a job and on the promise of good wages, managed to lure the girl into his cabin in the woods. Sandra was simply another missing youth according to the police; they couldn't have been further from the truth.

As the heat of the summer bathed the streets in sunshine, Olson increased his sinister activities. In the month of July, Olson claimed six more victims, not one of whom was over the age of eighteen. The police now realised that they had more than a list of missing children on their books and they enrolled over two hundred officers to scour the district for a possible serial killer. They were still not convinced that all the murders were connected and believed that they were possibly looking for more than one killer. They called in police psychologists to try and get inside the brain of a person who would kill so many juveniles. The only suspect they had at the time was a local man named Clifford Robert Olson, but they had no evidence.

A senior officer from the Serious Crimes Unit

came up with a simple plan on how to trap their suspect. He suggested taping a conversation between Olson and an officer, in which the officer would offer a substantial reward to Olson if he could give them clues that could lead to an arrest. They set up a meeting and surreptitiously hid a microphone underneath a seat in a local restaurant.

The officer was nervous but knew he had to remain calm if this was to be a successful liaison. The officer told Olson that there had been a few murders in the district recently and that he understood Olson might be able to help them. 'We're prepared to compensate you for whatever you're able to tell us to help us,' the officer said.

For quite a few minutes, Olson said nothing and coolly blew on his coffee before taking a mouthful. He thought long and hard before finally speaking. He told the officer that he would be prepared to give them information about the missing people if they would give him a salary of $3,000 a month. Olson was secretly getting a thrill out of the idea of giving the police information and if he could get money out of it as well, so much the better. The man suspected of several murders nonchalantly walked out of the restaurant into the sunshine, with a smirk on his face.

After his meeting with the officer, Olson decided

to pay a visit to his lawyer. While driving to his office he saw a petite girl walking along the street. The girl was seventeen-year-old Louise Chartrand, who looked exceptionally young for her age, and she immediately attracted Olson. Louise was on her way to her job as a waitress in a local restaurant when Olson stopped to offer her a lift. Using his charm he managed to convince her to get into his car, drugged her, and then headed off towards a gravel pit where he repeatedly hit her over the head with a hammer.

When Louise didn't arrive for her night shift, the restaurant phoned her parents to see if she was alright. One of Louise's sisters answered the phone and, aware that there had been a lot of homicides in the area recently, phoned the police straight away.

The long, hot summer of 1981 was getting everyone down, including the police who were getting nowhere with their investigations. Since the meeting with Olson, police had kept him under surveillance but he was proving to be a slippery fish. He only drove rental cars which he changed on a regular basis. He was always driving, and travelled over 20,000 kilometres in a period of just three months.

Then they got their lucky break. Olson had taken the ferry over to Vancouver Island and later in the day was spotted by two police officers driving erratically down a highway. They followed at a safe distance and watched as the car drove down a secluded dirt track. As they got towards the end of the track they noticed the car had stopped and that there was a man and two women standing outside the vehicle. The man was yelling at one of the women, telling her to 'take a hike!'

The police decided it was time to take action, but Olson spotted them moving through the thick undergrowth and bolted for the car. He managed to reverse the car down the track very rapidly, but was foiled by a police roadblock where the track met the highway.

Olson was taken back to the police station where he said he had only stopped in the forest because he needed to relieve himself. He was charged with dangerous driving and the police impounded the car while he was locked up for the night. Inside the rental car the police found an address book with the name of Judy Kozma (one of his victims) pencilled on one of the pages.

At the time of his arrest, only three of the children's bodies had been discovered little did the police know that in reality Olson had killed eleven juveniles.

August 1981 saw the Vancouver police task force working overtime to convict the man they suspected of murdering the local children. Still encouraged by the offer of money as a reward for information, Olsen promised to give the police a schedule to recover the bodies as long as the money was placed in safe accounts which he had set up. Olson eventually led them to all the bodies, even admitting to two more that the police knew nothing about. Aware that Olson was an accomplished escape artist, he was kept under secure guard at all times. The police were not prepared to let this one slip through their grasp.

The trial had been in progress for three days when Olson changed his plea to 'guilty'. As the police gave evidence, Olson didn't like the weak character they were portraying and in his sick mind he thought that if he admitted to the murders, the public would see him as a powerful and elusive killer. That is the way the mind of a psychopath works; they tend to hate feelings of inadequacy. In fact Olson showed all the traits of the classic psychopath – seeking thrills through bizarre antisocial behaviour, a constant pursuit of power and a complete lack of any guilt. He loved the publicity he received because of his crimes and even went on to write about it, giving disgusting and perverse accounts of his actions.

During the trial, his wife Joan was undergoing her

own ordeal. She was constantly taunted by people calling her names; she found it so hard to believe that anyone could think she had anything to do with her husband's behaviour. Her entire adult life she had been subjected to drunken beatings, not just by Olsen but by her first husband as well. This was not a side the public saw – Joan was just the wife of a serial killer who should be punished as well.

Olsen happily confessed to all eleven murders on the promise that his wife would receive any cash rewards. He was given eleven concurrent life sentences, but ironically, 'life' rarely means 'life' and he was eligible for parole in July 2006 having served twenty-five years of his sentence. His first application for parole was turned down, but he is eligible for a hearing every couple of years. He waived his right to a hearing in June 2008, but he can seek another hearing at any time and one will be scheduled for some time in 2010.

Henry Lee Lucas
and Ottis Toole

He is everybody's worst nightmare, the itinerant serial killer, murdering without motive in many different places and moving on as soon as he has done his dreadful work. The worst of these and the most prolific of all American serial killers was a one-eyed drifter named Henry Lee Lucas.

It all began before dawn on 15 June 1983 in the Montague County Jail in Texas. Joe Don Weaver, who was on duty that night, heard a commotion coming from one of the cells. When he went to check, he found Henry Lee Lucas, looking and sounding frightened. Lucas had been arrested for a minor firearms offence but he was also a suspect in two murders. Under close observation after trying to kill himself a few nights before, Lucas said there was a light in the cell and it was talking to him. Weaver looked around and, as he expected, saw no light. He told Lucas to quieten down and went back to his office.

Just as Weaver settled back into his office chair, he heard more shouts coming from Lucas's cell. He walked back and peered in through the slot in the cell door. Lucas said to him, 'Joe Don, I done some pretty bad things'. The police officer suggested praying if he found his conscience was weighing him down but Lucas asked for a pencil and some paper. Half an hour later he handed a letter to Weaver, addressed to Sheriff Bill F. Conway. It began, complete with spelling mistakes:

'I have tryed to get help for so long, and no one will believe me. I have killed for the past ten years and no one will believe me. I cannot go own [sic] doing this. I allso killed the only girl I ever loved…'
It was the break they had been waiting for.

When eighty-two-year-old widow Kate Rich had disappeared from her house, it emerged that she had been employing an odd-job man named Henry Lee Lucas and his common-law wife, fifteen-year-old Becky Powell. Lucas had been dismissed by Mrs Rich and had gone to stay in a local religious commune. Not long after, Becky Powell also disappeared.

Lucas had been arrested and questioned for days the previous October but he stuck to his guns; he knew nothing about Mrs Rich's disappearance. He also claimed that Becky had run off with a truck driver when they were hitchhiking back home to Florida.

Even polygraph tests had failed to implicate him and the sheriff had little option but to let him go.

A week later, however, the sheriff re-arrested the unshaven, smelly little tramp with a glass eye, rotten teeth and a thin, drawn face when it emerged that he had given Becky a gun to look after for him. As an ex-convict it was against the law for him to own a gun.

When Sheriff Conway arrived at the jail, Lucas told him that the light he had seen in his cell had told him to confess.

Lucas told the sheriff he had gone to Kate Rich's house and offered to take her to church but when she began asking questions about Becky's disappearance, he decided to kill the old lady. When they were in the car, he grabbed a butcher's knife he had brought along and stabbed it deep into her left side. It entered her heart and killed her. He dragged her body down an embankment, undressed her and raped her before stuffing her into a section of drainpipe that ran under the road. He returned later, wrapped her in a couple of plastic bags and drove the body back to the commune, the House of Prayer. He burned her in a stove in his room, burying what was left in a compost heap in the garden.

It is little surprise that Henry Lee Lucas turned out the way he did. Born into desperate poverty in rural Virginia in 1936, he lived with his seven siblings and his parents in a one-room shack. His father had lost his legs in a train accident and the family survived on what his mother Viola made from prostitution and selling moonshine whiskey. She often entertained her clients at home and had no shame about plying her trade in full view of her husband and children.

She was abusive, especially when she had been drinking, and the young Henry Lee frequently suffered at her hands. Once, when he was five, she hit him on the head with a piece of wood so hard that he was unconscious for three days after which he would suffer from headaches and blackouts. On another occasion, she had wounded him close to his left eye with a knife and after an incident at school, it was replaced with a glass eye. Henry Lee was inevitably antisocial and sullen.

He was taught about bestiality by one of his mother's lovers and had sex with the carcasses of dead dogs and sheep. He killed for the first time aged just fourteen. He wanted to know what it was like to have sex with a person, but they had to be dead for him to properly enjoy it.

In 1952, he was sent to a reformatory for robbing a shop and then, on his release, was almost immediately in trouble again, for which he received a sentence of four years in Virginia State Penitentiary. He escaped but was captured in Michigan. When he finally came out he stayed with one of his sisters in Tecumseh, Michigan.

His mother, although now aged seventy-four, remained the bane of his life and in 1974, while she was visiting her daughter, he got into a terrible drunken argument with her over a woman he was planning to marry. The anger of all the years of abuse boiled over and he grabbed a knife and stabbed her in the neck, killing her.

Convicted of second-degree murder, he was sentenced to twenty years in prison. He tried to kill himself and was sent to a psychiatric hospital. Released after serving half his sentence, he was soon inside again, sentenced to three and a half years for the attempted abduction of two young girls. Released again, he went to Pennsylvania where he married. It did not last long. She threw him out when she caught him sexually molesting her two young daughters.

He became a hobo, travelling to Florida where he hooked up with a man after his own heart – twenty-nine-year-old arsonist and serial killer, Ottis Elwood Toole. Toole had been seduced by his own sister, Drusilla, at the age of ten and had grown up bisexual. Abandoned by his father, he had been brought up by his mother, a religious fanatic who liked to dress her son in girl's clothes. Toole had also killed for the first time at the age of fourteen, driving his car over a man who had picked him up for sex. He liked nothing better than to watch the men he picked up have sex with his young niece, Becky Powell, and his sister, Drusilla. When he ran into Lucas, it was 1976 and he was hiding out in a rescue mission in Jacksonville, wanted by the police in connection with four murders.

Henry Lee Lucas told police that around this time he killed literally hundreds of people, Toole assisting him in 108 of the murders. 'I had no feelings for anybody; I came in contact with them, they had to die,' he later said. He described how he killed in many different ways in order to avoid creating a pattern that police would recognise. 'I killed them in every way there is except poison – there's been strangulations, there's been knifings, shootings and hit-and-runs'.

Becky Powell was on the run from a juvenile detention centre when Lucas met her and first had sex with her. When she ran away with Henry Lee, Ottis Toole was furious, venting his anger by killing nine people in six different states in the space of a year. He also went on an arson spree, setting forty fires. He was caught setting fire to a building in Florida and sent to prison for twenty years.

Lucas and Becky settled at the House of Prayer commune, but when she told him she wanted to go back home, he was initially reluctant. Nonetheless, they headed out to the road and stuck their thumbs out. As they stood there, he tried once again to persuade her to stay. It turned into an argument and he stabbed her to death with a carving knife before raping her corpse. He dismembered her, decapitating her and scattering the body parts in a field. Returning to the House of Prayer, he began to spin the story that she had climbed into the cab of a truck and gone off without him.

Lucas confessed all to Sheriff Conway but he also began what would become a pattern of confessing and then recanting. Nonetheless, the police took him seriously and he was flown to all the states where he said he had killed, answering questions about his murders. Two hundred and thirteen unsolved murders were cleared off police files as a result. He was having the time of his life. He was rarely handcuffed and was even taken to dine in restaurants outside prison.

By December 1983, investigators were able definitively to connect him with thirty-five murders. The following year, a police conference that brought together one hundred and seven officers from eighteen states increased the number of murders committed by Lucas and Toole to seventy-two. Additionally, they were suspects in seventy-one unsolved killings.

Henry Lee Lucas was ultimately charged with eleven murders but the one that brought him the death penalty was the one known as the Orange Socks Murder. In late October 1979, a woman's body was discovered in Williamson County in Texas and all she was wearing was a pair of orange socks. Lucas confessed to the murder but some gaps in the editing of the tapes on which he is seen and heard confessing encouraged suspicions that officers were feeding him information in order to clear up the case, a suspicion that had been prevalent amongst many sceptical officers. Records actually showed that Lucas was elsewhere at the time of the Orange Socks killing. The Texas Attorney General was certain that the guilty verdict in this case would later be overturned by the Supreme Court, but he was wrong. For his part, Lucas claimed that his confession to this murder amounted to 'legal suicide'. He wanted to die.

Ottis Toole died first, of cirrhosis of the liver in September 1996. At the time, he was serving six life sentences in a Florida prison.

But Henry Lee Lucas's attempt at 'legal suicide' would fail when the Texas Governor of the time, future President George W. Bush, distrusting his confession to the murder of the Orange Socks victim, commuted his death sentence to one of life.

Lucas eventually died of heart failure, aged sixty-four, on 13 March 2001.

TOMMY LYNN SELLS
THE 'CROSS COUNTRY KILLER'

Tommy Lynn Sells stopped his car in Guajia Bay, west of the city of Del Rio in Texas. It was four in the morning on the last day of the twentieth century. He quietly pushed the car door shut and crept across to a large trailer home. Inside slept Terry and Crystal Harris and their children. The family's Rottweiler began to get restless as he approached the home, so he went over to it, making reassuring sounds and letting the dog get his scent. It calmed down and lost interest in him.

He was carrying a long-bladed knife with which he tried to pick the lock on the trailer's back door, but he was out of luck. He crept around the trailer, on the lookout for a way in and found it, an open window at the front. Pulling over a metal tub, he climbed onto it, lifted off the screen from the window, pushed it open and clambered inside.

There was a boy in the room, fourteen-year-old Justin Harris, but Sells was in luck. Justin was blind and thought his siblings were messing around in his room. Sells sneaked out of the room and made for another next door. Flicking open his cigarette lighter, he saw that there was a little girl asleep, a seven-year-old friend of the family, Marque Surles. In the next bedroom lay the kids' mother Krystal, sharing a bed with her twelve-year-old daughter, Lori. The next room provided what he had been looking for and what he had travelled from Del Rio for – thirteen-year-old Kaylene 'Katy' Harris.

He went over to her bunk bed and woke the surprised girl up, placing a hand over her mouth to prevent her from screaming for help. He then slid the knife down her front, using its razor-sharp blade to slice through her shorts, panties and bra and began to fondle her. Katy managed to wriggle out of his grasp, however, screaming 'Go get Mama!' to someone else in the room. Sells looked up to see another girl asleep on the bunk above Katy. He jabbed his knife towards Katy to silence her, drawing blood before grabbing her again and standing behind her, drawing the knife across her throat. He sliced it across again and the girl in the top bunk, ten-year-old Krystal Surles, watched in horror as Katy slumped to the ground, gurgling sounds coming from her throat as she tried to scream. Sells wasn't finished with her, stabbing her prone body a further sixteen times, three of his thrusts so strong that the point of the knife came out through her back. He stood up and, as Krystal whimpered that she would be quiet, she wouldn't make a sound, he reached out and cut her throat. She slumped back on the bed but he had not killed her. Lying there, not moving, she heard him walk out of the room, believing her to be dead. She lay still as a car engine came to life and disappeared into the distance.

Krystal, thinking the worst, that everyone in the trailer must have shared a similar fate to her friend, ran to the front door, her hand at her bleeding throat and staggered a quarter of a mile to the nearest neighbour who immediately called 911.

In hospital, unable to speak, but communicating with pencil and paper, Krystal helped to create a sketch of the killer. He looked just like a man they had met at a Del Rio gas station. He was called Tom or Tommy, knew Katy's father Terry and had a job as a salesman at Amigo Auto Sales.

On 2 January, Tommy Lynn Sells was wakened early by knocking at the door of the trailer he shared with his wife and her four children. His three decades of killing were finally over.

Sells was as good as illiterate and had spent his life drifting, mostly dulling the pain of his inadequacies with booze and drugs. He wandered across the

United States, mostly travelling by train, leaving not a trace of himself; no credit cards, no bank account, no telephone. It was as if he didn't exist. His twenty or so victims, killed over three decades, wished he hadn't.

Tommy Lynn Sells just loved to kill. A big bearded guy with a serious mullet who seemed ordinary to the officers who arrested him in early January 2000, his crimes included rape and sexual mutilation. He killed with a variety of implements – knives, guns, a baseball bat – and used various items to garrot several of his victims. The variety of his murder methods, coupled with the fact that many of his crimes were totally spontaneous, absolutely unpremeditated, made it impossible to connect them with each other and rendered it almost impossible to catch him.

Tommy Lynn Sells was born in Oakland in 1964, one of a set of twins, the other being a sister by the name of Tammy Jean. His mother Nina already had two sons when the twins came along and three more boys would arrive in the years to come. The children's father was notionally the insurance agent William Sells, but one source relates how their actual father was a used-car salesman by the name of Joe Lovins. He was said to have helped Sells out with a bad money problem and in return Sells agreed to take on the children as his own. But this apparently kind act only hid an insurance scam whereby Sells' job provided health insurance for the children.

Nina Sells had family in St Louis and eighteen months after the birth of the twins she moved back there with the children. Not long after their arrival, however, the twins fell ill with meningitis. Tammy died but Tommy, although exhibiting the same symptoms as his sister, survived.

At the age of two, Tommy was sent to live with an aunt and remained in her care until the age of five, during which time his mother did not once come to visit him. When the aunt tried to adopt him, Nina was furious and took him back, but he was a wilful child and a regular truant from school.

At around the age of eight, he was befriended by a paedophile and a pattern of abuse began that would continue for a number of years until the man was caught. His mother, glad to be shot of him, had allowed him to spend many nights sleeping at the man's house and, in return, Tommy would receive gifts and treats.

The downward trajectory of his life continued – allowed to drink alcohol by his grandfather at the age of seven or eight, smoking marijuana at ten, sleeping naked with his grandmother at thirteen and attempting to rape his own mother.

By the age of fourteen he had already experienced

things most men never encounter in a lifetime and, bored with life, he took off across America. From 1978 to 1999, his life would be that of a transient, hopping freight trains, hitchhiking and stealing cars. Back and forth across the country he went, working in fairgrounds, cutting hair and labouring on building sites. And all the time he was killing.

He told of one murder he committed in 1985. It is typical of the many he committed during his life on the road.

While he was working with a carnival in Forsyth, Missouri, he met a thirty-five-year-old divorcee named Ena Cordt who had brought her four-year-old son to the fairground for a night out. Tommy and Ena seemed to hit it off and she invited him back to her house. There, he had sex with her, but later claimed that he discovered her stealing from his backpack. He picked up her son's baseball bat that was lying nearby and bludgeoned her to death with it. He next turned on her son and smashed his skull with the bat. Of course, the truth will never be known, but police officers suspected that he had actually followed the woman and her son home before breaking in, raping her and killing both of them.

Sells confessed to investigating officers that he had started killing at an early age. His first murder was at the age of sixteen when he shot a man dead in Mississippi in the course of a burglary. At seventeen, he claimed he had used an ice-pick to murder a man in Los Angeles. He described the murder of a woman near Little Rock in Arkansas in the early 1980s. Her body had been disposed of in an old bauxite mineshaft. Around the same time, another man was dead during a break-in. This latter claim was found to be incorrect, however. When police visited the man they found him to be alive and well. Tommy Lynn had missed.

He was at his most prolific in the late 1980s. In the two years from 1987 to 1989 he undertook a coast to coast murder tour, slaying a dozen people in seven states.

Autumn 1987 found him driving a stolen truck in Winnemucca, Nevada, when he saw twenty-year-old Stephanie Stroh standing beside the road hitching a lift back home to San Francisco. He picked her up, drove her towards Reno but pulled off the road and choked her to death. He threw her body into a hot spring, he said, but her body has never been found.

Later that year, he was responsible for a particularly gruesome multiple killing in Illinois. Hunters, walking in a field near the small town of Ina, found the body of Keith Dardeen, a bullet hole in his head and his genitals mutilated. When police went to the trailer in which he lived they made a grisly find. Dardeen's wife Elaine and three-year-old son had been beaten to death and Elaine had been raped and sexually assaulted with a baseball bat. In another room they faced the horrific sight of the couple's dead newborn daughter, born prematurely during the beating or even after death. She too had been bludgeoned with the baseball bat.

As ever, Sells' motive for these killings is unknown, although he claims that he met Dardeen at a truck-stop and after inviting Sells to his home, he had made sexual advances towards him. Relatives dismissed these claims as absurd.

During this time, Sells was a heavy user of drugs, heroin being his drug of choice. However, he would take anything he could get his hands on. These years were spent in a drugged haze.

In 1988 and 1989, he claims to have killed a teenage girl in New Hampshire, a woman and her three-year-old son near Twin Falls, Idaho, a fifty-one-year-old hobo in a knife fight near Tucson, a prostitute in Truckee, California, and a young female hitchhiker in Oregon.

In January 1990, he was in Rawlings, Wyoming when he was arrested for being drunk as he tried to hop a freight train. Unfortunately for him, he was also in possession of some stolen goods and was sent to jail for sixteen months. His incarceration may not have cured him of his urge to kill, but at least it got him off drugs.

Released from prison in 1991, he murdered Margaret McClain and her daughter Pamela in Charleston, West Virginia, and in May 1992 a woman who took him home after she met him as he begged on a street corner, had her kindness repaid with rape. She had fought back, however, getting her hands on his knife and slashing him twenty-three times before he picked up a piano stool and beat her. She survived her ordeal, however, and identified him. He was arrested and sentenced to two to ten years in West Virginia State Prison.

In jail he got married, to Nora Price, and when he was released in May 1997, the couple settled in Tennessee. Needless to say, Sells found it impossible to settle down and he left his new wife time and time again. During his absences, he picked up where he had left off in 1992. He strangled thirteen-year-old Stephanie Mahaney and threw her body into a pond near Springfield, Missouri, in October 1997.

By 1998, he was travelling with the Heart of America carnival, operating the Ferris wheel, and driving the truck that transported it. At Del Rio in Texas, he met twenty-eight-year-old Jessica Levrie, a mother of four children. He moved into her trailer in March, around the time that his wife Nora was giving birth to his son back in Arkansas. The child was put up for adoption.

He found employment at Amigo Auto Sales and bigamously married Jessica in October 1998. But he could not give up his old life and Jessica had to put up with frequent absences during which he committed a final series of murders. On 4 April 1999 he raped and stabbed to death a thirty-two-year-old woman in Tennessee, also killing her eight-year-old daughter. A fortnight later, working again with the carnival in San Antonio in Texas, he sexually assaulted and killed nine-year-old Mary Bea Perez who had disappeared during a music festival.

He got out of town and headed for Lexington, Kentucky where he abducted thirteen-year-old Haley McHone from a park and stripped, raped and choked her. He sold her bicycle for $20 and drank the proceeds. Arrested for being drunk that night, he was released and returned home to Del Rio, as if nothing had happened. But his spree was not over. In July that year, during one of his excursions, he raped and shot dead fourteen-year-old Bobby Lynn Wofford in Kingfisher, Oklahoma.

Sells first encountered the Harrises at Grace Community Church. His wife Jessica was a born-again Christian and had persuaded Tommy to accompany her and the children. It was there that he first noticed Katy, at thirteen just the right age for him. He became a friend of the family and had visited their trailer home several times before that dreadful night. That was how he knew that Terry Harris would not be home that night.

At his trial, Krystal Surles was a star. Looking him straight in the eyes, she recounted the events of that night. When asked, she identified him as her attacker and Katy's killer.

The jury declared Sells guilty and then voted for execution. Tommy Lynn Sells now sits on death row in the prison at Livingston, Texas awaiting an execution date. He claims to have actually killed around seventy people.

CARY STAYNER

Staff at the Cedar Lodge Resort in the small community of El Portal on the western slope of Yosemite National Park, cleaned the room on the morning of 16 February without uncovering anything suspicious. The occupants of the room, forty-two-year-old Carole Sund, her fifteen-year-old daughter, Juli, and sixteen-year-old Silvina Pelosso had checked out in advance and their room keys had been left on the desk in the room earlier that morning. They were returning to San Francisco airport where they would be meeting Carole's husband, Jens, who was flying out to a business meeting in Arizona. They were to accompany him and while he had his meeting, they were planning to explore the Grand Canyon.

Mrs Sund and her husband were both prominent real estate operators in Eureka, California and this holiday was partly to show some of the country to Argentinian student Silvina, daughter of a friend of Carole Sund. The three women had arrived at Cedar Lodge on 14 February and had spent the following day hiking in the park. That evening, they had rented a couple of videos from the lodge's reception and settled in for a night in front of the television. Tragically, that was the last that anyone ever saw of them. They failed to turn up at San Francisco Airport later on 16 February, and Jens Sund presumed that they had flown on to Arizona without him.

Next day, however, when there was still no sign of his wife and the two girls, he became concerned and informed the police. That concern increased when it was discovered that the 1999 Pontiac Grand Prix Carole had rented had not been returned to the rental agency.

It was initially feared that the women may have wandered off a trail and become lost or even that their car had skidded off the icy roads. An extensive search was launched of the area but as the days passed no sign was found of them.

After several days, Carole Sund's wallet, money and contents intact, turned up on a street in Modesto, California. It was bizarre and the FBI suspected there might be more to this than just a missing persons case. When the women had been missing for two weeks, the police announced formally that they believed that Carole, Juli and Silvina had been victims of a violent crime.

More than a thousand leads had come in but still they seemed no closer to solving the case. Jens

Sund offered a reward of $250,000 but still the case stalled.

Suddenly, on 18 March, a hiker walking close to Highway 108 in the Stanislaus National Forest in the Sierra Nevada Mountains of northern California stumbled upon a burnt-out red Pontiac. It was quickly identified as the car rented by Carole Sund and in the boot were the charred bodies of Mrs Sund and Silvina Pelosso. There was no sign, however, of Juli Sund.

They found her badly decomposed body a week later. Her throat had been cut.

The investigation intensified. Known sex offenders and the employees of Cedar Lodge were questioned. The FBI believed that the perpetrator was someone who knew the area because of the out-of-the-way location where he had dumped the car, a place where locals dumped old fridges and cookers and where it would not look out of place. Locals, meanwhile, were worried that a killer was in their midst.

A number of people with criminal records were considered to be suspects, but many of them had gone to prison for various offences since the disappearance of the women. The FBI stated that it believed the murderer was one of those people and that he or she was now out of circulation.

It was a statement they would regret three weeks later when, on 22 July, the body of a fourth victim was discovered only a couple of miles from Cedar Lodge.

Twenty-six-year-old Joie Ruth Armstrong, an employee of the Yosemite Institute, had been killed and decapitated close to where she lived in the Foresta community, a group of about thirty cabins that park workers lived in. She had failed to arrive at a friend's house and after the friend informed the police they found her car, packed and ready for the trip, parked outside her cabin. The terror returned to Yosemite as people realised that the killer was not, as the FBI had insisted, already behind bars.

Two days after Joie Armstrong's body had been found, the authorities announced that they were talking to a suspect.

Thirty-seven-year-old Cary Stayner was a janitor at the Cedar Lodge Resort and had already been questioned about the earlier killings. Stayner, a gifted artist, had a tragic past. His younger brother Steven had been abducted in 1972 by Kenneth Parnell and was held for eight years, finally escaping with another boy in 1980. He had then tragically died in a motorcycle accident in 1989. This traumatic event may have affected the eleven-year-old Cary, but by the time he took the job at Cedar Lodge, living in a small apartment on the top floor, he seemed well adjusted. He was clean-cut, pleasant and did not have a criminal record, apart from a conviction in 1997 for smoking marijuana.

After interrogating him and searching his truck, they released him, warning him not to leave El Portal while they undertook further enquiries. These included a search of his apartment where they found evidence linking him with the murder of Joie Armstrong. By now they were also developing a line of enquiry linking him to the Sund–Pelossa killings. Stayner was picked up and interviewed by FBI agent Jeff Rinek. Before he opened up to Rinek, Stayner made some demands. He told them he would tell everything in exchange for the reward money that had been offered being given to his parents; that he be sent to a prison near his parents' home and that he be provided with a large supply of child pornography. Nonetheless, he began to talk without being promised any of these things.

Stayner had noted the arrival of three women without a man at the Cedar Lodge on 14 February. The following night, as they watched Tom Cruise in *Jerry Maguire*, he knocked on their door, telling them that there was a water leak. Carole Sund was at first reluctant to let him in. The room was in a secluded part of the inn and she felt vulnerable.

When he said he would go and get the manager, however, she relented and opened the door. He thanked her politely and went into the bathroom where he fiddled with some pipes to give credence to his story. Exiting the bathroom, however, he suddenly pulled out a gun from his bag. He told them he was a desperate man and needed money to get out of the county, asking for their car keys and their purses. They handed the keys and what they had over to him. He then tied them up before ordering the girls into the bathroom. Returning to the room where Mrs Sund was lying on the bed, he took a rope out of his bag and wrapped it around her neck, pulling it tight and strangling her. He then carried her body out to the Pontiac where he dumped it in the boot.

Returning to the room, he fetched the girls from the bathroom and lay them on the bed where he began cutting off their clothes. He then began to sexually molest them. Silvina was getting hysterical, however, and he soon tired of it. He took her into the bathroom, threw her into the bath and proceeded to strangle her.

He returned to the bedroom where he remained for the next seven hours sexually assaulting Juli Stayner. But, as Staynor had suffered from impotence for most of his life and was unable to maintain an erection, it proved to be a frustrating night for him and a horrific one for the fifteen-year-old. Before daybreak, he wrapped her in a blanket and drove her to Lake Don Pedro where he pulled her hair away from her neck, pulled back her head and slit her throat. She did not die at once and Stayner later described how the dying girl had gestured to him to finish her off.

He explained that it made him feel as if he had power for once in his life.

He had sent the investigators a map showing where Juli's body was and had thrown away Carole Sund's wallet in Modesto simply to lead the investigation down a blind alley.

He went on to confess to the murder of Joie Armstrong whom he described as a 'fairly attractive girl'. He was passing her house carrying a backpack in which were a .22 revolver, a large knife and a roll of duct tape. He engaged her in conversation, about Bigfoot, the legendary ape-like creature that was said to inhabit the mountains of that area. As she went to go inside, Stayner said, she turned round. By this time he had pulled his revolver from his backpack and as she turned, he put it to her head. She panicked and he ordered her to go into the cabin. Inside, he gagged her and tied her up with the duct tape, as she struggled. He then forced her down her path and into his truck, throwing her into the back seat. She continued to struggle and as he drove off, she fell through the vehicle's window and out onto the road. He pulled out his knife and calmly slit her throat. He parked the truck and went back and cut off her head.

Later in his interview, Stayner told agent Rinek that he had fantasised about killing women for thirty years. He also added that he knew it would probably cost him his life. Rinek did not disabuse him of that belief.

The FBI immediately came under fire for what was viewed to have been a bungled investigation. Many thought that if the bureau had not decided that the killer was already in jail early on in the investigation, Joie Armstrong would not have died. Of the four suspects at that time, three had passed lie detector tests, their lawyers offering blood testing of their clients to support their innocence and one, it later transpired, had been working in another state at the time of the Sund–Pelosso murders.

Cary Stayner's trial began in Santa Clara County in May 2002 and he pleaded not guilty by reason of insanity. The defence produced a psychiatrist who maintained that Cary Stayner had a great deal wrong with him, citing the killer's obsession with Bigfoot, the prophecies of Nostradamus and his nightmares featuring disembodied heads. He had violent fantasies of childhood rape and possessed disorders such as paedophilia, voyeurism, social dysfunction and mild autism. He also described the Stayner family tree as blighted by sexual abuse and mental illness. It came down to whether Stayner was a cold-blooded murderer and sexual predator or a mentally ill victim of child abuse.

The jury had no doubts. On 26 August 2002, they took less than five hours to find Cary Stayner guilty of first-degree murder and on 9 October they recommended that he should be executed.

Cary Stayner now sits in the Adjustment Center on death row in San Quentin Penitentiary in California. He is working on an appeal.

PART THREE

SOUTH AMERICA

PEDRO ALONSO
LÓPEZ

In the hierarchy of monsters, he stands fifth, lagging behind only Thug Behram, Countess Elizabeth Bathory, Henry Lee Lucas and Harold Shipman in terms of number of murders committed. He was a Colombian-born serial killer who preyed on little girls across South America in the 1970s and 1980s.

The world into which Pedro Alonso López was born in 1949 was already a violent one. It was the period in Colombia known as 'La Violencia' which had started the previous year with the assassination of the popular Liberal politician, Jorge Eliécer Gaitán. Civil war broke out and more than 200,000 lives would be lost during the next ten years. It was the horrific way that the killings were carried out that made this period so notable. Guns were scarce and machetes, knives and swords were used instead. The various factions developed their own distinctive forms of corpse desecration as a signature. One group used what became known as the 'T-shirt cut' which involved severing the arms of their victims and decapitating them; another was characterised by the 'Necktie cut' in which the throat was split open and the tongue placed over the chest like a tie; the 'Flower Vase cut' involved the severed arms and legs being arranged inside an opened torso like a flower arrangement. Colombia's crime rate was a frightening fifty times higher than anywhere else on earth.

Violence was, therefore, a way of life in Colombia at the time and the young Pedro Alonso López was no stranger to it. His mother, a large overbearing woman who worked as a prostitute, ruled her household and her thirteen children with a rod of iron.

The streets of his home town of Tolmia were a terrifying prospect for a kid but it was to those streets that eight-year-old Pedro was consigned after his mother caught him raping a younger sister. However, no sooner had he stepped into the world outside than it seemed as if his luck was about to change. A man approached him, promising food and a bed. He went with him, but it was not to the comfortable house that he had expected. Instead the man pushed him into an abandoned building where he raped him countless times before throwing him back out onto the streets.

It was an experience that scarred him and from then on he would only venture out at night from the alleyways and deserted buildings in which he slept. He fed himself from scraps he scavenged in dustbins and from the local dump. By day, he remained out of sight, terrified that it would happen again.

After a year, he began to regain his confidence, leaving Tolmia and heading for Bogotá, the Colombian capital. There, he resumed his life of begging and scavenging food where he could find it. However, one day his luck really did change. He was approached by an elderly American couple who were living at the time in Bogotá. They had seen him on the streets and were distressed at his plight as he begged for food. They told him they could provide him with a warm meal and a place to sleep. Initially, of course, he was reluctant. He did not trust anyone any more. But, he was hungry and tired and decided to take a chance. He accompanied them to their house and was fed and given a bed.

Pedro stayed with the American couple, enrolling in a school for orphans and beginning for the first time to enjoy life. He seems to have been a magnet for trouble, however. In 1963, when he was twelve years old, one of the teachers at his school sexually molested him. Pedro's old fears came flooding back and he ran away, after stealing money from an office in the school. He was back on the streets begging and stealing whatever he could.

By his mid-teens, he had graduated to stealing cars which he would deliver to local 'chop shops' who paid him well. At last, he had found something at which he was very good and for the first time in his life he gained respect from his peers. Life was good again. Needless to say, it did not last. In 1969, he was arrested and sent to prison for seven years. He had been behind bars only two days when four of his fellow inmates brutally gang-raped him.

It was a defining moment for the eighteen-year-old. 'No one will ever touch me again,' he swore to himself. As if to emphasise that fact, he spent the next two weeks murdering each of his attackers with a crude knife he had fashioned out of kitchen utensils. Deciding that the killings had been carried out in self-defence, the prison authorities let him off lightly, adding just two years to his existing sentence.

In prison López developed a serious hatred of women. The cruelty he had experienced at the hands of his mother during his early years had scarred him. He was unable to mix or converse with women and his only contact was through pornographic magazines. He decided to take revenge on womankind when he got out.

Finally released in 1978, he took off on a journey through the neighbouring country of Peru. He launched his war on women, stalking and killing, he later claimed, at least a hundred young Indian girls. Of course, it is impossible to confirm his claim, but it is known that he was stripped, tortured and almost buried alive by a group of Ayacucho Indians in northern Peru on one occasion when he was caught in the act of kidnapping a nine-year-old girl. He was saved only by the intervention of an American missionary who happened to be passing. So, instead of killing him, they handed him over to the police. But they were unwilling to spend time on a complaint brought by the Ayacuchos and simply deported Pedro to Ecuador.

He continued with his itinerant lifestyle, travelling around Ecuador and heading north over the border into Colombia now and then. The authorities in the places through which he passed, noticed an escalation in the disappearances of young girls, but rather than ascribe them to the actions of a serial killer, they blamed them on the growing number of South American sex slave rings.

This began to change, however, in April 1980. Heavy rain had caused flash floods near the town of Ambato in Ecuador which had uncovered the remains of four children who had been reported missing. They had been in the water too long for a cause of death to be ascertained, but it was blindingly obvious that their deaths had been the result of foul play. A few days later, local man Carvina Poveda was shopping at the local market with his twelve-year-old daughter, Marie. Suddenly, when he turned his head for just a moment, a man tried to grab Marie and run off with her. Carvina screamed for help, pulling Marie away from the man, who took off. Before he could get away, however, the stallholders brought him down and pinned him to the ground until the police arrived. The man was Pedro Alonso López.

He remained silent in the face of questioning at the police station and the investigating officers became frustrated. They believed that this man could be responsible not just for trying to abduct Marie Poveda but also for the murders of the four girls found in the floods. They decided to dress up a local priest, Father Cordoba Gudino, as a prisoner and put him in a cell with Pedro for the night. The priest would gain his confidence and he would begin to talk.

The plan worked like a dream. Pedro rambled all night to the priest, describing horrific acts until the other man could take no more and asked to be taken out of the cell. Confronted with the virtual confession gleaned from him during the night, Pedro broke down and began to talk.

His tally of killings was astonishing. He claimed to have killed at least one hundred and ten girls in Ecuador, one hundred in Colombia and many more than one hundred in Peru – he spoke chillingly about his preference for South American girls. 'I like the girls in Ecuador,' he said. 'They are more gentle and trusting, more innocent. They are not as suspicious of strangers as Colombian girls.'

He justified his actions by saying that he was stealing the innocence of young girls just as his had been stolen at the age of eight. He explained how when he arrived in a village, he would search in the market for girls with a look that he described as 'a certain look of innocence'. He would stalk them for several days before making his move, luring them with a trinket or a mirror. He would take them to one of his secret places, in all probability a burial site where many other girls had met their end. The grave would already be dug. He would then cuddle the girl until sunrise next morning when he would rape her, placing his hands around her throat. Then, as the sun came up, looking straight into her eyes so that he could luxuriate in the exact moment of death, he would strangle her, his sexual pleasure enhanced by watching the life ooze out of her. 'It was only good if I could see her eyes,' he said later in an interview with an American journalist. 'It would have been wasted in the dark. I had to watch them by daylight. There is a divine moment when I have my hands around a young girl's throat. I look into her eyes and see a certain light, a spark, suddenly go out. The moment of death is enthralling and exciting. Only those who actually kill know what I mean.'

The horror was sometimes not even over then. Often he would stage gruesome tea parties, talking to the dead bodies of the little girls propped up across from him.

As he recounted his life to the officers it became clear to him that they did not believe him, so extravagant were his claims. To counter this, he offered to lead them to a number of his burial plots throughout the country. He was taken in leg irons and they drove in convoy across the country. Near Ambato they uncovered the bodies of fifty-three girls, aged between eight and twelve. They visited twenty-eight other sites but were unable to locate any more bodies. It was thought that animals had in all probability removed the bones or that they may even have been washed away by the floods.

Initially charged with fifty-seven murders, the number ascribed to him quickly escalated to one hundred and ten as he confessed to more. The director of prison affairs reckoned that three hundred would probably be too low an estimate – Pedro López probably murdered many more.

In late 1980, López was found guilty of many counts of murder and sentenced to life imprisonment.

Pedro Alonso López was released from prison in Ecuador on 31 August 1994 but rearrested an hour later as an illegal immigrant and handed over to the Colombian police who wanted him for the twenty-year-old murder of twelve-year-old Flora Sanchez. They declared him to be insane, locking him up in the psychiatric wing of a Bogotá hospital.

Astonishingly, he was declared sane and released on $50 bail in 1998 on condition that he continued to receive psychiatric treatment and reported once a month to a judge. He went on a nostalgic journey back home to see his mother for the first time in nineteen years. He told her he was there to collect his inheritance but she replied that she was poor and all she had was a chair and a bed. He said that would do and put them out on the porch, telling his heartbroken mother he was going to sell them and if no one bought them, he would set fire to them. A woman bought them and he left with the money. He disappeared into the countryside where he had killed so many of his victims and has not been seen since.

A warrant was issued by Interpol on behalf of the Colombian government for his arrest in connection with a murder in 2002. The man who had once claimed to be like God – 'I can give life or take it away' – had seemingly picked up where he left off.

LUIS ALFREDO
GARAVITO CUBILLOS

Luis Alfredo Garavito, known as 'La Bestia' (The Beast) is the killer and rapist of several hundred young boys in Colombia in the late 1990s. It is feared that the number of victims could rise to as many as three hundred, making him one of the world's most prolific serial killers. His victims were mainly poor children between the ages of six and sixteen. Garavito travelled extensively throughout Colombia and his victims were found in many different parts of the country.

Born in 1957 in Genova, the oldest of seven brothers, he was physically and mentally abused by his father as a child. He also claims to have suffered sexual abuse. He began to kill in February 1998 when the naked bodies of two children were discovered lying beside each other on a hillside near Garavito's home town of Genova. The following day, a third body was found nearby, although this one differed from the others in that it was in a fairly advanced state of decomposition. The three bodies had their hands tied and the area in which they lay was stained with blood. A knife was found not far from them. The neck of each corpse had been cut and the genitals of each had been severed. All three showed signs of anal penetration and a bottle of lubricant lay on the ground. It was unknown how long they had been there and, sadly, cost precluded the analysis of the DNA of the stains that surrounded the bodies.

Colombia was a dangerous place at the time. Several serial killers were thought to be operating and some even wondered if these victims might have lost their lives at the hands of the 'Monster of the Andes', the mass killer Pedro Alonzo López, who had murdered several hundred young girls in the 1970s and 1980s. This suspicion was quickly dispensed with, however. The victims had been killed fairly recently and López only killed girls.

It was quickly ascertained that the first two boys to be found were from the local town, were aged eleven and thirteen and had been close friends. They were from poor backgrounds and had spent their days working in the streets, supplementing their families' income by selling fruit, sweets and chewing gum. Investigating officers, trying to learn the movements of the boys on the day they disappeared, were told by the mother of one that he had told her that he was going to help a man move some cattle.

Police started to examine other cases in Colombia of children who had disappeared or had been found murdered. There were hundreds of them but, frustratingly, resources being so limited, identification of many of the children had been impossible and, in most cases, no one had even bothered to record the injuries that had killed them. Comparison with the bodies found near Genova was, therefore, rendered almost impossible.

They paid particular attention to a series of four child murders that had been carried out on children aged between eight and ten in 1995 in the Valle region of the country. There were similarities in that all the children came from poor backgrounds and were uneducated and, interestingly, as in the Genova case, they had all disappeared shortly before noon. Even more interesting was the fact that they had also been discovered on the slope of a hill, close to their home town, lying on the ground, unburied. It looked like this serial killer's signature was being established. Once he selected his spot, he killed there, again and again.

On 22 April 1999, the police had a stroke of luck that made the impossible task of finding this killer a whole lot easier. On that day, in a street in the town of Villavicencio, a homeless man saw a man trying to abduct a boy. The boy got away from his assailant and the man fled. However, when his description was passed around town, he was spotted by taxi drivers who confronted him and handed him over to the police.

Asked to identify himself, he gave the name of a politician from another town. Even though the officers were unable to disprove his claim, they remained highly suspicious, especially as he fitted the description given by the boy. Amongst his clothing they discovered telephone numbers that soon led them to his true identity – Luis Alfredo Garavito. Critically, they found that he was listed amongst the suspects in the case of the murdered children.

The case against him became even clearer when one of his family turned up and handed police a box containing cryptic notes and passport-size photos of many of the dead children, cut out of the identity cards they had been carrying. A calendar with indecipherable notes on it was also found. It turned out to be a list detailing his victims and the dates on which they met their ends.

When confronted with this evidence, Garavito broke down and immediately started to confess, admitting to the murders of one hundred and forty boys – a number that has since risen to closer on three hundred – and the sexual assault of many others.

The public were shocked when they learned that

one man had been responsible for so many deaths. Until that point it was being suggested that satanic cults might be responsible or that the boys had been killed to feed the growing trade in human organs.

Garavito generally selected his victims carefully – they had to have the right colour of skin and bone structure. Having introduced himself, wearing one of his many disguises – priest, street vendor, poor farmer – he bought them fruit juice or a piece of cake in a local shop before asking them if they would like to take a walk with him. Or he might enlist their help in carrying a crate of oranges, in looking after some cattle or in harvesting sugarcane. If he spotted a child who was addicted to drugs, he would offer drugs, and if there were boys who liked games, he would pay for them.

He had evolved his method of luring them. In the beginning he had simply offered money, but this, of course, just made the boys suspicious. He changed his approach to a mixture of promises and a slightly greater amount of cash – more than a day's work which would buy the child in question a day's holiday from their life of drudgery. Most of the killings took place at weekends when children could be guaranteed to be hanging around in the market place.

Decapitation, or attempted decapitation, also formed part of his modus operandi. There were notches in the fourth vertebrae of the necks of his victims, often made, it seemed, with an old knife that probably had notches in its blade. He left the internal organs in place but often stabbed his victim repeatedly. He only dismembered bodies when they had to be cut up in order to be transported more easily from a house and occasionally he would place the bodies in a bag, weigh them down with stones and toss them in a river. An empty bottle of cheap Schnapps was usually found at the crime scene; the killer obviously liked a drink.

On one occasion he had almost been caught. When one boy disappeared, his mother had immediately launched a search, learning that a man had been seen buying her son and his friends sweets in a shop. Garavito was questioned and admitted to having been with the boy but claimed that after that he had not seen him again. Her son was found five days later, decapitated and with his severed penis stuck in his mouth. Four days later, Garavito killed another boy in a nearby town.

Pedro Luis Garavito was found guilty of 138 of the 172 cases with which he was charged and the sentences for those cases totalled 1,853 years in prison. Colombia, however, has a maximum prison sentence of thirty years and he could, conceivably, be released within the next ten to twenty years.

The fact that he has also cooperated with the authorities in finding so many of his victims has reduced this thirty-year term to twenty-two years. Many Colombians are understandably horrified at the prospect of his release and are working to ensure that he remains locked up for the remainder of his life. In 2006, a judicial review stipulated that his prison sentence could indeed be extended and his release delayed.

He is held in isolation from other prisoners because there is little doubt that otherwise he would be killed immediately. He is terrified of being poisoned and accepts drinks only from certain people.

He continues to help find the bodies of his victims and insisted sensationally in a 2006 television interview that he wants to launch a political career with the aim of helping abused children.

ADOLFO DE JESÚS CONSTANZO

On 6 May 1989, Adolfo de Jesús Constanzo, his *madrina* or head witch Sara Aldrete, his lover Martin Quintana Rodriguez and professional hitman Alvaro de Leon Valdez who went by the nickname El Duby, were holed up in an apartment in Mexico City. The whole world, it seemed, was searching for them and there was nowhere left to run. Realising it could only end one way, Aldrete had tried to find a way to save herself by tossing a handwritten note out of the window into the street below. It read, 'Please call the judicial police and tell them that in this building are those that they are seeking. Give them the address, fourth floor. Tell them that a woman is being held hostage. I beg for this, because what I want most is to talk – or they're going to kill the girl'. It was picked up by a passer-by who thought it was just a joke and failed to pass it on to the authorities.

On the same day, however, a loud argument broke

out in the apartment, accompanied, some have said, by gunshots. Anxious neighbours called the police. As what seemed like the whole Mexico City police force converged on the scene, Constanzo let loose with a Uzi machine gun. The police returned fire and for forty-five minutes the air was thick with gunfire. Miraculously, only one policeman was injured but inside the apartment things were getting desperate. Suddenly, Constanzo handed his weapon to Valdez and ordered him to shoot him and Quintana. El Duby was horrified and told him he could not do it. Constanzo slapped him hard on the face and told him if he failed to obey he would ensure that everything went badly for him when he got to hell. El Duby believed that Constanzo did, indeed, have that power. Constanzo and Quintana embraced and El Duby raised the Uzi and shot them dead.

Hearing gunfire from inside the apartment, police stormed the building. They found the two dead men and arrested Aldrete and El Duby. Adolfo de Jesús Constanzo's reign of terror was finally over. It was the end of an extraordinary life of witchcraft, human sacrifice and brutal murder.

He could make you invisible, they said. Or bullet-proof. You could evade your enemies or the police with his help and he could make problems go away, for a fee. He was worshipped like a god by those who fell under his spell and they were not always simple, impressionable people. His followers included sophisticated society figures – doctors, wealthy property directors and musicians. Of course, there were also elements of the lower echelons of Mexico City society, such as the transvestites who performed in the local nightclubs. At least four members of the Federal Judicial Police were members of his cult. Salvador Garcia was head of the Mexico City drug squad and Florentino Ventura commanded the Mexican branch of the international police organisation, Interpol. For them, too, he was a connection to the spiritual world and for him they just offered more ways to make money and become even wealthier than he already was.

He had been born in Miami in 1962 to a fifteen-year-old Cuban immigrant called Delia Aurora González del Valle who would have three children by three different fathers. When her first husband died, she moved to Puerto Rico and remarried. The young Adolfo, meanwhile, was baptised and served as an altar boy. The Catholic religion was not the only one in their lives, however. His mother had an interest in Palo Mayombe, a religion that had developed in Cuba amongst slaves from Central Africa. Some said that Aurora was a witch and those with whom she did not get on were liable to find headless goats or chickens on their doorsteps.

At the age of nine, Adolfo was introduced to the rituals of the Santeria cult, a religion practised by immigrants. It welded together elements of various belief systems. Then, aged fourteen, he began to receive instruction from a Palo Mayombe priest who taught him much more than religious ritual – he also gave him lessons in drug dealing and hustling. He travelled to Haiti and Puerto Rico, learning about voodoo.

His mother claimed that around this time her son began displaying an ability to predict the future. She said that he foretold events such as the 1981 shooting of US President Ronald Reagan by John Hinckley, but his fantastic talent did not stop him being arrested a couple of times for shoplifting.

The family returned to Miami when Adolfo was ten years old, but his stepfather died not long after. His mother married again to a drug dealer who was also involved in the occult.

In 1983, when he was twenty-one, a modelling assignment took Constanzo to Mexico City where the handsome young sorcerer, who had already demonstrated bisexual tendencies, had soon recruited Martin Quintana Rodriguez, Omar Chewe Orea Ochoa, and homosexual psychic Jorge

Montes as servants and lovers. They would be the first members of the extraordinary cult that would form around Constanzo in the next few years.

In 1984, he decided to settle in Mexico, living with Quintana and Orea and attracting other disciples as his reputation for magic grew. His services included telling the future and providing limpias, ritual cleansings for people who believed they had been cursed by their enemies. It was lucrative business and he built up a clientele of some thirty-one regular customers who paid $4,500 for a single ritual. If you wanted a sacrifice, you paid according to the creature used – $6 for a rooster, $30 for a goat, $450 for a boa constrictor, $1,100 for a zebra and, top of the range, African lion cubs for $3,100 each.

His predictions were much sought after by wealthy drug dealers, who wanted to know the most fortuitous time for a shipment or a meeting. If you were really in trouble he could make you invisible or bulletproof. One Mexico City drug dealer is reputed to have paid Constanzo $40,000 for his services over a three-year period. Part of the paraphernalia of his trade was the *nganga*, a cauldron into which were put blood and bones. Constanzo and his henchmen raided Mexico City cemeteries, collecting human remains to feed his *nganga*.

In 1986, the head of Interpol, Florentino Ventura,

introduced Constanzo to the Calzada family, the heads of one of Mexico's leading drug cartels. It proved a profitable entrée for the sorcerer, who began to make good money from them and their contacts. By early 1987 he was living in an expensive Mexico City condominium and was the owner of a fleet of luxury cars, including an $80,000 Mercedes Benz. He supplemented his income with his own scams, once posing as an American Drug Enforcement Agency agent to rip off a coke dealer in Guadalajara for $100,000.

Constanzo was changing, however. No longer were animal bones and blood enough to satisfy the demands of his sorcery and his ever-hungry *nganga*. He started to sacrifice humans. Twenty-three people are estimated to have been ritually slaughtered by him and his disciples but it is feared that the true number is much greater, especially as many of the people upon whom he preyed were small-time drug dealers, transvestites and impoverished peasants whom no one would miss and on whom the authorities were not prepared to waste any time.

Constanzo wanted a greater share of the action with the Calzadas and asked for a partnership in the cartel. The leader of the family, Guillermo Calzada, refused, however; a decision that he and his family would live to regret. At the end of April 1987,

Guillermo and six members of his family vanished. In their headquarters were found the trappings of ritualistic ceremony. Six days later, their mutilated corpses, minus brains, sexual organs, fingers, toes, ears and hearts, were discovered in the Zumpango River.

The *nganga* was happy.

In July 1987, Constanzo took a shine to Sara Aldrete, a twenty-two-year-old Mexican woman who was studying at Brownsville University in Texas. She was the girlfriend of Brownsville drug dealer Gilberto Sosa, but Constanzo wooed her away from her boyfriend, making her his *madrina*, or high priestess. She threw herself into the cult and had soon become very important to Constanzo, finessing his sacrifices and rituals by adding her own twists.

Those sacrifices became increasingly elaborate and sadistic when he moved his base to Rancho Santa Helena, about twenty miles from the city of Matamoros. On 28 May 1988, drug dealer Hector de la Fuente and farmer Moises Castillo were used to feed the *nganga* when they were shot dead. Constanzo was not satisfied, however. On a visit to Mexico City, he ordered his disciples to kill a transvestite, Ramon Esquivel, dismember him and dump his remains on a city street corner.

Drug dealers still sought his help. In the same

year, he had been introduced to another drug-running family run by the brothers Elio and Ovidio Hernandez. In August 1988, Ovidio and his two-year-old son were kidnapped by rival dealers and Constanzo was called in to deal with the kidnappers and get Ovidio and his son back. A human sacrifice was staged at Rancho Santa Helena on 12 August and the following day the two were returned unharmed. The sacrifice had sent a message to the superstitious kidnappers and, terrified of what might happen to them, they had opted for the return of their victims. Ovidio was initiated into the cult shortly after, cementing the sorcerer's ties with the powerful Hernandez drug cartel.

Constanzo was at the height of his powers.

His sacrifices were not just limited to enemies. Jorge Montes, his long-time follower, fed the *nganga* in November 1988 after he had been caught snorting a line of coke, strictly forbidden by Constanzo. On 14 February 1989, rival drug dealers Ezequiel Luna, Ruben Garza and Ernesto Diaz were sacrificed and on 25 February, when the sorcerer decided on a whim that he wanted a sacrifice, his new cult member, Ovidio Hernandez, offered up his own fourteen-year-old cousin, Jose Garcia.

The beginning of the end was marked by a sacrifice that gravely disappointed Constanzo. The victim had not screamed for mercy in the way he so enjoyed. His next sacrificial victim had to be a white man, he ordered.

Mark Kilroy, a twenty-one-year-old American student, was visiting Mexico with some friends when he was abducted outside a Matamoros bar. Constanzo was happy with the sacrifice and equally happy a couple of weeks later when Sara Aldrete's former boyfriend, Gilberto Sosa, joined the American in the *nganga*.

Constanzo, however, had miscalculated, failing to anticipate the furore that would be created by the disappearance of Kilroy. Family members and even Texan politicians began to put pressure on the Mexican government to find out what had happened to him. It rapidly escalated into an international incident. Meanwhile, it would actually be the stupidity of one of Constanzo's disciples that would bring him down.

The Mexican authorities were having one of their periodic clampdowns on drug-running. Road blocks had been set up everywhere and when Serafin Hernandez drove past one without stopping, police cars set off in pursuit. He had stupidly believed the sorcerer had rendered him and his vehicle invisible. He also believed the nonsense about being bulletproof and invited officers to try to shoot him when they finally caught up with him and another cult member, David Martinez. The two were driven back to Rancho Santa Helena where drugs and firearms were discovered. Another two followers of Constanzo were rounded up and the four were questioned about the cult's activity. Police discovered the *nganga* in which were bubbling away blood, spiders, scorpions, a dead black cat, a turtle shell, bones, deer antlers and a human brain. Excavation of a patch of ground revealed fifteen corpses.

A manhunt was launched for Constanzo and the senior figures in the cult and sightings were reported from as far away as Chicago, but he had already returned to Mexico City, hiding out in the apartment where he would meet his end in the arms of his lover.

El Duby was sentenced to thirty years in prison and Sara Aldrete was given a six-year sentence for criminal association. Towards the end of that sentence in 1994, her long-delayed trial on multiple murder charges resulted in a sixty-year prison term.

In prison, just before he died of AIDS, Omar Orea said, 'I don't think that the religion will end with us, because it has a lot of people in it. They have found a temple in Monterrey that isn't even related to us. It will continue'.

JUANA BARRAZA
THE LITTLE OLD LADY KILLER

It was so extraordinary that it was hardly believable – a female wrestler who went around killing little old ladies. Forty-eight-year-old Juana Barraza was indeed a female wrestler in wrestling-mad Mexico, working under the professional name of La Dama del Silencio, the Lady of the Silence. The only silence that mattered to her, though, was the silence of death, the ultimate silence that she imposed on her eleven certain victims in Mexico between 2003 and 2005. In truth, she may have imposed that silence on more than forty murder victims attributed to the same killer.

She was born in 1956 into great poverty in the rural state of Hidalgo, north of Mexico City, and had the kind of horrendous upbringing that is likely to result in a very disturbed human being. She never learned to read or write and was given away by her alcoholic mother at the age of twelve in exchange for three beers. The man who bought her so cheaply raped her repeatedly and eventually she became pregnant and gave birth to a baby boy.

Needless to say, Barraza harboured an immense amount of resentment towards her mother and it seems likely that the women she killed were substitutes for her.

She eventually had four children and tried to be a better mother to them than hers had been, but she experienced the tragedy of losing her oldest son who died after being beaten with a baseball bat by muggers. Her second child, a girl, married early and left home, leaving Barraza with her two youngest children, a thirteen-year-old boy and a girl of eleven. She scraped a living from street-vending, domestic work and stealing, but even though life was tough, she is remembered by neighbours as being friendly. Meanwhile, she was busy killing little old ladies.

All of her victims were sixty years old or more and most of them lived alone. She killed them by bludgeoning them with a heavy object or by strangling them with tights, electric flex or the stethoscope she often carried. She robbed them of totemic items such as religious statues or rings, but these were taken, in the classic manner of the serial killer, as trophies rather than for financial gain. Disturbingly, in some cases there was also evidence of sexual abuse.

The *Mataviejitas* (Little Old Lady Killer), as she became known, spent time getting to know her victims before killing them, gaining their trust and friendship. She might help them carry their shopping home from the market or ask if they had any cleaning work. While she was still on the loose police thought that she was possibly posing as a government official, offering the vulnerable women the opportunity to sign up to welfare programmes.

The investigation was a difficult one and the pressure on the authorities to find the *Mataviejitas* was intense. At one point they were convinced that they were actually searching for not one, but two killers. There was also a strange coincidence that distracted them for some time; at least three of the killer's victims owned a print of an eighteenth-century painting, *The Boy in the Red Waistcoat* by French artist Jean-Baptiste Greuze. Half a million leaflets were distributed, appealing for help and warning of the danger. Elderly ladies were told to beware of strangers who approached them in the market or outside the church, offering to take them home or to help them in some way.

The authorities were heavily criticised by the media for dismissing newspaper talk of a serial killer as just 'media sensationalism', even as late as 2005, when it was obvious to everyone else what was going on. They had witnesses, or at least people who had seen someone suspicious leaving victims' houses around the time of the murders. In one instance, she was spotted leaving the flat of her latest victim, eighty-five-year-old widow Guadalupe Oliveira, in the Tlatelco suburb of Mexico City. She was described by a witness on that occasion as being a large woman wearing a red blouse. Police and many Mexicans, unable to conceive of a woman carrying out such dreadful acts, speculated that it had actually been a man in drag.

It ended on 25 January 2006 when Barraza tricked her way into the house of an elderly woman called Ana Maria de los Reyes, asking if she might have a glass of water. Once inside the house, she strangled the woman with her stethoscope. As she was leaving, however, the old woman's lodger was returning home. He identified her and she was arrested.

News of the arrest spread fast and there was huge relief in Mexico City. News spread, too, of her career as La Dama del Silencio. Wrestling in Mexico is known as *Lucha Libre*, literally 'free wrestling'. Wrestlers wear masks and costumes and use nicknames, and enjoy the adoration of the Mexican public. Her wrestling added a neat populist twist to the case. Juana had often been seen in the front row of major wrestling bouts and she also organised wrestling events for small-town festivals. Occasionally she would climb into the ring herself in her guise of La Dama del Silencio. Mexican wrestlers are split into two categories – *técnicos*, who are the good guys and fight according to the rules and *rudos*, the wrestlers who break the rules, and get the crowd going. It hardly needs saying, but La Dama del Silencio was a *rudo*, 'to the core', as she later said.

She was charged with ten murders but pleaded guilty to one – Ana Maria de los Reyes. 'I only killed one little old lady. Not the others,' she told the court on her first appearance. 'It isn't right to pin the others on me'. When they asked her why she did it, she said simply, 'I got angry'. Evidence was piling up against her, however. Fingerprints placed her at the scene of at least eleven of the murders.

Within hours of her arrest, Barraza was paraded in front of the television and press cameras. She posed beside a plasticine bust that had been made of the prime suspect in the case from the description of a witness and, unsurprisingly, it bore some resemblance to her. Photos were released by the police of her taking part in a re-creation of the murder of Ana Maria de los Reyes, and excerpts from her interrogation were released to the media. This was even before she had been remanded in custody. It was a circus and there was a great deal of criticism of the police's handling of the case. One human rights expert said that 'the media has become the great judge'.

At her trial in spring of 2008, the prosecution alleged that she had killed as many as forty elderly ladies. Her lawyers attempted to have her declared mentally unfit, but psychologists had established that she had been completely aware of her actions. She told the court about her upbringing and explained that her actions were a direct result of her mother's treatment of her.

Nonetheless, on 31 March 2008, she was found guilty on sixteen charges of murder and aggravated burglary, and eleven separate counts of murder, and sentenced to 759 years in prison.

In Mexico sentences are served concurrently and she is likely to have to serve fifty years in prison. Juana Barraza will be eligible for parole at the age of one hundred, when she, herself, will be a little old lady.

PART FOUR

AFRICA

RAYA AND SAKINA

In November 1919 the shadow of the First World War continued to be cast across the Egyptian city of Alexandria where criminality was rife. Prostitution and alcohol had been legalised by the occupying British forces and alongside them rose an unhealthy trade in drugs, rampant theft, racketeering and murder. The authorities seemed powerless to do anything about the rising tide of crime. One journalist of the time asked where the police were, especially in the light of the series of killings and disappearances of women that started in 1918 and continued unabated for several years. 'Where is the sword of government that should fall on the necks of bloodthirsty criminals?' he wrote. 'Where is the vigilant eye of justice that should never wink? Where is the mighty hand of authority?' The government, he maintained, 'has been too intent upon training the hordes of its secret political police to concern itself with training forces necessary to safeguard our internal security or personal safety. It is time for us to ask it to address the dangers posed by that negligence. The recent murders are a great calamity, the horrors of which have blackened the forehead of the twentieth century'.

Indeed, the authorities in Alexandria did have other fish to fry. Stone-throwing children were attacking the forces of the British Empire who were trying to maintain security in the country, keeping their minds and efforts off the murderous activities of a number of individuals operating in Alexandria at the time.

Women were disappearing on a daily basis and all had in common the fact that they were wearing gold jewellery or were carrying cash. Some were reported to have been last seen in the company of a woman named Sakina. She was in fact questioned a number of times, but the police were never able to pin anything on her.

On 20 December 1920, the dismembered remains of a woman were found at the side of a road. The body was in such a poor state that it was impossible to identify it. Even the piece of black cloth and black-and-white striped socks found nearby were no help. Around the same time, the owner of a building in Labban uncovered a skull and the remains of a woman while he was clearing a drainage well underneath his house. Once again, the authorities suspected

Sakina, who had lived in the building until recently. Sakina and her sister Raya originated from Upper Egypt. While working as a prostitute, Sakina had met and fallen in love with Abdel-Aal and the two had eloped and moved to Alexandria. Meanwhile, Raya had been widowed and, as was the custom in Egypt at the time, married her late husband's brother, Hasaballah, a thief and hashish smuggler. When Hasaballah fell foul of the authorities in Kafr Al-Zayyat, the couple were banished and moved in with Sakina and her husband in Alexandria's Azarita district.

In Alexandria the two women proved resourceful, opening a string of brothels. The first was in Souq Al-Asr, known to them as 'The Camp' due to its proximity to a British camp full of British soldiers, potential customers. Another followed near to the Al-Fahham Mosque, a third was close to the Akhwas Mosque, a fourth was opened in the Al-Uyuni area and a fifth was set up near the Labban Bakery. They took no chances. It was customary to obtain protection for such establishments. They took on a tough-nut named Orabi Hassan to deal with troublemakers or anyone failing to pay his bill.

Alexandria was not the only place in Egypt where criminality was running wild. The town of Tantra, too, had its problems with drugs, prostitution and racketeering. Rather more ominously, it also had the problem of disappearing women and in November 1920 Mahmoud Allam was sentenced to death for the murder of a number of these. He and his wife had been killing prostitutes and other women in order to steal their jewellery.

Sakina was immediately under suspicion for the murder of the woman found under the house in Alexandria and when a police officer visited her house his suspicions were immediately aroused by the strong smell of incense. She excused it saying that when your house is also a brothel there are always some strange smells that have to be dealt with. Not satisfied with her answer, the officer immediately informed his superiors and a senior police officer was dispatched to carry out an investigation.

Walking around the house, the officer noticed that some of the floor tiles were newer than others. He ordered them to be lifted and immediately this was done, a terrible smell arose from the earth below. They began to dig and made a grim discovery. The space beneath the floor had been used as a grave for three women.

An immediate search was ordered of all the houses in which Sakina and Raya had lived. This uncovered the remains of a total of seventeen women, most of whom could not be identified as they were prostitutes or runaways. Meanwhile, the women were arrested and interrogated, Sakina, the younger of the two, holding out longer than her sister who confessed immediately, helping police to find the bodies.

Witnesses began to come forward. One woman described how, a few months earlier, she had seen Hasaballah and Abdel-Aal, the two husbands, enter Sakina's room with a woman known as Zanouba, 'the poultry woman'. A lot of drinking was done through the night and then, as dawn approached, the woman said, there was a loud scream. She had asked Sakina about it next morning but her enquiry was brushed aside. Six weeks later, she continued, a similar incident occurred when Fatima, a one-eyed woman who was a servant-broker, spent the night carousing with Sakina, Raya and their husbands. Again there was a scream in the middle of the night and again Sakina brushed away her question about it the next day.

Zanouba, it later emerged, knew a little too much about what was going on and was killed in order to prevent her using her information against them.

The women ensnared their victims very easily. They would go to the market and be on the lookout for any woman wearing a lot of jewellery. Once she had been singled out, Raya would approach the woman and casually engage her in conversation about the prices or quality of the goods on offer in the shop they were in at the time. The conversation would cleverly be worked around to the fact that she had come into possession of some goods that she was selling at better prices than the ones on offer in the market. She would then invite the woman to her house to have a look at what she had to offer.

At the house, each member of the gang had a role to play. The victim would be given drugged drinks and when she became disorientated they would pounce. Abdel-Aal would grab her feet while Orabi and another man, Abdul Razik, would pin her arms behind her back. Meanwhile, Hasaballah would press a towel against the victim's nose and mouth, suffocating her.

Their first victim had been Raya's neighbour, Hanim. Raya had become irrationally jealous of her after she had purchased some beautiful new jewellery ,and she, her husband and Razik and Orabi killed her. Raya went off to fetch Sakina to tell her what she had done. When they returned to the house, they found the men digging a grave and Hanim's body lying, eyes wide open, under a nearby bench. When Sakina expressed her horror, her sister threatened her with the same fate as Hanim. She calmed down and was given a share of the spoils for her trouble – three Egyptian pounds.

Egyptians were horrified by the barbarity of the murders, and the lengthy trial attracted dramatic headlines in the Egyptian press. The women's humanity was questioned and at one point, when a newspaper printed the headline 'Raya and Sakina in the Zoo!', thousands of people flocked to Alexandria's zoo believing that the two women were being displayed in a cage like animals.

There was great controversy over whether women should be liable for the death penalty. No woman had ever been executed in Egypt, but there seemed to be no reason why they could not be sentenced to death if found guilty, as seemed inevitable.

The trial lasted for three days, from 10 to 12 May, and apart from the sisters, their husbands, their two accomplices, Orabi and Razik, there were four other defendants who had been involved in some way. The defence was almost non-existent and the defence lawyers merely resorted to trying to push the blame away from their client onto one of the others. Three of the defendants were acquitted, while the goldsmith who bought the stolen jewellery from them was sentenced to five years in prison.

On 16 May 1921 Raya and Sakina, along with their husbands and two accomplices, were sentenced to death by hanging. They were the first women to be executed in Egypt.

DAISY DE MELKER

The staff at the Children's Memorial Hospital in the Braamfontein area of Johannesburg where Daisy de Melker worked, believe that she never really left the place. They say her ghost still walks the corridors and when it appears at the bedside of a sick child, that child is going to die.

She certainly was no stranger to death – it stalked her throughout her life. The problem was that on more than one occasion she was responsible for it.

She was born Daisy Louisa Hancorn-Smith in 1886 in Seven Fountains, about twenty-five miles from the town of Germanstown in the British Cape Colony in what is now South Africa. Her parents had emigrated from England to try to make their living from farming, but life was tough for Daisy and her ten siblings.

She was a bright child, but was born with a cleft palate which made her speech indistinct. When she was about eight years old, her father went to Rhodesia to see whether he could make a better living there, having learned that land was extremely cheap. Two years later Daisy joined her father and two brothers, but by the age of thirteen she was back in Cape Colony, attending the Good Hope Seminary in Cape Town, a very good school.

Returning to Rhodesia after completing her education, Daisy made the acquaintance of a young Englishman named Bert Fuller, an Assistant Commissioner of Native Affairs. He was well paid and would one day be the recipient of a good pension. He lived in rent-free government accommodation, drove a car and enjoyed the services of a cook, a gardener and a housekeeper. The two fell in love but Daisy was not yet ready to settle down. She returned to Cape Colony to train as a nurse, working for three years at the Berea Nursing Home in Durban.

In 1906, she returned to Rhodesia where Bert was waiting for her. They announced their engagement and set a date for the wedding. Meanwhile, Bert had been transferred to Matetsi, near the Victoria Falls, a wild, steamy place where the temperature could get as high as 110°F. Daisy was living in Bulawayo but visited Bert in Matetsi frequently. She found him in poor health when she visited, but his illness was put down to the harsh frontier life in which bugs and disease were rife. On one visit she asked for the wedding to be postponed until October 1907 so that she could complete her nursing training. Bert had no problem with this and, realising the new responsibilities he was about to assume, he decided to make a will. Daisy was to get everything – whatever money he had and the substantial amount in his pension fund.

No sooner had Daisy arrived back in Bulawayo than she received a telegram informing her that Bert was very ill and unlikely to live. She returned immediately to learn that he had been diagnosed with blackwater fever. Not long after, he died. He was buried in March 1907.

In December that year, she became the beneficiary of Bert's estate. She had nothing to do with his death, but she liked what it had brought her.

Back in Cape Colony, now aged twenty-two, she found work as a nurse at a hospital in Johannesburg. Around this time she met Alf Cowle, a thirty-six-year-old plumber from the Isle of Man who earned good money working for the Johannesburg municipality. On 3 March 1909, Daisy and Alf were married, signing a pre-marital contract that made all their assets jointly owned, and moved into a house in Turffontein. It was not the most salubrious of areas and did not help Alf's already fragile constitution. He had a bad back and his weak stomach had never really become used to the spicy foods and fatty meats that were served up in the Cape.

In 1910, Daisy gave birth to twin boys who died

in infancy, but a year later she had a son, Rhodes Cecil – named after the founder of Rhodesia, Cecil Rhodes – who became the most important thing in her life. Lester followed in 1913 and two years later Eric was born. Lester died at the age of four, however, of an abscess on his liver. She had now lost four people close to her in just ten years. That number became five when her other son, Eric, died a few weeks after Lester, of an unknown ailment.

After thirteen years of marriage, Alf was not a well man. He had consulted several doctors, tried numerous drugs and concoctions, but did not seem to be getting any better. On 8 January 1923, he began to vomit and sweat; he was constipated and crying out with the pain. Daisy gave him some Epsom salts she herself had mixed and then called the doctor. There was nothing to be done, however; by the end of that day he was dead, aged forty-nine. An autopsy attributed his demise to Bright's Syndrome – a kidney disease – that had led to a cerebral haemorrhage.

Daisy was thirty-seven years old and a widow for the second time. She was also going to be in need of money, without Alf's weekly wage packet. That came in the shape of Alf's will which left her more than £1,800, a quite substantial sum. She also had possession of the house in which they had lived. She still wanted to work, however, even with such a tidy sum in the bank, and, unable to return to nursing after such a long time away, found a job as a porter at the Children's Memorial Hospital.

Meanwhile, her son Rhodes was a big problem. Spoiled since childhood, he was hopeless and lazy at school. She spent a lot of money getting him into good schools but they did not seem to make him a better scholar. Exasperated, she enrolled him at a plumbing college but he would even fail at that.

Her next husband was another Englishman. Bob Sproat was a plumber like Alf Cowie and, like his predecessor, earned good money, a prerequisite, of course, for Daisy's husbands. They married in July 1926 and once again Bob signed a wedding contract that left everything to Daisy, should he die. But Bob, like Alf, was not in good health from the beginning, suffering from stomach cramps and chronic indigestion. A year after their wedding, he collapsed with a pain in his side. A month later, he collapsed again in severe pain. The doctor diagnosed indigestion and gave him medicine. On 8 October, he fell ill again and the doctor was called. He gave Bob something to ease the pain.

Daisy, meanwhile, summoned both Billy Johnson, a friend of Bob, and his brother William. She told the latter that he should come to what she described as his brother's 'deathbed'. During that night, as they sat at his bedside, Bob remembered that he had not made a will since the one that he had made in England leaving everything to his mother. He told Billy that he wanted to leave everything to Daisy and repeated this to William when he arrived. That morning William drew up a new will that Bob signed.

Suddenly, however, he got better and was even well enough to go to work a few days later. It did not last. A month later, he died suddenly after complaining of feeling unwell, his death certificate attributing his death to arteriosclerosis and a cerebral haemorrhage.

Daisy inherited almost £5,000 and celebrated by taking her son Rhodes on holiday to England for three months. They brought back a shiny new motorbike for Rhodes and Daisy settled into the life of a well-off widow. Rhodes, meanwhile, drifted from one menial job to another until he found employment as a mechanic in Swaziland. He was still a wastrel, however, and on her visits he always asked her for money. Always insistent on everyone leaving a will, she persuaded him to write one, making her the beneficiary.

From 1928 until 1931, Daisy was alone but at the age of forty-five she decided it was time to find a new husband. In January 1931 she married former South African rugby star, forty-seven-year-old Sid de Melker, another plumber, who worked at a gold mine. His health, in contrast to her previous husbands, was excellent.

Rhodes, however, was beginning to feel unwell. Having lost his job in Swaziland, he had moved in with Daisy and Sid but managed to find another position as a mechanic. He was by this time an unpleasant and increasingly violent individual who argued with everyone in the house, including Sid's daughter who also lived with them. On one occasion he even hit his mother. But he was suffering from chronic stomach cramps and was diagnosed with malaria. When he became really ill, Daisy stayed by his bed for three weeks, caring for him, and eventually he began to get well. On 2 March 1932, however, he complained of a headache. The following day, he came home early from work and went to bed. Three days later he died, aged just twenty.

A month later, Daisy received a cheque for £100 from the African Life Insurance Company. It was from a policy that she had taken out on Rhodes when he was a child. It would have matured the following year when he turned twenty-one. She also made sure she got his outstanding wages of fifteen shillings from the garage where he had worked.

Waste not, want not, she thought. Unbeknown to Daisy, however, William Sproat, Bob's brother, had become increasingly suspicious about his brother's death and took those suspicions to the police. They exhumed the bodies of Alf Cowle, Rhodes and Bob Sproat. They were found to contain strychnine and arsenic.

Daisy was arrested and when her house was searched, thermos flasks containing arsenic residue were found. A friend of Rhodes from the garage came forward to say that he had become unwell after drinking some coffee from Rhodes' flask. When asked who had made the coffee for Rhodes, he told them that it was his mother, Daisy. She had obtained the poison from a pharmacy in the area where she had formerly lived, claiming it was to be used to kill stray cats who were knocking over her dustbin at night and making a terrible noise. Crucially, she used her old address when signing the poisons register which was required when obtaining a substance such as arsenic.

Her trial, starting on 17 October 1932, was a sensation, the public gallery filled with women who glared at her throughout the proceedings. She scowled back at them and occasionally shouted at witnesses. She was certain she was going to be acquitted and saw herself selling her story to Hollywood. She was already behaving like a Hollywood star, smiling seductively for the photographers who gathered outside the court.

Forty days later, however, she was stunned when the judge announced to a packed courtroom that she was guilty of poisoning her son – he was the only case they could definitely prove to be murder – and that she would be 'taken from here to a place of execution where you will hang by the neck until you are dead'.

On 30 December, at Pretoria Central Prison, Daisy de Melker walked the fifty-two paces from her cell to the gallows chamber in which was a beam from which dangled seven nooses. She was positioned under one of them, her feet being pushed apart to fit into two white footprints painted on the floor. The noose was slipped over her head and a hood followed. The hangman pulled the lever, the trapdoor opened and Daisy de Melker fell through to her death.

The men of 1930s South Africa could sleep easy in their beds.

MOSES SITHOLE

The first body was found by a police reservist walking his dog in a field on 4 January 1995. She was semi-naked and badly decomposed. She would never be identified.

On 9 February, the second turned up, completely naked this time, but with her clothes piled up on top of her and weighed down with rocks. From her fingerprints police established her to be twenty-seven-year-old Beauty Nuku Soko who had disappeared the previous month on her way to visit her sister in Klipgat.

A month passed before the next one was found. On 6 March, construction workers digging a ditch in the township of Atteridgeville, saw the breasts of a woman protruding from the earth. It was twenty-five-year-old Sara Matlakala Mokono who had gone missing three days earlier en route to a meeting with someone who had promised her work.

The grisly monthly instalments continued with the discovery of yet another body on 12 April. Twenty-five-year-old Letta Nomthandazo Ndlangamandla was found in Atteridgeville, her hands tied behind her back with her bra. She had been strangled. Her clothes were found nearby but her panties had disappeared. Like Sara Mokono, Letta had left to meet a man in Pretoria about a job offer. With her had been her two-year-old son, Sibusiso. He was found dead about sixty-five feet away from her with a head wound, although it seems likely that he had died of exposure. Police surmised that he had been left alive and, frightened of leaving his mother's body, had stayed close to her until he had succumbed to the elements.

The killer's methods were noted by a local newspaper to be similar to those of David Selepe, who had strangled eight women in the township of Cleveland. Selepe, however, had recently been shot dead by police. There was little doubt that there was a new serial killer on the loose.

This was emphasised even more on 13 May when the body of Esther Moshibudi Mainetja was found in a field of corn, near Hercules in Pretoria West. She was naked and her killer had strangled her with items of her clothing. The last sighting of her had been the previous evening when she had been seen leaving a café, presumably on her way home.

Women were disappearing at a frightening rate and by the time the next body turned up, five had vanished. Francina Nomsa Sithebe was found on 13 June, slumped against a tree in a sitting position. She was still wearing her dress, but her panties and handbag strap had been used to tie her to the tree by the neck.

Three days later, nineteen-year-old Elizabeth Granny Mathetsa's naked body was found in Rosslyn, nine miles north-west of Pretoria. She had been missing since 25 May. Thirty-year-old Ernestina Mohadi Mosebo was found, raped and strangled, in Rosherville on 22 June, and on 24 June, Nikiwe Diko's body turned up in Atteridgeville. Missing for more than two months, Nikiwe, like many of the others, had been lured to her death by a job opportunity. By the time she was found, her body had been savaged by wild dogs and lay in pieces. Her hands had been tied using her panties and her pantyhose had been pulled so tightly around her neck that there were bone fragments embedded in it. The killer had pushed a stick into her vagina.

The authorities threw resources at this horrific series of crimes and soon a crucial witness emerged. Absalom Sangweni, who lived in a caravan in Beyers Park, Boksburg, described seeing a man and woman walk into the veld on 17 July. He had actually shouted to them to tell them that their way would be blocked by a fence but the man replied that he was aware of that but that he knew the area. The couple disappeared. A little later, Sangweni was still watching when he saw the man reappear alone. He described him as carrying something shiny in his hand and that he seemed furtive as if he wanted to get away from the area as quickly as possible. He did, in fact, start to run. When Sangweni went to investigate, he found the woman out in the velt. She had been assaulted and was not moving. He went to a payphone at a nearby supermarket and informed the police. She had been strangled with her belt and was later identified as Josephine Mantsali Miangeni, a twenty-five-year-old mother of four. As with the others, she had left home to meet a man about the possibility of work.

A special task force was set up to investigate these harrowing acts. They were puzzled about the bewildering array of different methods the killer had used. Some victims had been tied up, some had not. Some had had their hands tied in front of them, some behind. Were these women all killed by the same man or could there be more than one serial killer out there?

While police pondered this question the bodies continued to pile up. Twenty-one-year-old Granny Dimakatso Ramela was found clothed and strangled the day after Josephine Miangeni was found. Twenty-eight-year-old Mildred Ntiya Lepule, was driven to Pretoria by her husband to meet a man about a job offer. He, and no one else, ever saw her alive again. On 26 July she was found in a canal near the Bon Accord Dam, close to the town of Onderstepoort, north of Pretoria. She had been strangled with her pantyhose and her panties had been pulled over her face.

The murderer seemed to be honing his technique as he went on. Now he was garrotting his victims, using a stick to tighten their clothing around their throats. It was a disturbing development.

On 8 August, twenty-five-year-old Elsie Khoti Masango was found, again near Onderstepoort, and the following day another body was found. It had been burned in a veld fire and has never been identified. Three more turned up before the end of the month, two of which have also never been identified. Another body was found on 12 September. Four days later, the first of ten bodies was found at the Van Dyk Mine near Boksburg.

By now, of course, the media were in a frenzy, and when this killing field was discovered the area was inundated with reporters as well as police officers. Even South African president, Nelson Mandela, visited the scene.

This site brought several interesting elements to

the investigation. Firstly, its proximity to Boksburg Prison seemed significant, although no one was really sure why. Secondly, scattered around the area were a number of objects of ritualistic significance – red and black candles, mirrors, feathers, knives and so on, items normally linked with traditional healing. They might or might not have a connection with the killings. One chilling new discovery was that the killer had refined his method still further. These victims' hands had been tied to their necks; the more they struggled, the more they strangled themselves. It was a cruel and pitiless way to die.

Police announced that these deaths were linked to the ones in Atteridgeville and offered a large reward for information leading to the arrest of the perpetrator. They began to believe that more than one person may have been involved on at least some of the murders. The killer, they reasoned, was a very organised, intelligent person who was growing in confidence with every murder. They believed that he may have been hurt by a woman sometime in his past and now he was raping and killing her over and over again to punish her and make himself feel better.

In a handbag found near the Boksburg killing field, police found an identity card that named a woman, Amelia Rapodile. When the people with whom she worked were questioned about her, they said that she had had an appointment with a man named Moses Sithole on 7 September. She had not been seen again after that date. They found an application form for an organisation run by Sithole – Youth Against Human Abuse. Sithole had offered her a job with the organisation. The phone number on the form led them to Sithole's sister, Kwazi, who lived in Wattville, near Boksburg. She told them that he did not live there and, indeed, she had no idea where he was.

Another victim was identified as Tryphina Mogotsi and the link with Moses Sithole became even stronger. He had also offered her a job with Youth Against Human Abuse after which she had disappeared.

As they looked for Sithole, the killer, unfazed by the tremendous media coverage and heightened police activity, had the gall to strike again just a week later. Twenty-year-old Agnes Sibongile Mbuli disappeared on her way to meet a friend and was found dead on 3 October at Kleinfontein railway station, near Benoni.

The day she disappeared, however, Tamsen de Beer, a reporter at the *Star* newspaper, took a call from a man, calling himself Joseph Magwena, claiming to be the Gauteng killer, Gauteng being the name for the province in which the killings had been taking place. 'I am the man that is so highly wanted,' he said. He went on to say that he was ready to give himself up. She informed the police.

He called her four times, proving his involvement by providing details of the crimes that only the killer and the investigating officers would know. He explained that he had begun to kill after a woman falsely accused him of rape for which he went to jail and while incarcerated he was badly abused by fellow prisoners. He described how he killed the women and said that many of his victims saw the other victims before they, too, died. He denied that he had carried out the Cleveland killings and the killing of Letta Ndlangamandla and her son. He loved children, he said.

He provided the last resting place of a victim who had still not been found and police were convinced that Joseph Magwena was a pseudonym of the man they were searching for, Moses Sithole. A picture of Sithole was published in the national press but, as if to taunt the police, another body turned up the following day at the Village Main Reef Mine near Johannesburg.

Sithole emerged from hiding a few days later to phone his brother-in-law, Maxwell, asking him to get him a gun and arranging to meet him at a factory in Benoni. Maxwell went straight to the police.

At nine in the evening of 18 October, when Sithole arrived at the factory, as arranged with Maxwell, he became suspicious and fled, followed by a policeman who had been posing as a security guard. The policeman, Inspector Mulovhedzi, shouted to Sithole to stop, blindly firing two bullets at him in a dark alleyway. He missed and Sithole came running at him, wielding an axe. The inspector fired at his legs but Sithole kept coming. Finally, after he had been struck on the hand by the axe, Mulovhedzi succeeded in hitting his attacker. Sithole fell to the ground, shot in the stomach and the leg. Police were initially worried that it would be a repeat of the Selepe case and that their suspect had been killed before his case could come to court, but Sithole survived.

On 23 October 1995, Moses Sithole was charged with twenty-nine murders and five days later, the press revealed that he was HIV-positive. Under questioning in his hospital bed, he was uncooperative until a female officer entered the room. At that point he began to describe a number of his crimes, masturbating as he did so. He said he only killed in daylight and that he only chose the 'pretty ones'. While they died, he would masturbate. He denied that he had worked with an accomplice and claimed that there had been copycat killings.

A fresh newspaper frenzy erupted on 30 September 1996 when it was announced that Sithole would be charged with thirty-eight counts of murder, forty counts of rape and six counts of robbery.

Like many serial killers, Moses Sithole's childhood had been troubled. His father had died when he was five and he and his five siblings had been abandoned by their mother at a police station. Placed in an orphanage, Sithole claims to have been mistreated and ran away after three years. He moved in with his older brother Patrick and worked at a series of menial jobs on farms and in the gold mines around Johannesburg. Gradually, however, he drifted towards killing as a way to take revenge on the father who had died, the mother who had abandoned him and the woman who, he claimed, had falsely accused him of rape.

The trial, a long and very expensive affair, began on 21 October 1996. On 5 December 1997, he was found guilty of all charges and sentenced to fifty years' imprisonment for each of the thirty-eight murders committed by him, twelve years for each of the rapes and five years for each of the robberies. These sentences were ordered by the judge to run consecutively, meaning that his total sentence ran to 2,410 years. The judge stipulated that he should serve at least 930 years before being eligible for parole, meaning that he will never be released. He is held in C-Max Pretoria Central Prison's maximum security section.

STUART WILKEN

He was a rare serial killer – one that diversified.

Normally serial killers will focus their murderous intent on one distinct type of person – young boys, women who wear high heels, prostitutes, blondes and so on. Stuart Wilken, however, killed adolescent boys and prostitutes. He said he killed the boys because he wanted to send them to a better place, far from the violence and neglect of this world. It has been suggested that perhaps he saw himself in them and was symbolically saving himself. As for the women, it is more difficult to say, although he might have been taking revenge on them for abandoning him. It would not, after all, be the first time a serial killer had tried to eradicate womankind because he perceived himself to have been betrayed by one or two of the female gender.

The baby that would become the murderer of eight people was born in the town of Boksburg in South Africa on 11 November 1966. Just six months later, he was abandoned by his mother in a phone box, along with his two-year-old sister. They were discovered by a domestic servant who took them to the house of her employer who took them in. It would have been better, however, if they had been left in the phone box. The man who took them in, known as Doep, would introduce the young Stuart to the callousness and depravity that would characterise his life.

The abuse was horrendous. Stuart was burned on the genitals with cigarettes and was forced to eat with the man's domestic animals from their bowls. Doep's astonishingly depraved behaviour included bestiality with his animals, after which he would force Stuart to lick his unwashed penis.

Eventually, the people who lived next door to Doep took pity on Stuart and took him in. He was in a pitiable condition, suffering from malnutrition and his body infested with lice. The neighbours were called Wilken and it was at this point that he was given the name Stuart. Soon, he had moved to Port Elizabeth with the Wilkens.

He went to school, but the casual brutality that had become the norm in his life continued there. He was inadequate both academically and socially, failing to pass third grade three times and being bullied and made fun of because he was an orphan. Incredibly, his teacher did nothing to stop the other pupils from humiliating him; in fact, he encouraged them. Finally, when Stuart could take no more, he attacked his teacher. His punishment was to be severely beaten by the school principal in front of his schoolmates.

He was no easier at home, often biting his adoptive mother and being aggressive and violent towards her other children. As punishment he was often locked up in his room where he would take his temper out on the furniture, smashing lights and knocking over tables and chairs. He said that on occasion he was locked in a cupboard and he was even punished for wetting the bed.

Even when he was sent home from school for fighting back when another boy attacked him, his mother punished him. It is no wonder that he developed into a strongly independent boy, determined to make his way in the world without the help of adults whom he saw as failing him at every turn.

Even the Church let him down. At the age of nine, after attending Sunday school, he was invited by the deacon back to his house. The man raped him.

When his adoptive father died later that same year, his mother felt unable to cope with Stuart. He was smoking marijuana by this time and seemed to be followed by trouble everywhere he went. She arranged for him to be accepted by a reformatory for difficult boys where life became even worse. He was sodomised by the other boys and was often locked up naked in a small cell as a punishment. He ran away many times, but never got far. Finally, when he was sixteen, he enrolled in the South African army, but even that did not work out for him. After just four months he was discharged after a suicide attempt. He moved back home with Mrs Wilken in the town of Despatch, not far from Port Elizabeth.

It seemed that stability might be entering his life when he married his first wife, Lynne, in December 1985. They had a daughter named Wuane but afterwards, according to his wife, Stuart began to behave oddly. He refused to have anything but anal sex with her and it would very often be done in very uncomfortable positions. He assaulted her frequently and she had him arrested for smoking marijuana. For his part, Wilken claims that she became a prostitute after the birth of their daughter. The inevitable result was divorce.

He met and married another woman, Veronica. To the two sons she already had, the couple added another two daughters but this marriage also foundered, especially when Veronica's parents accused Wilken of sodomising her sons. Wilken moved out and lived rough, sleeping in the bushes at Happy Valley, a Port Elizabeth park.

Stuart Wilken had become a killer long before this, his first murder being committed while he was still married to his first wife Lynne, in February 1990. He sodomised and then strangled fifteen-year-old Monte Fiko, a street urchin, at Cilliers Secondary School in Sydenham.

He killed again, eight months later, on 3 October. Following a furious argument with Lynne, he picked up a twenty-five-year-old prostitute, Virginia Gysman, and paid her to go with him to Dagbreek Primary School where they had sex. When he tried to penetrate her anally, she began to struggle. He strangled her with her clothing and climaxed as she died. Her body was found next day, lying in the school playground.

A few months later, on 10 January, he picked up another prostitute, thirty-seven-year-old Mercia Papenfus, who had been touting for business at a local hotel. He took her to a park but she refused to have sex until he had first paid her. Wilken flew into a furious rage and strangled her. As she lay dead, he sodomised her.

It would be nine months before he would once again feel the urge to kill, returning once again to murdering adolescent boys. It was a fourteen-year-old boy, again living on the streets. He agreed to provide sex for payment but once again Wilken lost his temper when the boy asked for his money. The two struggled and the boy attempted to escape, but Wilken was too strong. He sodomised him and then experienced an orgasm as he wrapped his hands around the boy's neck and squeezed the life from him.

Another unidentified street child followed sometime between June and September of 1993. He was sodomised and strangled and his body was dumped in a ravine.

On 27 July 1995, Wilken returned to killing prostitutes. Forty-two-year-old Boniswa Zweni was sodomised and strangled in Prince Alfred's Park. Having killed and sexually assaulted her, however, he was still not satisfied. He sexually assaulted her with a knife, stabbing her repeatedly. He then cut off her nipples, put them in his mouth and ate them.

His penultimate victim was his own daughter Wuane, from his first marriage. The last sighting of the little girl, on 29 September 1995, was by her half-sister who saw her with Wilken, who had been visiting his first wife. They were seated on the pavement close to her home.

Wilken took Wuane to Happy Valley park where he later claimed he examined her vagina and found that she was no longer a virgin. He became distressed and, wishing to protect her from the kind of things that had happened to him in his life, strangled her. He would return at night to sleep with her decomposing corpse, talking to it and covering it with a tarpaulin when he was not around.

His last murder would present police with an opportunity to catch a serial killer they did not even realise they were chasing.

On 22 January 1997, twelve-year-old Henry Bakers disappeared. His mother initially thought he had decided to spend the night at his grandmother's house in nearby Missionvale, as he frequently did. However, when there was still no sign of him by Friday morning, she went to her mother's house where she was told that Henry had left for home on Wednesday, two days previously.

The frantic mother contacted the police who discovered that after leaving his grandmother's house, Henry had played with a friend in a nearby park. The friend had to run an errand for his parents but on his return saw Henry with Stuart Wilken in a nearby street. Henry and his mother knew Wilken and he had even lived briefly in their house during a rough patch in his marriage. When the boy asked Henry where he was going, Wilken interjected that it was none of his business.

The police became concerned, as they were already investigating the two cases of sodomy on her sons that had been brought against him by his second wife Veronica. Furthermore, his daughter Wuane had disappeared in 1995 and they noted that, like Henry Bakers, she had last been seen with Wilken.

When he was arrested on 28 January 1997 and brought in for questioning, Wilken told investigating officers that he had been with Henry on Wednesday, but they had separated after a while and he had no idea what had become of the boy. He claimed to have spent the night at the house of a lady friend. He was released but when his alibi was found to be a lie, he was rearrested.

When the officer in charge of the investigation told Wilken that they knew he had killed two children and that he had returned to their bodies to sodomise them after death, Wilken cracked. 'I am sick,' he said. He admitted to the murder of Wuane and Henry, and added that he had returned to the boy's body that morning to have sex with it.

He told them that Henry had asked Wilken about sex and he had taken him to a field at the edge of the park where they had met. He had stripped Henry and then committed fellatio on him before sodomising and strangling him, climaxing as he did so. He said that Henry had told him he was being beaten at home and that he wanted to free the boy from the torture he was going through by sending him to God.

He described how he returned to the decomposing bodies of the boys he had killed, rubbing vinegar and butter on their feet to put police sniffer dogs off the scent. He also inserted rolled up pieces of newspaper into their anuses to keep maggots out so that he could continue to have sex with them. He vehemently denied raping Wuane, however, or having sex with her body after she was dead.

He also described how he liked to be looking into the eyes of his victims as he strangled them, watching as the life oozed out of them.

Stuart Wilken was charged eventually with ten counts of murder and five of sodomy. At his trial, he became sexually aroused on more than one occasion by the testimony being presented, once indicating as he was being led to the toilet that he was going there to masturbate.

Found guilty of seven murders and two counts of sodomy, he received seven terms of life imprisonment. He currently languishes in St Albans prison in South Africa, victim of hallucinations and delusions of persecution. He claims that he is haunted by the ghosts of his victims.

You really could not blame them.

PART FIVE

AUSTRALIA

ERIC EDGAR COOKE

The city of Perth in Western Australia lies more than 1,600 miles away from the nearest major city, Adelaide. Perhaps, back in the 1960s, it was this isolation that made its inhabitants so relaxed. It was the kind of place where people rarely bothered to lock the doors of their houses or their cars; they were friendly and trusted each other, always ready to lend a helping hand.

That all changed one summer night in 1963 when Eric Edgar Cooke unleashed a one-man crime wave, a spree of senseless killing that shocked Perth, changing the city and its inhabitants forever.

Cooke had already killed, in 1959, when he broke into a house owned by a divorced woman who lived alone. As she slept in her bedroom, he searched the rest of her house for cash and valuables. Finding none, he entered the bedroom but was surprised to find the woman awake. She leapt out of bed and struggled with him until he fumbled in his pocket for the small knife he carried in case of emergencies. He plunged it into her body several times, killing her.

He had never had much of a chance. Born in Perth in 1931, with a cleft palate, he underwent a successful operation to improve his looks. But his speech was never quite right and he was inevitably bullied at school. Things were not much better at home. His father was a violent alcoholic who beat his wife, son and two daughters regularly with both fists and a belt. His father hated Eric so much that if his mother seemed to be paying too much attention to him, she was beaten for it.

Needless to say, he became a withdrawn, quiet child, with few friends. He also began to suffer from headaches and blackouts which were not helped by a bad fall from a bicycle and injuries received when he unwittingly dived into a pool of shallow water when he was fourteen. He was examined by doctors who, initially suspecting some kind of brain damage, carried out an exploratory operation. None was found.

Cooke was kicked out of a number of schools for disruptive behaviour and by the age of fourteen had dropped out of the education system altogether. He found work, but as his father often spent his wages on booze, all his earnings had to be given to his mother to help feed and clothe herself and his sisters.

Life went from bad to worse. At sixteen, he made the mistake of trying to protect his mother from one of his father's drunken beatings. He ended up in hospital for three weeks, telling doctors that he had been in a fight with other boys.

Eventually, he was called up to do his national service and finally learned something. Unfortunately for Perth and a number of its inhabitants, it was how to use a rifle.

He had already begun his criminal career before going into the army. Giving all his earnings to his mother left him little to live on and he had resorted to housebreaking to bolster his wages. It was easy with all those unlocked doors. While the occupants watched television, he would sneak in and raid their purses and wallets. Not only would he steal, however. He became a peeping tom, enjoying watching women get ready for bed or making love with their husbands.

Demobbed from the army, he carried on where he had left off, breaking and entering and sometimes, when he got bored or found nothing worth stealing, vandalising the house he was in or even setting fire to it. Eventually, however, he was caught, his fingerprints connecting him with numerous burglaries. He went to prison for three years.

In 1953, aged twenty-two, he married an eighteen-year-old British immigrant by the name of Sally and he would have seven children with her, although even now his bad luck continued – one of his sons was born with a developmental disability, while a daughter was born without a right arm. He was working, however, as a truck driver, although at the weekend he pursued his criminal activities to bring in some extra cash.

The law caught up with him again in 1955 when he was given two years' hard labour for stealing a car. In 1960, having got away with the killing of the divorcee, he returned to prison. In spite of his record, however, the police believed him to be harmless.

How wrong they were was about to become evident.

That summer Saturday night in 1963 at around two in the morning, Nicholas August, a married man, was sharing a drink in his car with barmaid Rowena Reeves. Suddenly, Rowena thought she saw a man and August leaned out of the window and told him to 'Bugger off!' thinking he was a peeping tom. When August chucked an empty bottle at the figure in the dark, Rowena noticed that the man had a gun in his hands, and was alarmed to see that it was aimed at them. She pushed her companion's head down as a bullet whizzed into the car, grazing his neck and thudding into her forearm. August fumbled with the keys and switched on the engine as quickly as he could. He pushed his foot down hard on the accelerator, gunning the car past the shooter and almost hitting him. By the time they reached the local hospital, Rowena had slipped into unconsciousness through loss of blood, but, fortunately, both survived.

The night was still young, however, and Eric Cooke's next victim wasn't so lucky.

An hour after Nicholas August and Rowena Reeves had been attacked, a couple of miles away, fifty-four-year-old George Walmsley was awakened by the sound of his doorbell. Puzzled as to who would be at the door at this time in the morning, he got out of bed, went to the door and opened it. Immediately, a bullet smashed into his forehead. He was dead before he hit the ground.

A little later, at a boarding house located just around the corner from where George Walmsley had died, a nineteen-year-old student, John Sturkey, who was sleeping on the building's verandah was discovered shot between the eyes.

But it was not over yet. When Brian Weir failed to show up for work at the Surf Life Saving Club next morning, one of his colleagues went to get him out of bed, thinking he had merely overslept. He found Weir in bed alright, but his sheets were soaked in blood and there was a bullet hole in his forehead.

He lived, but suffered serious brain damage before dying three years later.

The press went crazy and a large reward was offered for information leading to the arrest of the person they were calling the 'Maniac Slayer'. It was the random nature of the shootings that terrified people most. They had no idea where and when he would strike next and took to sleeping with loaded guns by their beds.

All went quiet for three weeks.

Joy Noble was making breakfast one Saturday morning in her West Perth home when, glancing out of the kitchen window, she was horrified to see a naked young woman lying on the grass in her garden. Initially, she feared that it was her daughter, and first made sure that she was safe and well before investigating. The body was that of Lucy Madrill, a twenty-four-year-old social worker who lived in a neighbouring street. She had been raped, strangled and, bizarrely, dumped on Joy Noble's lawn. The police were flummoxed, but, with absolutely no evidence to support the theory, claimed that the murderer must have been an Aborigine.

Cooke laid low for the next six months before shooting dead, on 10 August 1963, an eighteen-year-old science student, Shirley McLeod, leaving the child she had been babysitting unharmed. The gun was different, but the investigating officers had no doubt that their man had just claimed his fourth victim. They began to fingerprint every male in Perth over the age of twelve and there was talk of closing down the alleys that ran down the backs of houses. Doors in the city were now firmly locked at night.

It was a stroke of luck rather than a great piece of detective work that finally enabled them to trap their man. On Saturday 17 August an elderly couple were out picking flowers in a wooded area in the pretty Perth suburb of Mount Pleasant when they spied a rifle concealed in some bushes. It turned out to be a Winchester .22 and police determined it was the weapon that had been used in the recent killings. They reasoned that their killer would almost certainly return to collect the weapon, staking out the area for two weeks before he finally turned up. Eric Cooke was arrested, handcuffed and at last taken into custody. The entire city breathed a sigh of relief.

At first, he denied everything, but gradually he began to open up, admitting to some two hundred and fifty break-ins and car thefts, and remembering the smallest details of crimes committed years previously. He told how he had abused women while they slept, and even described how one girl thought she had fallen out of bed and banged her head when really he had hit her with an object but, before he could continue his assault, he had been scared off. He told them of hit-and-runs that he had deliberately perpetrated, running people over and then speeding off without stopping.

He had obtained the Winchester during a burglary while the owners of the house were watching television in the lounge. He had taken it and some cartridges thinking he could sell it, but instead shot the babysitter, although he claimed to have absolutely no memory of the incident, only realising what he had done when it was reported on the next day's television news.

He confessed to the murder of Lucy Madrill, telling officers that she had woken up when he made a noise as he robbed her house. He had struck her and then strangled her with the flex of a lamp. He had then raped her lifeless body before dragging her from her house with the intention of stealing a car and dumping her body somewhere. Finding only a bicycle, however, he had left the body on Joy Noble's lawn and cycled home.

All he could say about the fateful night the previous summer when he had shot five people, was that he had done it because he 'wanted to hurt somebody'. He had stolen the gun and a car, and had driven around until he found Nicholas August and Rowena Reeves. He had merely been spying on them but lost his temper when the bottle was thrown at him. The rest were just pieces of opportunism. The only shooting he claimed to regret was that of John Sturkey. Ultimately, he conceded that he was 'just a cold-blooded killer'.

He confessed to the 1959 murder of thirty-three-year-old Patricia Vinico Berkman, lover of local radio star Fotis Hountas. She had received multiple stab wounds to the head as she lay in bed in her apartment in South Perth. Furthermore, he claimed to have killed wealthy twenty-two-year-old socialite Jillian Brewer later that same year. A twenty-year-old deaf mute, Darryl Beamish, had confessed to killing her but later claimed that he had been forced to make the confession. Nevertheless, he was found guilty and given a death sentence. Cooke, however, cast doubt on that verdict by recalling tiny details about the flat. He also solved a mystery about the murder. When the woman's body was found, all the doors to the flat were locked from the inside and there was no sign of forced entry. Cooke explained that he had stolen one of the dead woman's keys when he had broken into the flat a few months previously. The appeal court judges did not believe Cooke's confession, but at least Beamish did not hang; his sentence was commuted to life imprisonment.

Eric Edgar Cooke had no such luck. He was hanged in Fremantle Prison on 26 October 1964, the last man to be hanged in Australia.

Unlucky to the bitter end.

WILLIAM
'THE MUTILATOR'
MACDONALD

He became a killer on the spur of the moment, he later claimed. It was 1960 and William Macdonald, a thirty-six-year-old emigrant from England started drinking with fifty-five-year-old Amos Hurst in a hotel near Roma Street in Brisbane, Australia. They repaired to Hurst's room in the hotel and continued the session, both becoming extremely drunk. Macdonald suddenly felt an uncontrollable urge to strangle Hurst and put his hands round his neck and squeezed until blood spurted from the other man's mouth. Macdonald punched him hard in the face and let him slide to the floor. He was dead.

He removed his clothes and lay him on the bed before carefully washing the blood off his clothes and hands. He left the room, calmly walked out of the hotel and returned to his lodgings.

He worried for a few days until, picking up

a newspaper, he found an obituary of Hurst. He was astonished to read that he had died of a heart attack. No mention was made of him being strangled. It seemed that Hurst's death had initially been considered to be suspicious but the coroner was unable to establish conclusively whether the bruising on his neck had killed him or whether he had received it in a fight before his death. They opted for the fight and, to his delight, Macdonald had got away with murder.

William Macdonald had always been different to the rest. Born Allen Ginsberg in Liverpool in 1924, his childhood had been a lonely and solitary one – as is often the case with serial killers. He had almost no friends and was unable to form lasting relationships.

Eventually, his life going nowhere, at the age of nineteen he enlisted in the British Army. It was there that he would have the experience that would define his life and tell him who and what he was. He was raped by a corporal who threatened to kill him if he told anyone. There was no problem for Macdonald, however, because not only did he enjoy the experience, he wanted more. He was, he discovered to his surprise, homosexual.

He had suffered from behavioural problems

since an early age and while still a child had been diagnosed as schizophrenic. The same problem resulted in his discharge from the army and in 1947, aged twenty-three, his behaviour was becoming so erratic that his brother had him committed to an asylum. It was an experience filled with horror that ended when his mother obtained his release. He still heard voices and suffered from delusions, however, but when he sought help the only treatment once again was for him to be incarcerated in an institution. It made little difference. When he was released three months later, the same old voices were still echoing in his head. Resolving to make a major change in his life, in 1949 he changed his name by deed poll from Allen Ginsberg to William Macdonald and emigrated to Canada. Six years later, he relocated to Australia, just one of the thousands of Britons hoping to find opportunity in the wide open spaces Down Under.

Sex was still a problem, however. In Australia, as it had been in Britain and Canada, homosexuality was a criminal offence. Sexual liaisons had to be sought in grubby public toilets or in secluded areas of public parks. He had not been in the country for very long before he was arrested for soliciting sex in a public toilet with a man who happened to be an undercover police officer. Macdonald was put on two years' probation.

Murder seemed to give him just as big a thrill as sex, however, and having got away with one, he decided to look for another victim. He purchased a knife and before long was getting drunk with a potential target in a bar. They bought a bottle of sherry and took it to a local park to continue their carousing. The other man fell to the ground, dead drunk. Macdonald felt the urge to kill again, straddling the other man's comatose body and pulling out his knife. Before he plunged it into his companion, however, he felt the urge suddenly leave his mind. He slipped the knife back into its sheath and walked away, leaving behind a very drunk but very fortunate man.

He adopted another new identity – Alan Edward Brennan – when he moved to Sydney in 1961 and was employed as a sorter by the Australian Postal Department. Soon, he was a well-known figure in the public toilets and cruising sections of the city's parks.

On one venture into a park, Green Park in the Sydney suburb of Darlinghurst, he befriended a man named Alfred Greenfield. He lured Greenfield to a well-known hangout for drinkers, the alcoves at the nearby Domain Swimming Baths, by telling him he had some booze secreted there. When they arrived and found a secluded spot, Macdonald waited until Greenfield was comatose, pulled on a plastic raincoat and drew his knife. He stabbed Greenfield in the neck and body repeatedly until he was certain he was dead. He then removed his trousers and underpants and sliced off his genitals which he later threw into Sydney Harbour. He took off the blood-splattered raincoat, wrapped the knife in it and went home.

When the body was discovered next day there was outrage. The media went into great detail about the shocking nature of the killing and dubbed the perpetrator 'the Mutilator'.

The police, however, were puzzled. It was a crime without any obvious motive. There was speculation that it may have been a crime of passion, sparked by jealousy, but nothing emerged to support that theory. The investigation stalled, even with a $2,000 reward for information.

The next one, on 21 November, was easy. Forty-one-year-old Ernest Cobbin was already drunk when Macdonald met him and it did not take much to lure him to the toilet of a nearby park. Even drunk, however, Cobbin must have been puzzled when his companion slipped on a plastic raincoat, especially as it was not raining. His bemusement did not last long, however, because Macdonald pulled out a knife with a six-inch blade that he had recently purchased and plunged it into his throat. Again and again he stabbed Cobbin, spraying the toilet cubicle with blood from his severed jugular vein.

As Cobbin lay dead, the blood from his neck reduced to a trickle, 'the Mutilator' pulled down his trousers and underwear and sliced off his victim's penis and testicles. This time he wanted to be close to them before disposing of them, however. He took them home, washed them and took them to bed with him. Next day, he threw them off Sydney Harbour Bridge.

The media went crazy but the police still had nothing to go on. It was another murder with no motive. The victim had no enemies and there were no witnesses. Months passed and they were no closer to finding the serial killer whose actions were hogging the front pages of every newspaper in Australia.

The urge came on Macdonald again on 31 March 1962. He found a drunk man, Frank McLean, on a Sydney street and suggested conspiratorially that they go into an alley for a drink. When they turned the corner into the unlit Bourke Lane, Macdonald suddenly pulled out his knife and stabbed the 6ft tall McLean in the neck. McLean was a strong man and began to fight but Macdonald was able to punch him in the face and force him to the ground where he stabbed him frenziedly. When the big man lay dead in front of him, he sliced off his genitals and crept out of the alley. The stolen body part would end up in the waters of the harbour.

The case terrified the inhabitants of Sydney and the media frenzy continued. The authorities, under huge pressure to find the serial killer who was on the rampage, turned to clairvoyants. They then thought that he must be a doctor because of the neatness of the mutilations he had carried out. The reward was increased to $10,000 but they seemed no closer to apprehending him.

Macdonald lost his job at the sorting office but decided to open a delicatessen. He found suitable premises and moved into the apartment above. The urge to kill was never far away, though.

James Hackett was a vagrant who had the misfortune to bump into Macdonald in a bar one night. Macdonald now had a place of his own to which he could take his victims and he invited Hackett back to his home. As usual, when Hackett had drunk himself into oblivion, Macdonald pulled out a knife and thrust it into the comatose man's neck. Hackett woke up, however, and a desperate struggle ensued. When Macdonald was stabbed in the hand in the midst of the fight, he became enraged, stabbing Hackett repeatedly in the heart, blood spraying everywhere. He made a futile effort to cut off Hackett's penis, but, exhausted, fell into a deep sleep where he sat.

Next morning he awoke to a room resembling a slaughterhouse. There was blood on the walls and the ceiling and there was so much of it slooshing about on the floor that it threatened to seep through to the ceiling, of his delicatessen below.

First of all, he had to do something about his hand which had been badly cut in the fight. He cleaned himself up and went to the local hospital where the wound was cleaned up and stitched. Returning to the horror of that room, he dragged Hackett's corpse downstairs and left it in a space under the shop. He spent the remainder of the day scrubbing and cleaning, trying to remove every stain. But it was impossible. The stains would not come off the walls or out of the floorboards where the blood had soaked into the wood. There was only one option open to him. He had to flee. He packed his bags and travelled to Brisbane where he found lodgings in a boarding house. He dyed his hair black, grew a moustache to disguise himself and waited for the news that Hackett's body had been discovered and that they were looking for him.

The days passed, however, and there was nothing. Eventually the body was found, but Macdonald's amazing luck was in. It had decomposed so badly that it was impossible to establish the cause of death or to accurately identify it. The police simply presumed that it was the body of the shop-owner, Brennan, and closed the case. Once again, he had got away with murder.

Macdonald could have carried on but for one fatal mistake. He foolishly returned to Sydney and was spotted by a former workmate who was astonished to see Alan Brennan, whose funeral he had attended six months previously, walking nonchalantly and very much alive along a Sydney street. He approached him, but Macdonald fled. The police were informed and the following day the newspapers had the story. 'Case of the Walking Corpse' ran one headline.

Macdonald went to Melbourne where he found work on the railways, but his disguise did not hide him for long. The police were now certain that he was 'the Mutilator' and it was only a matter of time before he was arrested.

William Macdonald was inevitably found guilty and given a life sentence, but in 1964 was declared insane after beating another inmate to death and sent to a psychiatric hospital for the criminally insane.

By 1980, he was considered sane enough to be returned to a mainstream prison where he remains to this day. Ironically, 'the Mutilator', one of Australia's most vicious serial killers, claims to have no desire to be released on parole because he believes the streets of Sydney are not safe.

PAUL CHARLES DENYER

Killing was part of his vile nature. As a child, he began by slitting the throats of his sister's teddy bears. From that, he graduated to slitting the throat of the family kitten and hanging it from the branch of a tree. It was later discovered that he was also responsible for disembowelling a friend's cat and then slitting the throats of her kittens. He was fascinated by blood, gore and death, and spent his spare time watching slasher movies like *Halloween*, *The Stepfather* and *Fear*. It was only a matter of time before his urge to kill animals became an urge to kill humans. In a seven-week period in 1993, he would stab and slash to death three young women and violently assault another, a forty-one-year-old woman who was lucky to escape with her life.

Denyer was born in Sydney, Australia in 1972, the third of six children. The family had emigrated from England and settled in Campbelltown, a south-western suburb of Sydney. His parents told how he had rolled off a bench as a baby and banged his head, but it is unknown whether this had any effect on his later development into a monster.

At kindergarten, it was noted that he found it difficult to mix and make friends, but by the time he went to primary school, he seemed like a normal kid. Life changed in 1981, however, when his father found a job as manager of a steakhouse in the South Oakleigh suburb of Melbourne. The children were unhappy with the move, particularly nine-year-old Paul who had settled in well at school and did not relish making new friends and establishing himself in a new school. He was right. The move did not suit him and he became a loner, with no friends and little interest in his schoolwork.

His size did not help. He had grown into a large child, taller and fatter than his classmates. He was also developing an unhealthy fascination with knives and clubs, of which he had a large collection. He made lethal slingshot guns that fired pebbles and ball-bearings. It was around the age of ten that he began attacking his sister's teddies and the family cat.

His first brush with the law came shortly before his thirteenth birthday when he was arrested for stealing a car. He was released with only a warning, but a couple of months later he was charged with theft, wilful damage and making a false report to the emergency services. He was charged with assault at the age of fifteen after forcing another boy to masturbate in front of some other children.

Aged twenty, finally, he met a girl called Sharon Johnson while he was working at a supermarket. He lost that job when he deliberately ran a convoy of empty shopping trolleys into a woman and child, knocking them down and injuring them. He applied to join the police force but his application was rejected because he was by this time grossly overweight. He was fired from his next job in a marine workshop because he spent all his time making the knives and daggers with which he was still obsessed.

People started calling him 'John Candy' because his size matched that of the large Hollywood film star, but by 1993 he was a social misfit who was unable to hold down a job of any kind.

Meanwhile, his fascination with death and killing had been increasing, fed by a diet of slasher movies, especially *The Stepfather*, the story of American mass murderer John List, which he watched continuosly.

In 1992, he and Sharon had moved into a flat in the city of Frankston. Sharon had to work two jobs to keep them afloat, while Denyer remained at home with nothing to do but cause trouble.

The first incident occurred when a neighbour

arrived home one night to discover that her flat had been broken into. Clothing had been ripped and slashed and thrown around the apartment, and her pictures were smashed. Then another tenant of the block reported a peeping tom. Worst of all was what happened to another neighbour, Donna, who lived with her fiancé, Les, and their baby in an apartment in a nearby block.

One night in February 1993, Les and Donna came home with their baby late at night to find that someone had scrawled in blood on the wall next to the TV the words 'Dead Don'. In the middle of the kitchen floor they discovered the disembowelled body of Donna's cat Buffy with a picture of a bikini-clad woman over it. The cat's entrails had been spread around the kitchen and the words 'Donna – You're dead' were written in its blood on the wall. It was a horrific scene.

The flat had been ransacked and Donna's belongings were everywhere. Cupboard doors had been smashed and a picture of a half-naked woman, stabbed through the middle, was put in the baby's cot. On the mirror on the dressing table in Donna's bedroom was sprayed in shaving foam the words 'Donna and Robyn'. What made it even more bizarre was that she had no idea who 'Robyn' was.

Needless to say, Donna did not spend another

night in the flat. She moved in with her sister Tricia until she could find a new place to stay. Tricia's neighbour was Paul Denyer.

Denyer reassured her that she would now be safe and boasted that if the police ever found out who was responsible he would personally take care of him. Meanwhile, the urge to do more than torment people had taken hold of Denyer. He claimed his first victim on 11 June 1963.

Elizabeth Shavers was found, partially clothed, on Saturday 12 June, having been reported missing when she failed to come home the previous night by the uncle and aunt with whom she was staying. Naked from the waist up, her bra around her neck, she was found in Lloyd Park on the Cranbourne Road in Langwarrin, not far from Frankston. Her throat had been cut and she had been stabbed viciously six times in the chest. Four deep cuts ran from her breasts to her navel and there were four more running at right angles to those, forming a grisly pattern across her abdomen. Her nose had been broken and there were cuts and scratches on her face. The post-mortem would confirm that she had not been sexually assaulted.

Police were unable to establish a motive for the murder. Elizabeth had no enemies and was not involved in drugs or dubious relationships. The only conclusion they could arrive at was that she had been killed randomly or someone had attempted to rape her and it had gone tragically wrong.

The investigation was extensive. Officers knocked on thousands of doors in the area and the bus driver and people who had been travelling on the bus she took that night were questioned. Nothing turned up.

Just under a month later, they had another seemingly random incident to investigate. Fortunately this victim survived, however. On 8 July, forty-one-year-old bank clerk Roszsa Toth was attacked by a man as she made her way home from work. Her assailant had a gun and dragged her into a nature reserve. She fought for her life, however, biting his fingers down to the bone and scratching him. He, meanwhile, pulled out clumps of her hair as he struggled to bring her under his control. She succeeded in fighting him off and staggered onto the road to stop a passing motorist. Her attacker fled into the night to lick his wounds. When police arrived at the scene to investigate, they found nothing to indicate who the man was. All they knew was that her fight had saved her life.

Twenty-two-year-old Debbie Fream was not as strong as Roszsa. She was found next day by a farmer near Carrum Downs. Reported missing later on the night that Roszsa Toth had been attacked, she bore twenty-four stab wounds to her neck, chest and arms and had been strangled. Debbie had given birth to a son just twelve days previously and had disappeared after driving to a local shop to buy a bottle of milk.

The police were now convinced that there was a serial killer on the rampage in Frankston. The bars of Frankston were deserted at nights and women locked and barricaded their doors. Every man became a suspect. The media followed every minute detail of the massive manhunt that had been launched, and a help centre, Operation Reassurance, was opened to advise women living locally how to protect themselves and what they should do if attacked.

He was expected to strike again and he did on the afternoon of 30 July. Seventeen-year-old Natalie Russell was cycling home from college in Frankston when she disappeared. A frantic search was launched, but her brutally wounded body was discovered eight hours later in some bushes next to a cycle track that ran between two golf courses. She had multiple stab wounds to the face and neck and her throat had been cut. Again, she had not been sexually assaulted but the savagery of the attack was shocking.

Denyer had made a fatal mistake, however, that would bring his career as a serial killer to an end. A tiny piece of skin was found on Natalie's neck and when analysed was found not to be hers. It had to be the killer's. There had also been a sighting by a police officer of a yellow Toyota Corona near the cycle track that afternoon at around three o'clock, which was the time that the coroner estimated Natalie had died. Not only that, the policeman had written down the registration of the car from its registration label because it had no plates.

Everything began to happen very fast. When the number was fed into the police computer, it brought up a report by a postman who said he had earlier seen a man in a yellow Toyota who seemed to be trying to hide. The car also popped up as having been seen in the vicinity of where Debbie Fream's body had been found. The car belonged to Paul Denyer.

When they called at Denyer's flat at 3.40 p.m. the next day, he was out. They pushed a card through his letterbox asking him to contact them. At 5.15 p.m. they received a call from Sharon, but so as not to arouse her or Denyer's suspicion, they said that it was no more than a routine enquiry. Shortly afterwards a large team of officers arrived at Denyer's apartment.

When he opened the door, he expressed surprise at the large police presence, but calmly invited them in. The first thing the detectives noticed were the cuts on his hands. He, of course, provided alibis and stated

361

that although he had been in the vicinity of a couple of the killings, he had absolutely nothing to do with them. When they asked him about the scratches, he explained them away by saying he had got his hands trapped in a fan while working on his car.

Denyer was taken to Frankston police station for further questioning and denied everything until the early hours of the next day. When they asked him for samples to run a DNA test, he knew the game was up, however. Suddenly, he blurted out, 'Okay, I killed all three of them'.

His confessions were chilling. Of the killing of Elizabeth Shavers he said, 'Walked in a bit of bushland beside the main track in Lloyd Park. Sat there, you know, stood in the bushes for a while just – I can't remember, just standing there I suppose. I held the "gun" to the back of her neck, walked across the track over towards the other small sandhill or something. And on the other side of that hill, she asked me if she could, you know – go to the toilet, so to speak. So I respected her privacy. So I turned around and everything while she did it and everything. When she finished we just walked down towards where the goal posts are and we turned right and headed towards the area where she was found. I got to that area there and I started choking her with my hands and she passed out after a while.

You know, the oxygen got cut off to her head and she just stopped. And then I pulled out the knife ... and stabbed her many times in the throat. And she was still alive. And then she stood up and then we walked around and all that, just walking around a few steps, and then I threw her on the ground and stuck my foot over her neck to finish her off'.

Asked why the killing of Natalie Russell had been so savage, he told a tale of brutality and horror that places him amongst the worst killers in not just Australian history but in criminal history.

He had been waiting for a victim for about twenty minutes when she showed up. He sneaked up behind her, grabbed her and put a knife to her throat, cutting himself in the process and leaving behind the piece of skin that would convict him. She struggled at first but he stopped her by telling her he would cut her throat if she continued. She then told him if it was sex he wanted he could have it, if it meant he would let her live. But Denyer found this repulsive, offended by what he viewed as her loose morals. He forced her to kneel in front of him and then to lie on the ground. She struggled again and he cut her face. As she kneeled on the ground in front of him again, he wound a strap around her neck to strangle her but it broke. He then threw her to the ground again as she struggled once more and cut her throat, a small cut, he said. He then stuck his hands down her throat, 'grabbed her chords and I twisted them'. As she started to lose consciousness he cut her throat properly – 'one big large cut,' he told the disgusted officers, 'which sort of cut almost her whole head off. And then she slowly died'.

He then explained that as he walked back to the Toyota, he saw the officers taking down the details of his registration number. He had simply turned round and walked home.

He told them he 'just wanted to kill', adding later that he hated women, or at least all women apart from his girlfriend Sharon Johnson.

Paul Denyer pleaded guilty to all charges and on 20 December 1993, was sentenced to three terms of life imprisonment with no possibility of parole.

In prison, Denyer has begun dressing as a woman and has also filed requests to learn what the Victorian government's policy is on gender reassignment surgery for prisoners.

It seems that the man who hated women now wants to become one.

IVAN MILAT

Belanglo State Forest is situated south of the town of Berrima in the Southern Highlands of the Australian state of New South Wales. Open to hikers, it is about three kilometres from the Hume Highway that runs between Canberra and Sydney. On 19 September 1993, a couple of people orienteering noticed a foul smell emanating from what appeared to be a pile of rubbish. They warily walked towards it and to their horror discovered that the rubbish was, in fact, human remains.

When police were called in they immediately began to speculate that these remains might have something to do with backpackers who had mysteriously disappeared in the area in the past few years. Four Germans, a couple of English girls and two Australians from the state of Victoria, had all vanished into thin air and not a trace had been found of them since.

Their speculation was confirmed to be correct when it was announced that two bodies had been found and that they belonged to the two English girls, Caroline Clarke and Joanne Walters. They had been killed by a powerful individual, undoubtedly a man, and Joanne had been stabbed with such power that her spine had been cut and two ribs had been completely severed. Caroline had also been stabbed, but he had also shot her in the head several times. Chillingly, it was found that she had been shot from three different directions as if the killer had used her head for target practice.

He seemed to have hung around for a while. There was a fireplace, built with stones, and a number of cigarette butts lay around on the ground. Trying to build a profile, police surmised that the killer was a local man who knew the area. Given that Caroline had been killed in what seemed to be an execution style and had not been sexually assaulted, it seemed likely that he was the kind of man who liked to exert control over people. The murder of Joanne had been very different, however. The killer – or killers; they believed that more than one person had possibly been involved – had launched a frenzied attack on her that had a sexual element. Her shirt and bra were pushed up and the zipper of her jeans was undone, although the button was still fastened. She was wearing no underwear and it was presumed that the killer had taken it away with him as a trophy.

According to the profiler, the girls had been killed purely for pleasure.

Police knew that they were looking for a very dangerous killer and a massive search of the area was launched. Nothing further was found, however, and the police announced that they were confident that there were no more bodies in the forest.

They were wrong.

A few months later, as Bruce Pryor was driving along an unfamiliar and unused road in the forest, he came to a bare, rocky spot in which was a small fireplace built from rocks. He stopped the car and climbed out to stretch his legs and take a look around. On the ground, not far from the fireplace, he noticed a bone which, if he were not mistaken, resembled very closely a human thigh bone. He walked around to see if there was anything else and sure enough, hidden amongst some undergrowth, he saw something gleaming white. He took a closer look and was horrified to discover a human skull.

The clearing hid two bodies that were soon identified as the missing Victoria couple, James Gibson and Deborah Everist, who had disappeared on a backpacking trip in 1989. Strangely, James's backpack and camera had been found seventy-eight miles north of Belanglo Forest after they had disappeared. It seemed as if the killer had dumped them there in an effort to divert attention from the forest and confuse the investigation.

Only the couple's bones remained, but it was soon evident that they had each received multiple stab wounds. Deborah's skull had been fractured several times and there were slash marks on the forehead of her skull. Her bra was found and it had a stab wound through one of its cups. Police also found a pair of tights that looked as if they may have been used to tie up one of the victims.

Embarrassed at having been wrong in their assertion that there were no more bodies in the forest, the police launched another massive search, accompanied by special sniffer dogs.

It was established that the bullets and casings found at the scene of James's and Deborah's deaths had been fired from a Ruger repeating rifle. The bad news was that this was one of the most popular rifles in Australia, with around 5,000 of them in private ownership. Nonetheless, gun clubs and local gun-owners were questioned. One man provided officers with descriptions of a couple of vehicles he had seen in the forest the previous year. He claimed that he had seen a man and woman in one of them and that he had thought for a moment that they were bound but could not be sure. He knew the name of the owner of the vehicle. It was Alex Milat.

Meanwhile, however, the search revealed more bodies. Twenty-six days after the last two had been found, a search team entered a small clearing where they found a pair of women's pink jeans and a length of blue and yellow rope. There was also the trademark fireplace. One officer stopped as he almost stepped on what looked like a human bone. A little further on lay a human skull. On closer inspection, the officer noticed something wrapped around its forehead – a distinctive purple headband.

German backpacker Simone 'Simi' Schmidl had travelled the world and had last been seen hitch-hiking on the Hume Highway out of the town of Liverpool in the direction of Sydney. Now her bones lay in the forest, partially clothed, her shirt and underclothes pushed up around her neck. She had died from multiple stab wounds. The pink jeans were not hers, though. They belonged to another German girl, Anja Habschied, who had gone missing with her travelling companion, Gregor Neugebauer, from Sydney's Kings Cross area just after Christmas 1991.

Gregor had been strangled and shot, and the bullets matched up with the ones that had been used in the other killings. Anja's death had been most horrific of all, however. Her top two vertebrae and her head were missing. She had been decapitated with a sharp instrument such as a sword or a machete. She had been made to kneel for it to be done. The killer had turned her death into a horrific ritual execution. This was one of the most extraordinary series of murders that had ever been encountered. Serial killers generally find a method that works for them and stick to it. This serial killer seemed to want to experiment with a variety of methods – beating, strangling, decapitating, stabbing and shooting. Men and women had been sexually assaulted in some way. Their zippers were often down but always the top button of their trousers was fastened. The killer also appeared to spend time with his victims, piling on the cruelty and confirming the sadistic nature of the murders.

The authorities were flooded with information but began to develop suspicions about the Milat family and Ivan Robert Marko Milat in particular. He was born in 1944 into a large Yugoslavian immigrant family, but little is known about his childhood except that his family lived in an isolated, rural spot and he had thirteen siblings. From an early age, he had an interest in guns and hunting, and he and his brothers had gained a reputation for wildness and lawlessness. They had had many brushes with the law.

In 1971 Ivan Milat had been arrested and charged with raping two woman hitchhikers but he was acquitted due to insufficient evidence.

Astonishingly, he could have been arrested for kidnapping backpackers some time before the bodies were found. On 25 January 1990, Englishman Paul Onions was on his way to find work fruit-picking in the Riverina area, a couple of hundred miles south-west of Sydney. Onions had taken a train from Sydney to the city of Liverpool and had then walked out of the city to hitchhike on the Hume Highway.

After a few hours by the side of the road, he walked to a small shopping centre to buy a drink and as he stood there drinking, a well-built man came up to him and asked if he was looking for a lift. Paul was delighted to accept and was soon sitting in a four by four beside the man, who told him his name was Bill. Bill threw a lot of questions at Paul about his time in Australia and at first seemed pleasant enough. As the journey went on, however, Bill started to become irascible, making racist comments and making Paul feel uneasy. Eventually the man went silent and seemed morose.

Just outside the town of Mittagong, Paul became even more uneasy as Bill's driving seemed to be getting erratic. He seemed edgy and was constantly looking in his rear-view mirror. Suddenly, he stopped the truck, saying he wanted to get some cassette tapes from the back. He climbed out, ordering Paul to remain in the vehicle. Paul was puzzled because there was a pile of cassettes in a space between the seats. He decided to get out as well but, as he did so, Bill growled at him to get back in. He did as he was told, but when Bill climbed back in he reached down beneath his seat and drew out a large black revolver and pointed it at Paul. 'This is a robbery,' he snarled at him, also pulling out a length of rope. Paul made a grab for the door handle, pulled the door open and leapt from the car. He jumped into oncoming traffic that swerved wildly to avoid him. A van approached and, waving his arms, he threw himself in front of it, forcing its driver, Joanne Berry, to stop. He ran round, opened her passenger door and jumped in. He screamed that the man in the four-wheel drive had a gun. Joanne considered for a split second. In the back of the van were her sister and her four children. She slammed her foot hard on the accelerator and sped off to the nearest police station.

Tragically, however, no one took any action. Paul made a statement and waited to hear something but there was no contact. He returned to England and put it down to experience. Then in 1994, the police called him and asked him to return to Australia. There was someone they wanted him to take a look at.

Early on the morning of 22 May 1994, police spread out around the Milat property. They shouted to Ivan to come out and give himself up. He had nowhere to run and was under arrest shortly after.

Inside they discovered a huge amount of evidence implicating him in the murders, including sleeping bags, clothing and camping equipment. There was also an arsenal of guns and ammunition. A long, curved sword was later found in a locked cupboard at the house of Milat's mother. It had probably been the weapon that was used to behead Anja Habschied.

Milat was charged with seven murders and with the attack on Paul Onions.

His trial was the most sensational in Australian legal history, especially when Milat claimed that he had been framed by other members of his large family. However, he was found guilty and given seven life sentences.

Having sworn that he would try to escape at every opportunity, he almost succeeded in 1997. The breakout was foiled and Milat's accomplice was found mysteriously hanged in his prison cell next morning.

Ivan Milat has been questioned about countless other disappearances and it is almost certain that he had killed a number of times before 1989. His brother, Boris, in hiding from the other members of his violent family, has told the media, 'the things I can tell you are much worse than what Ivan's meant to have done. Everywhere he's worked, people have disappeared, I know where he's been'. No further charges have been made, however.

THE SNOWTOWN MURDERERS

As they killed, they played a CD of the song *Selling the Drama* from Live's album *Throwing Copper,* turning the murder into a ritual of sorts, although they didn't call it murder. It was 'playing'. Playing for high stakes, too. They murdered nine people in Australia's worst case of serial killing, in the seven years during which the slaughter took place, making $95,000 from welfare and credit card fraud. Now and then they even turned on each other, in order to keep their secrets within the circle.

Their first murder was relatively straightforward – a twenty-two-year-old homosexual, Clinton Trezise, was hit on the head with a heavy instrument, possibly a hammer, and then buried in a shallow grave in a remote spot in the agricultural hinterland of Lower Light, about fifty kilometres north of Adelaide.

Gradually, however, they became more elaborate, not to mention more horrific, in their methods. Dismemberment, removal of limbs, de-fleshing and torture all became part of the game of death they enjoyed playing. It was so gruesome that when the case eventually came to trial, three jurors had to drop out, unable to bear the gorier parts of the testimony, while others required counselling after the conclusion of the trial.

At the centre of it all was thirty-two-year-old John Justin Bunting, a man filled with hate. When he was young, he whiled away his time by burning insects in acid, and as a teenager was linked to neo-Nazi groups. As an adult, his hatred was directed at homosexuals and paedophiles. At his home in Waterloo Corner Road, in the northern Adelaide suburb of Salisbury North, Bunting devised a large chart on a wall in one of the rooms. On it, using paper and lengths of wool, he had created a network of the names of people he suspected of being paedophiles or homosexuals. Now and then, he would vent some of his anger and disgust by selecting one of the names at random and making an offensive telephone call to them.

The police had become concerned about the number of missing persons cases in the Adelaide area and a task force, named Chart, was assembled to try to get to the bottom of them. The trail led to a disused bank in the town of Snowtown, one hundred and fifty kilometres north of Adelaide.

Once, it had been a bustling small town branch of the State Bank of South Australia, home to the savings and mortgages of the farmers who owned local farms and the businessmen who serviced the needs of the families who lived in the area. Now, it was long closed and dust had settled on its fixtures and fittings. It had recently been used for other purposes, however. On 20 May 1999, as police entered the red-brick building in the town's main street at the culmination of their long and complex missing persons investigation, anticipation hung heavy in the air. They would not be disappointed.

The main area of the bank contained electrical and computing equipment, but as police opened the door to the bank vault's ten centimetre-thick metal door, a horrific smell was unleashed from within. Behind the door they found the source of the stench. Six black plastic barrels stood there ominously. Inside them was acid in which floated human body parts from eight different people. The remains included fifteen human feet.

At the same time, police found evidence in a rented house not far from the bank, home to a suspect in the case. The occupants had very much kept themselves to themselves and neighbours were unable to provide any information about them.

In the early morning of the following day, police

raided houses in the northern suburbs of Adelaide. Three men – John Bunting, twenty-seven-year-old Robert Joe Wagner and forty-year-old Mark Ray Haydon – were arrested and charged with the murder of an unknown person between 1 August 1993 and 20 May 1999. It was almost certain that more charges would be made as the investigation proceeded. They were remanded in custody until 2 July 1999.

The media, of course, were having a field day, speculating wildly about the motives for the killings. Some suggested that the neo-Nazi links of one of the accused might provide the reason, while others posited that there might be psychosexual motives. To the police, however, it seemed clear that there was a financial motive behind them. They believed the answer lay in social security payments. The Australian agency responsible for these, analysed the list of missing persons provided by the police and discovered that a number had never been reported to them as missing or dead. Their payments, therefore, were still being issued and were being collected years after their real beneficiaries had disappeared.

On 2 June, police raided another property in the northern suburbs and arrested nineteen-year-old James Spyridon Vlassakis. Vlassakis had met John Bunting when he was just fourteen after his mother moved in with him. He worshipped him and was entirely in thrall to Bunting's overwhelming personality. He attempted to kill himself twice during his first week in custody, adding even more sensational elements to an already sensational case. For his own safety, they locked Vlassakis up in James Nash House, the South Australian Department of Correction's maximum security psychiatric clinic.

Meanwhile, more houses were raided and searched, possibly as a result of information provided by Vlassakis.

Six of the eight bodies found in the Snowtown bank vault had been identified by 3 June but the names were withheld. Furthermore, another body was still expected to be found. Police searched back through cold case files until they discovered that an as-yet unidentified corpse had been found by a local farmer in a field in the rural agricultural area of Lower Light, fifty kilometres north of Adelaide, on 16 August 1994. As DNA cross-matching was begun, police raided another two properties, one in Riverland, near the Murray River, the other to the north of Adelaide.

The names of some of the dead began to be released to the media and the public, revealing a fascinating network of relationships with the accused. The Acting Police Commissioner stated that this was a group that 'preys upon itself'.

Forty-year-old Barry Lane was a convicted sex offender and transvestite who went under the name 'Vanessa'. He had lived for eight years with one of the accused, Robert Wagner, at 1 Bingham Road in Salisbury North, just a street away from John Bunting's house at Waterloo Corner Road, where bodies would later be found. Wagner would help to kill Lane.

Lane had also had a relationship with Clinton Trezise whose disappearance had begun the investigation. John Bunting, for his part, was engaged to Gail Sinclair, sister of another victim found at the bank, Elizabeth Hayden, who was the wife of another accused man, Mark Hayden.

The remains found at Lower Light were identified as those of Clinton Trezise. It was a significant breakthrough.

The search for bodies was not over, however. On 23 June, the former address of John Bunting, on Waterloo Corner Road, was searched. Officers used ground-penetrating radar, developed from technology created by the British Army for finding land mines during the Falklands War. It had already proved its worth in criminal investigation during searches of the property owned by English serial killer, Fred West.

A concrete slab, once covered by a rainwater

tank, outside the house's back door was smashed and the device was wheeled over the exposed earth. It showed that an area about two metres square had been disturbed sometime in the recent past. A short while later, a body was found buried a couple of metres down. It had been dismembered, put into two plastic bags and buried, and had been in the ground for three or four years. The ground radar discovered a second body a few days later, beneath the location of the first. This one was not wrapped in plastic.

Another of the accused, Mark Hayden, had lived in Elizabeth East with his father, close to Waterloo Corner Road. Haydon was remembered by neighbours as quiet and unassuming and would spend most of his time under the bonnet of his car. Neighbours also remember his rough-looking visitors but there was never any noise or trouble. In 1995, Elizabeth Sinclair arrived, marrying Hayden a couple of years later. In 1998, the couple moved to another north Adelaide suburb, Smithfield Plains. Shortly afterwards, Elizabeth Hayden disappeared. On 22 November, Mark went to pick up two of her sons who had been at the house of Elizabeth's brother, Garion, and informed him that he and Elizabeth had had a row and she had left him. Next day he claimed that she had run off with a boyfriend and before leaving had cleaned out a bank account held jointly by him and his father.

Mark seemed unconcerned, even by the fact that she had emptied his bank account, and Garion and his wife became suspicious. They also doubted the story because, after a fairly miserable life during which she had had eight children by a number of different men, Elizabeth seemed to be settling down with Mark. Three days later Garion reported his sister missing to the police.

Robert Wagner and Barry 'Vanessa' Lane also lived not far from Waterloo Corner Road. Lane's flamboyant dress – pink shorts in summer, for instance – and his record of paedophile convictions made the house a target for local children and the two men built a high fence around the building and kept four Doberman Pinchers to keep people away. Wagner, illiterate and dependent upon Lane, was a white supremacist with a loathing for gays and Asians, and a member of the far-right group National Action.

In July 2000, Wagner, Bunting and Haydon pleaded guilty to four charges of murder in the Adelaide Supreme Court and were sentenced to life imprison-ment with a twenty-six-year non-parole period.

JOHN WAYNE GLOVER

They called him the 'Granny Killer' or the 'Monster of Mosman'. He was a vicious serial killer who specialised in the particularly brutal killing of elderly women. His method was always the same. He would select his victim and force her into an alley or secluded spot where he would proceed to pulverise her with his fists and a hammer in a frenzy of violence and horror. When she lay in a bloody heap at his feet, he would remove her underwear and would then strangle her with her own pantyhose. This last act was the calling card that identified the killer as the same one in all six cases.

John Wayne Glover was not the type. A large, friendly man in his late fifties, he was considered an ordinary family man who loved his wife and two daughters and could be trusted with anything. He lived in a comfortable house in the fashionable and well-off Sydney suburb of Mosman, right beside Sydney Harbour. He worked as a sales rep for the

Four 'n' Twenty Pie Company and was a volunteer with the Senior Citizens Society. A real good bloke, as the Aussies would say. But in reality he was a heartless killer who spent the easily won proceeds of his murders on gambling and booze.

Glover, born in Wolverhampton in England, had been convicted of various petty crimes in 1947, being discharged from the British Army when these emerged. He emigrated to Australia in 1956, initially living in Melbourne. He had always had problems with older women, perhaps suggesting reasons for his later activities. He had never got on with his mother Freda, a woman who had had several husbands and many relationships. In Australia, when he married Jacqueline 'Gay' Rolls in 1968 and moved into his well-off in-laws' house in Mosman, he encountered another older woman with whom he did not get on – his mother-in-law Essie Rolls, a cantankerous, domineering individual.

His offending did not stop when he emigrated. Not long after arriving Down Under, he was convicted on two charges of theft in Victoria, and in New South Wales he was also convicted of stealing. In 1962, aged twenty-nine, while employed as a television rigger with the Australian Broadcasting Commission, he was arrested for the assaults of two women in Melbourne as well as theft.

These assaults presaged his later, more vicious assaults. The victims were beaten about the face and body and forced to the ground as he frenziedly ripped the clothes from their bodies. On each occasion, the screams of the women alerted local people to what was happening and Glover was forced to flee before he could rape or kill them.

After the second of these attacks, residents reported seeing a young man running into a nearby garden and police cornered Glover and arrested him. He told them that he had had a fight with his girlfriend and had been feeling very emotional. He was released on bail the following morning. As he was leaving the police station, however, he was intercepted by two other police officers who wanted to ask him some questions about a similar assault a few weeks previously. He confessed under their questioning and was charged with that attack, too. He was lucky, however, receiving only a three-year suspended sentence.

He was in trouble again in 1965, picked up on a peeping tom charge. Sentenced to three months, he served only six weeks before being paroled. It would be many years before he broke the law again, apart from a minor shoplifting charge in 1978. Not everyone is convinced that he was squeaky clean during that time, however, and there are at least five unsolved murders between 1965 and 1989 that involved similar methods to those later used by Glover.

In 1982, he was dismayed to learn that his mother Freda was following him by emigrating from England to Australia. He was even more upset when he learned that Freda planned to move into the Mosman house as a companion to Essie. His wife and her parents knew nothing of Glover's criminal past and he was certain that Freda could not be trusted to keep it quiet. Fortunately for him, however, he succeeded in dissuading her and she went to live in Gosford, one hundred miles north of Sydney, just far enough away. She died in 1988 of breast cancer and he was diagnosed as having the same condition, an extremely rare occurrence amongst men. He underwent a mastectomy but developed prostate problems that rendered him impotent. It would later be said that he changed around this time as a result of his health problems.

On 11 January 1989, eighty-four-year-old Margaret Todhunter was walking in a quiet road in Mosman when Glover drove past. He parked his car and, when he was certain no one could see him, walked up to her and punched her in the face, snatching her handbag in which was $209. He took to his heels with the handbag as she shouted after him. Given what happened to Glover's other victims, she could consider herself very lucky.

Gwendoline Mitchellhill was not quite so lucky a couple of months later.

On 1 March, Glover spotted Mrs Mitchell hobbling along with the help of a walking stick. He opened the boot of his car and took out a hammer, tucking it into his belt, out of sight. He followed at a safe distance and when she arrived at the secluded entry to the retirement village where she lived, he raised the hammer above his head and brought it down heavily on her skull. He continued to bludgeon her about the head and body before grabbing her purse which contained $100. She was still alive when she was found but was dead by the time the emergency services arrived on the scene.

The two attacks had the police puzzled and they were not even certain that they were connected. Finally, they reasoned that it was just another mugging – there had been many in the area – that had gone very wrong.

It was ten weeks before Glover killed again. Lady Winifred Ashton had been playing bingo at the social club that Glover also frequented and was walking home when Glover saw her. He again followed her into the foyer of her apartment building where he attacked her with the hammer. She was a frail little old lady who was suffering from cancer at the time, but she put up a fight. However, Glover bashed her head continuously on the concrete floor until she was unconscious. He then removed her pantyhose and, pulling it tight around her thin neck, strangled her. He had established a calling card that would tell police that it was the same man carrying out these horrific crimes. He also arranged her shoes and walking stick neatly at her feet. He found $100 in her purse and returned to the social club to buy drinks with it and play the poker machines to which he was addicted.

The police now knew they were dealing with a serial killer, a homicidal maniac who was heartless enough to unleash his violence on defenceless old ladies. Although he never had any interest in sexually assaulting the women he killed, he now very strangely started assaulting elderly, bed-ridden women in the nursing homes he visited in his capacity as a pie salesman. He began on 6 June by putting his hand under the nightdress of seventy-seven-year-old Marjorie Moseley at a retirement home in Belrose. When the police were called, she was unable to describe her assailant and they made no connection between these crimes and the murders.

He did it again on 24 June at another retirement home, when he lifted an elderly lady's dress and fondled her buttocks, and in the neighbouring room he stroked another woman's breasts. Staff, alerted by the woman's shouts, came running and questioned Glover but he left without being held or his identity being established.

On 8 August, he assaulted Effie Carnie in a back street of Linfield, not far from Mosman, not killing her but stealing her groceries. He impersonated a doctor on 6 October, putting his hand up the dress of a woman patient in a nursing home at Neutral Bay, a harbourside suburb, but again escaped.

On 18 October he started a conversation with eighty-six-year-old Doris Cox and walked with her into the secluded stairwell of her retirement village. Suddenly, he smashed her face against the wall, using all of his strength. He rummaged in her purse, but finding nothing, left her for dead and went home.

Unfortunately, Mrs Cox's description of her attacker had police looking for a considerably younger man than Glover. It was a lucky break for him, especially when police began to think that they were probably looking for a local teenager with a grudge against grandmothers. Police concentrated all their efforts on this and Glover was free to continue his attacks.

On 2 November, he offered to carry home the groceries of an elderly woman in Lane Cove, about ten miles from Mosman. The woman offered him a cup of tea in return but he declined. On his way back to the main street he passed eighty-five-year-old Margaret Pahud and, turning, hit her on the back of the head with a blunt instrument, probably his hammer. When she collapsed to the ground he struck her again on the side of the head, killing her. He grabbed her handbag and took off after neatly arranging her clothes as usual. Shortly after, he was buying drinks in the social club with the $300 he had found in her purse.

Twenty-four hours later, eighty-one-year-old Olive Cleveland became his fourth victim. He engaged her in conversation on a bench near her retirement village in Belrose. When she stood up to go home, he grabbed her from behind and pushed her down a ramp onto a secluded lane. He beat her and slammed her head continuously against the concrete until she lost consciousness. He then removed her pantyhose, wrapped it around her neck and strangled her. Having tidily rearranged her walking stick and clothing, he removed $60 from her handbag and headed for the club. An increasingly worried state government increased the reward they were offering for information from $200,000 to $250,000.

Although they were not yet being linked to the

murders, on 11 January 1990 there was a significant breakthrough in the investigations into the molestations of the elderly women in nursing homes. Glover had visited the Greenwich Hospital that day in his work outfit. With an official-looking clipboard in his hand, he entered the hospital's palliative care ward which was occupied at the time by four elderly women. He pulled up the nightdress of one of them and touched her indecently. When she screamed for help, a hospital sister arrived and found Glover. He ran out of the ward, but she managed to get the registration number of his vehicle and the police were called.

Glover was identified as the attacker and he was asked to come to the police station to answer some questions. When he failed to appear, they called his house to be told that he had tried to take his own life and was in the Royal North Shore Hospital. He refused to answer any questions but handed staff of the hospital a note saying, 'no more grannies ... grannies' and 'Essie started it'.

When the note was passed to the squad investigating the Granny Killings, they knew they had their man. But they did not have any evidence and unless he talked, he would have to be allowed to go free. They decided not to alert him to their suspicions and put him under surveillance.

He still managed to kill one last time. On 19 March, he visited sixty-year-old divorcee Joan Sinclair, a friend of his. Police officers watched him enter the house at around ten o'clock but by one o'clock there was no sign of him leaving and there appeared to be no movement inside the building. Increasingly concerned, at six o'clock they entered the building where they found Sinclair's battered body, naked from the waist down and with the tell-tale pantyhose tied around her neck. Glover's hammer lay in a pool of blood on a mat. Glover was found unconscious in the bath, which had been filled with water. He had washed down a handful of Valium with a bottle of whisky and had then slashed his wrists.

Glover survived and at his trial pleaded not guilty on the grounds of diminished responsibility, blaming his action on the aggression he felt towards first his mother and then his mother-in-law. However, the prosecution argued successfully that Glover had been well aware of what he was doing and had tried to trick the police into believing they were dealing with a sexually motivated murderer. In fact, it was claimed, Glover needed his victims' money to feed his addiction to the poker machines at the social club he attended.

Sentenced to life imprisonment without parole,

he hanged himself in his cell on 9 September 2005.

Just days before he killed himself, Glover handed a sketch to his last visitor. It was a drawing of a park and in amongst the palm trees was the number nine. This figure is believed to represent the number of murders that he had committed but had never been charged with.

PETER DUPAS

According to friends, twenty-eight-year-old Nicole Patterson was one of the nicest people you could meet. A consulting psychotherapist who dedicated much of her time to helping disadvantaged young people, especially those with drug problems, she had turned the bedroom of her home into a consulting room and had placed adverts in the local papers, looking for clients. Unfortunately, one of those who read the advert was a man called Peter Dupas, a serial sex offender who had also turned killer.

Dupas's record stretched back to 1968 when he was just fifteen. He had been born in Sydney into a normal family in 1953, the youngest of three children. However, he had arrived many years after his siblings and his parents were more like his grandparents than his parents in terms of their age. He grew up, consequently, like an only child and, as a result, was spoiled and made to feel inadequate by an overprotective mother and a father who was something of a perfectionist. While he was still young, the family moved to Melbourne.

His time at school was difficult. He was overweight and was teased a great deal about it, being nicknamed 'Pugsley' after a character in the television show, *The Addams Family*. He was also a poor learner and frequently bottom of his class.

On 28 October, home from school and still wearing his school uniform, Dupas knocked at the door of his twenty-seven-year-old neighbour who at the time was nursing her five-week-old baby. He asked her if he could borrow a sharp knife as he was helping his mother to peel potatoes for that evening's dinner. She handed him the knife, remarking on how good he was to help his mother in this way. Dupas suddenly lunged at her with the knife, stabbing her in the stomach. He threw her to the floor and straddled her, still stabbing away at her with the knife, striking her hands with which she was trying to fight him off. She was being cut on the hands, face and neck. As she grabbed the implement, trying to break it, he gasped between breaths, 'It's too late, I can't stop now, they'll lock me up'. He put his hand across her mouth to stop her screaming and began to bash her head on the floor. Suddenly, almost as quickly as he had begun, he stopped.

Dupas was taken to a psychiatric hospital to be assessed, and it was concluded that he was 'caught in an emotional conflict between the need to conform to the expec-tations of his parents and the unconscious urges to express his aggression and his developing masculinity'. He was put on probation for eighteen months and ordered to undergo psychiatric treatment.

He left school and became an apprentice fitter and turner at the General Electric Company in Melbourne's Notting Hill suburb, but he was in trouble with the law again on 10 March 1972, when he was caught spying on a woman taking a shower. In November 1973, he was questioned by police after driving his car alongside another and leering continuously at the driver's twelve-year-old daughter. A few weeks later, he was arrested for rape.

On 5 November, he had knocked on the door of a house at Nunawading, claiming to the woman who answered that his car had broken down. She went off to search for a screwdriver and he entered the house where he threatened her and her eighteen-month-old baby at knifepoint. He had then raped her. It was not the first time he had tried this trick. On one occasion, he had stole some money and left, while on another, his terrified victim told him that her husband would be home at any minute and he fled.

The police knew he was dangerous and that his

crimes were gradually escalating. One described him as 'an evil, cold, baby-faced liar' who he thought would eventually kill if he was not stopped.

He was not wrong.

They discovered that he was very meticulous in the planning of his attacks. He selected his victims carefully and was cold and calculating in his preparation. Dupas was released on bail but remanded to a psychiatric hospital, Mont Park. He was allowed to visit home occasionally and was arrested again for a number of incidents at the nearby Rosebud Beach during these visits. He entered women's toilets where he watched girls showering. A witness tipped off the police and he was caught in the act. Again, he was admitted to Mont Park as a voluntary patient, remaining there until 22 February 1974.

Mont Park psychiatrists could find no serious psychiatric disorders but they intimated that he could suffer from personality problems in future. He got off lightly, being fined $140.

He was not treated so leniently when he was tried for the rape of the woman in Nunawading. Describing it as one of the most appalling rapes imaginable – a woman in her own home, with a young baby whom he threatened to harm if she resisted – the judge sentenced him to nine years' imprisonment of which he had to serve five years before parole could be considered.

Little had changed when he was released on 4 September 1979 after serving five years and eight months. During a ten-day period just two months after his release, wearing a balaclava, he attacked four women and threatened them with a knife. The balaclava and the knife would become his clothing and his weapon of choice from this point on.

The first of these four women was raped in a public toilet in Frankston. The next three managed to escape rape, but one was stabbed in the chest as she struggled with him. He was picked up and confessed to the attacks, claiming that he was glad to have been arrested. He could not excuse himself in any other way than by telling investigating officers that he 'gets the urge ... it just comes over me'. He continued: 'I can't help myself. I have had this problem for about six years. I don't know if it was because my girlfriend left me or what it is. I just find it hard to mix with people and I haven't many friends'.

An array of charges were thrown at him, including rape and malicious wounding, but, astonishingly, the judge gave him a lighter sentence than the previous one, sending him to prison for just six and a half years, again with five having to be served before he could be considered eligible for parole.

Released in February 1985, Dupas took only four days to reoffend. He attacked and raped a twenty-one-year-old receptionist while she sunbathed on a secluded Melbourne beach. The distraught victim had sought help from a couple of men and they caught up with Dupas as he walked to his car.

Arrested once again, police quizzed him about the murder of a mother of four, Helen McMahon, who had been beaten to death in the sand dunes at Rye Beach, coincidentally at the very same time as one of Dupas's home visits from prison.

This time, the judge – the same one who had presided when he had been tried for the rape of the woman in Nunawading – threw the book at him. He told the court that all efforts to rehabilitate Dupas had 'failed miserably' and described Dupas as 'walking around with a loaded time bomb in his pocket'. He sentenced him to twelve years, with a minimum of ten to be served before parole could be considered.

In prison they tried to deal with his problems, giving him medical treatment to try to reduce his sex drive. Surprisingly, he got married in 1987 while still an inmate, to a nurse sixteen years older than him. He was considered to be getting better, leaving his problems behind him. A psychiatrist said, 'he understands himself better and has become more assertive'.

He was released in March 1992 after serving seven years, and kept out of trouble for eighteen months. On 23 September 1993, however, he attacked a fifteen-year-old girl horse-riding at Knyeton. The girl quick-wittedly pushed her horse between herself and Dupas and managed to escape unharmed.

Just over three months later, on 3 January 1994 ,he attacked a twenty-six-year-old bank teller at 11.30 in the morning as she sat in a cubicle in a public toilet in north-western Victoria. He burst into the cubicle wearing his trademark balaclava and wielding a knife. She resisted his orders to turn and face the wall and struggled with him violently, receiving numerous cuts on her hands. Abruptly, he stopped, turned round and calmly walked back to his car, parked nearby.

The woman's boyfriend, an off-duty police officer, sped off in pursuit along with other people, capturing Dupas after his car ran off the road. In the boot of the vehicle was found a chilling collection of tools of the rapist's trade – a roll of tape, knives, a black balaclava, condoms and, most worrying of all, a shovel and a sheet of plastic. He was prepared, it seemed, for every eventuality, even murder.

Tragically, there was not enough evidence to charge him with attempted rape and he was charged, instead, with false imprisonment, a much lesser charge. He pleaded guilty and went to jail for two years and nine months.

Back on the streets in September 1996, he was on his own. His wife had left him and he moved into an apartment in Brunswick, working in a factory. Shortly after, he moved in with a woman, telling her nothing of his violent past.

More women were murdered around this time. Recovering forty-year-old heroin addict and prostitute Margaret Maher was found dead in October 1997 in long grass in Somerton. She had been stabbed repeatedly and her breasts had been mutilated.

A month later, twenty-five-year-old Mersina Halvagis was also found with numerous stab wounds at Fawkner Cemetery where she had been putting flowers on the grave of her grandmother.

On the last day of 1997, ninety-five-year-old Kathleen Downes, who had been crippled by two strokes, was found stabbed to death in her room at Brunswick Lodge Nursing Home. Interestingly, a number of phone calls had been made from Dupas's home to the nursing home in the weeks before the killing, but police were unable to establish a link between the calls and the murder.

Nicole Patterson was his last victim. She was killed on the morning of 19 April 1999 and was found on the floor of her consulting room, naked from the waist down and with her clothes ripped. The wounds on both hands suggested that she had put up a desperate fight for her life. Disturbingly, both of her breasts had been sliced off and taken away as there was no trace of them at the scene. Her wounds reminded investigators of the wounds suffered by Margaret Maher two years previously.

A neighbour said she had heard a shout at about 9.30 that morning and had seen a man walk away from the house about ten minutes later. It was obvious to police, however, that he had been very careful. The house had been cleaned from top to bottom and there were no finger- or footprints.

The killer had been careful but had missed one vital piece of evidence. In Nicole's appointment book there was listed an appointment with a man called 'Malcolm' for nine that morning. Next to the entry was a mobile phone number.

The phone number did, indeed, belong to a man called Malcolm, a student. But he had never heard of Nicole Patterson. Officers asked him to list everyone to whom he had given his mobile number in the recent past and on that list was the name of none other than Peter Dupas for whom Malcolm had recently done some odd jobs.

When they went to Dupas's home, they

discovered a bloodstained jacket on which was the DNA of Nicole Patterson. He had arrived for the appointment at nine, hoping, he told her, to cure a gambling addiction, but had attacked her as she made coffee for them both. He had killed her and then meticulously cleaned up before taking the body parts as souvenirs and leaving. He was placed in the vicinity around this time by CCTV footage taken at a nearby petrol station.

Naturally, he denied everything, as he always had when arrested, claiming that the police had planted the evidence. The jury failed to be convinced, however. On 17 August 2000, he was found guilty and sentenced to spend the remainder of his life in prison with no possibility of parole.

In prison, he has been questioned about the murders of Margaret Maher, Mersina Halvagis, Helen McMahon and Kathleen Downes. He denies it all, as ever.

CATHERINE AND DAVID BIRNIE

Four young women had gone missing in Perth in the last twenty-seven days. They were all unconnected and from good homes, with no record of drugs or even any secret love affairs that might have given a reason for their disappearances. In a couple of cases relatives had received letters and phone calls from them saying that they were alright, but after that, nothing. The officers investigating the disappearances were convinced they had a serial killer on their hands.

They seemed to have had a breakthrough in the investigation when it was announced that a naked and very distressed young woman had staggered into a shopping centre in Willagee and had been taken to Palmyra police station. They thought that it might be the last girl to go missing, Denise Brown, and hurried to Palmyra to interview her. It wasn't Denise Brown, but the sixteen-year-old girl they found was able to tell them a horrific story and finally solve the case for them.

She told them that she had been abducted at knifepoint the previous evening as she walked along a street near her home. A couple had asked her for directions and when she stopped to help them, the man had pulled a knife. They had driven her to a house in Willagee where she had been raped repeatedly after being tied up and chained to a bed. While the man raped her, the woman had watched. She had listened in horror as they talked about injecting cocaine into his penis.

Earlier that morning, the man had gone to work and the woman had forced her to make an agonising call to her parents to tell them she was staying with friends. Shortly afterwards, there was a knock at the door and when the woman went to answer it, the girl had leapt from an open window. She provided comprehensive descriptions of her attackers, their address and their telephone number.

A short while later, Catherine and David Birnie were in custody.

Each of their lives was a car crash from the start. Both born in 1951, they first met when they lived next door to each other as children. Catherine's mother had died in childbirth when she was two years old and she was bundled off to live with her father in South Africa. Two years later, however, she was back in Australia, being cared for by her grandparents. She grew into a lonely little girl who was not allowed out to play with the other kids.

David Birnie's early life was not much better. His family was well known as a particularly dysfunctional one. There were rumours of incest and his parents were both chronic alcoholics. By the time he was a teenager he had already acquired a catalogue of juvenile offences. In his early teens he trained as an apprentice jockey, but during this time he broke into an elderly lady's house, naked but for a stocking over his head, and committed the first of his many rapes. The next few years were spent in and out of jail for a series of crimes.

Catherine and David were reunited in their late teens. Soon, however, they had embarked on a burglary spree for which he was locked up for nine months and she was put on probation. In July 1969, further charges led to three years being added to David's jail-term and a further four years being added to her sentence.

Birnie escaped from prison a year later and the two teamed up again before being rearrested just under three weeks later and charged with fifty-three counts of stealing, receiving, breaking and entering, and a range of other crimes. He got two and a half years and she went to prison for six months.

When Catherine was released she found work as a live-in domestic for a Fremantle family. There she fell in love with and married the son of the house, Donald McLaughlin, with whom, over the course of the next thirteen years, she had six children. The marriage, however, was not a good one, and Catherine was desperately unhappy. In her heart she still longed for David Birnie.

She had found Birnie again and for the last two years with her husband she had been seeing her old lover. Finally, one day, she just rang Donald and told him she wasn't coming home. She moved in with David at Willagee and, in a show of love, changed her name by deed poll to Birnie.

David Birnie was addicted to sex and possessed an extensive library of porn videos. He is described by his own brother as having to have sex four or five times a day and he also describes how he liked to have it. He would inject 'that stuff you have when they're going to put stitches in your leg. It makes you numb. He put the needle in his penis. Then he had sex'. But sex, no matter how kinky, was not enough for this dysfunctional couple. They began to debate how they could get even more of a thrill, and rape and abduction began to feature in their fantasies. They first made their fantasies real on 6 October 1986.

Mary Neilson, a twenty-two-year-old student, knocked on their door. Birnie worked in a yard selling spare parts for cars and she had been there earlier in the day looking for new tyres for her car. Birnie had told her that if she called at his house he could do her a better deal.

Birnie asked her in and as she walked into the hallway of the house, he grabbed her and put a knife to her throat. He took her into a bedroom where she was tied up, gagged and chained to the bed. Then, with Catherine watching, Birnie raped her repeatedly. That night they bundled her into their car and drove to the Gleneagles National Park. He raped her again and then strangled her with a length of nylon cord. When she was dead, he stabbed her. He had read somewhere that a stab wound allows the gases to exit the decomposing body. They buried her in a shallow grave.

Two weeks later, fifteen-year-old Susannah Candy was abducted as she hitchhiked on the Stirling Highway in Claremont. Back at the house, she was raped and this time Catherine climbed into bed with David and joined in. When they tried to strangle Susannah, however, she fought back and they had to force-feed her sleeping pills to calm her down. When she lay quiet, Birnie told Catherine that she had to prove her love for him by strangling the girl. Without hesitating, she took each end of the nylon cord and pulled it tight. They buried her close to where Mary Neilson lay in the State Forest.

When thirty-one-year-old Noelene Patterson ran out of petrol on the Canning Highway in East Fremantle, on her way home from work as a bar manager at a golf club, she hoped someone would pick her up. She had been an air hostess for nine years before spending two years doing the same job on the private jet owned by Australian media tycoon Alan Bond.

When the Birnies stopped, Noelene was pleased to accept their offer of a lift but a knife was immediately put to her throat and she was tied up. She was an attractive girl and Birnie's obvious attraction to her irritated Catherine. After he had raped her, she was supposed to be killed, but he postponed the murder. Catherine, furious at her man's attraction to another, better-looking woman, took a knife and held it to her chest, telling him he had better choose between her and the girl. It was three days before Birnie finally agreed to kill Noelene. He strangled her and she was driven to the forest where she was buried close to their other two victims.

Twenty-one-year-old Denise Brown was waiting for a bus when she was taken. The same procedure was followed as with the other girls but as she was being driven to her death the following day, the Birnies spotted another potential victim, a nineteen-year-old student. They stopped to offer the girl a lift but she was suspicious, especially when she noticed that the woman in the front seat was sipping from a can of rum and coke. She thought it was a bit early in the day to be drinking and refused the lift. As they pulled away, however, she did see a small person seemingly asleep on the back seat of the car – it must have been Denise Brown, she later told police officers. She had been lucky.

Denise Brown, of course, had not been so lucky. Still alive when they reached the forest, she had been raped again in the car before being dragged out and raped yet again. While he was doing it, he pulled a knife and plunged it into her neck. She was still not dead, however, and Catherine found a bigger knife and, handing it to Birnie, urged him to stab the girl again. Finally, convinced she was at last dead, they buried her in a shallow grave. But, as they were shovelling earth onto her supine body, she suddenly sat up in her grave. Birnie picked up an axe and swung it at her skull. He then swung it again, smashing her skull open. They finished the job of covering her up and drove home.

However, the extremely violent nature of this murder was too much even for a callous woman such as Catherine Birnie, which probably explains why their last victim remained alive long enough to escape. She later told police, 'I think I must have come to a decision that, sooner or later, there had to be an end to the rampage. I had reached the stage when I didn't know what to do. I suppose I came to a decision that I was prepared to give her a chance. I knew it was a foregone conclusion that David would kill her, and probably do it that night. I was just fed up with the killings. I thought if something did not happen soon it would simply go on and on and never end'.

There was uproar when the news broke and furious Australians called for the reintroduction of the death penalty. They were even angrier when Catherine was seen stroking David Birnie's hands as they stood in the dock at their trial. Their relationship was put under the microscope and one psychiatrist talked of Birnie's evil influence over Catherine as 'the worst case of personality dependence I have seen in my career'. They both pleaded guilty and were sentenced to life imprisonment with a recommendation by the judge that they never be released. They never saw each other again but exchanged 2,600 letters during their first four years behind bars.

On 2 October 2005, David Birnie, one of

Australia's most notorious serial killers, was found hanged in his cell at Perth's Casuarina Prison. Because no one came forward to claim his body, Birnie was given a secret pauper's cremation at the expense of the taxpayers. His apparent suicide came almost nineteen years into his life sentence – possibly because his former lover had cut off all contact with him; or just possibly because he felt some remorse.

PART SIX

ASIA

TSUTOMU MIYAZAKI

Tsutomu Miyazaki was the cruelest of murderers. Not content with merely abducting children and brutally killing them, he liked to taunt the parents of his victims with chillingly silent phone calls or postcards containing gloating messages He left a box on the doorstep of the parents of his first victim, four-year-old Mari Konno. Inside were fragments of charred bone, ten baby teeth and photographs of the clothes their daughter had been wearing the day she disappeared. Typed on a single piece of paper were the chilling words 'Mari. Bones. Cremated. Investigate. Prove'. He was taunting those searching for him and shattering the lives of those left behind to mourn.

When the box was turned over to the authorities, there was doubt as to whether the ashes and bone fragments actually belonged to Mari and this fact was made known at a high-profile press conference. Miyazaki, avidly following media reports on the killings, was affronted. He fired off a three-page letter to the Konno home, and the newspaper the

Asahi Shimbun received a copy as well as a Polaroid photo of the little girl. The letter bore the title 'Crime Confession' and was signed 'Yuko Imada', a play on the Japanese words for 'Now I'll tell'.

I put the cardboard box with Mari's remains in it in front of her home,' the letter said. 'I did everything. From the start of the Mari incident to the finish. I saw the police press conference where they said the remains were not Mari's. On camera, her mother said the report gave her new hope that Mari might still be alive. I knew then that I had to write this confession so Mari's mother would not continue to hope in vain. I say again: the remains are Mari's.

A media frenzy broke out and questions began to be asked about the police investigation into the disappearance of the little girl. The authorities immediately upgraded it from merely a missing person enquiry to a murder investigation, and manpower and expertise were brought in. Handwriting experts examined the writing in the letter, but failed to establish the sex of its author.

Meanwhile, the parents of the dead girl buried her on 11 March 1989, more than seven months after her disappearance. Her father Shigeo Konno acknowledged that her hands and feet had not been in the box with the rest of her bones and pleaded with her killer. 'When she gets to heaven,' he said, 'she won't be able to walk or eat. Please return the rest of her remains'.

He did not comply with that request, but there was a letter waiting for the Konnos when they returned home from their daughter's funeral. Again signed 'Yuko Imada' and headed 'Confession', it cruelly taunted them, describing their Mari's dead body. 'Before I knew it, the child's corpse had gone rigid. I wanted to cross her hands over her breast but they wouldn't budge ... Pretty soon, the body gets red spots all over it ... Big red spots. Like the Hinomaru flag ... After a while, the body is covered with stretch marks. It was so rigid before, but now it feels like it's full of water. And it smells. How it smells. Like nothing you've ever smelled in this whole wide world'.

Tsutomu Miyazaki inhabited a strange, lonely world, remote from the real one, immersed in a universe of videos and comics, the only things that really mattered to him. His removal from the world resulted in the deaths of four little girls and in him being nicknamed 'The Little Girl Murderer'.

He had been born prematurely in 1962 in

Itsukaichi, a Tokyo suburb. At birth, the joints in his hands were fused together, a disability that caused him a great deal of distress as he grew up. He was bullied on account of this difference to everyone else and responded by retreating into his own world, becoming incapable of making friends. All he had were the comic books that he would read into the night, long after everyone else had gone to sleep.

He was initially a good student and had the honour of being the first pupil from his junior high school to gain entry to the Meidai Nakano High School. After a couple of years, however, he had lost interest in his studies, failing to get into Meiji University where he had planned to study English and become a teacher.

Instead, he went to college where he took a photo technician's course and in 1983, aged twenty-one, found a job at a printing plant owned by one of his father's friends. He worked hard for three years, saving a large sum of money, before moving back home to live with his parents and two sisters.

His father owned a newspaper, the *Akikawa Shimbun*, and was a prominent figure around town. But he had little time for his son, partly because his work meant he was away from the house for long hours while his son was growing up, but mainly because Tsutomu was not the easiest person to get along with, as his two younger sisters would readily confirm. They hated him.

The only person with whom the boy had any kind of relationship was his grandfather Shokichi. He was the only person who took any interest in what he was doing.

Relationships with women his own age were non-existent. Some said that he was physically immature and self-conscious, although he is reported by some to have had a higher-than-average sex drive.

Rather than make friends with girls, he resorted increasingly to pornography for his thrills and as the display of pubic hair was banned by Japan's obscenity laws, but the showing of the sexual organs was not, he became obsessed with child pornography. He would also photograph girls playing tennis at college, focusing on their crotches.

When his grandfather died in 1988, something seems to have snapped inside Miyazaki. It seemed that any ties with society and normal behaviour were severed by the old man's death, and Miyazaki now felt able to do whatever he wanted, no matter how unspeakable it might be. There was nobody left to let down.

Mari Konno was last seen on 22 August, walking with a man towards the Iruna River. A description was provided that fitted Miyazaki – a round, pudgy face and wavy hair. But there was no sign of the little girl. A few days after she had vanished, however, her parents received their first communication from the unknown abductor. 'There are devils about', its chilling words read. The postcard was dismissed by police as the work of a crank. Meanwhile, they interviewed thousands of people and posters were put up across Japan. All to no avail.

As the hunt for Mari began to lose momentum, Miyazaki struck again. On 3 October, he persuaded seven-year-old Masami Yoshizawa to get into his car in Hanno in the Saitama Prefecture. He drove her into the hills and strangled her close to the scene of his first murder. He then undressed her and sexually abused her corpse. When the dead body seemed to shudder, he took fright, ran to his car and sped off.

Once again, thousands of interviews were under-taken and posters and flyers were distributed, and although it seemed as if the two cases were linked, the police found not a single clue.

Miyazaki killed for a third time that year on 12 December. Four-year-old Erika Namba was returning home from a friend's house when she was lured into his Nissan Langley. When he drove off she became frightened and started to cry. Stopping shortly before seven in the evening in the car park at the Youth Nature House in Naguri, he ordered her to undress and began photographing her. But tiring of her sobbing, he climbed on top of her and strangled her, his body holding her down as she struggled for her young life. He wrapped her in a sheet and put her in the boot. He was a little over-excited, however, and shortly after driving off, as he turned a corner, the wheels of his car slipped off the road into a drainage ditch where it became stuck.

He began to panic but was close to woods where he could dispose of Erika's body. Making sure no one was around, he opened the boot, lifted out her tiny body and walked into the woods where he dumped her out of sight.

Returning to the car, however, he was shocked to find two men standing beside the Nissan. They asked if he had a problem and as he casually dropped the sheet into the boot, he explained that he had become stuck in the ditch. They helped get the car out and he drove away. It had been a close shave.

When Erika's distraught parents reported their daughter missing, the police immediately connected her with the other girls. A special operations centre was set up to coordinate enquiries. The following day, her clothing was found behind the Naguri Youth Nature Centre and her body was located a day later, nylon cord binding her hands and feet. Police searched the area but little more was found until the two men who had helped Miyazaki get his car out of the ditch came forward. Crucially, however, they identified the vehicle as a Toyota Corolla and not a Nissan Langley. The police wasted valuable time and resources checking around 6,000 Toyota Corollas. Police now knew that a serial killer was on the loose, the three girls all having lived within thirty kilometres of each other. Then the phone calls to his victims' parents began. Silence hummed at the other end and when the phone was not picked up, it would ring relentlessly and cruelly for as long as twenty minutes.

Like the Konnos, the Nambas received a post-card made up of words cut from magazines and newspapers. 'Erika. Cold. Cough. Throat. Rest. Death' it read.

By the end of the year, the area was in a frenzy of fear and suspicion. Children were not allowed out on their own and they were accompanied by their parents everywhere they went.

On 6 February, Miyazaki delivered his gruesome box to the Konnos, but it would not be until the following summer that he would kill for the final time.

On 6 June 1989 he was disappointed to find the tennis courts at Ariake near Tokyo Bay closed. He had been hoping to photograph the girl tennis players. In a park not far away, however, he came upon five-year-old Ayako Nomoto playing on her own. He asked her if she would pose for some photos before leading her to his car. As he photographed her in the back seat, she commented on his deformed hands, driving him into a rage. He pulled on a pair of vinyl gloves and strangled her, before putting tape over her mouth and nose to make sure and tying her hands with rope. He wrapped her in a sheet and placed her in the boot of the car.

He drove her to his house, and there he laid her tiny body on a table, spread her legs and taped her vagina apart. He spent the next few hours photographing it and masturbating.

Two days later, the smell of the decomposing body became so bad that he had to get rid of it. Using a knife and a saw, he hacked off her head, hands and feet, knowing that the absence of these body parts would make identification difficult. Four days later, he hid the torso near a cemetery. Meanwhile, he barbecued her hands in his backyard and ate the flesh. He threw the remains into woods in front of his house. A couple of weeks later, however, he began to worry about the body parts being so close to his home. He brought them back into the house, hiding them in a store room. Later, he disposed of the bones in the woods and burned everything else.

It was his own stupidity that would finally bring Tsutomu Miyazaki to justice.

On Sunday 23 July, when he tried to abduct a little girl, her sister ran to get her father. When the father arrived on the scene, to his horror he found Miyazaki photographing between the little girl's spread legs. There was a struggle but Miyazaki managed to escape. Astonishingly, however, he returned to the scene of the crime a little later to get his car and the police were waiting for him. He was arrested on a charge of forcing a minor to commit indecent acts.

Seventeen days later, after police searching his home found videotapes and photographs of his victims, Miyazaki confessed.

He underwent years of psychological evaluation, but eventually, although he was said to be suffering from multiple personality disorder and schizophrenia, he was declared sane and sentenced to death.

Tsutsomu Miyazaki, a cruel and heartless killer of innocent little girls, was hanged in Tokyo on 17 June 2008.

JAVED IQBAL

Each killing cost around 120 rupees or £1.70, he estimated. The method never changed. The boy would be given a drugged drink and when he became groggy, Iqbal would rape him. Then, as the boy lay disorientated on the floor, Iqbal would place a chain around his neck and slowly pull it tight, strangling him. The body would then be dissected and the pieces would be thrown into a vat of hydrochloric acid which would dissolve them, leaving a thick, gory sludge. It did not pay to hurry the process and he waited until every last piece of bone, every hair had disappeared. The sludgy remnants would be poured down a nearby drain, but the neighbours began to complain about the smell and he was forced to enlist his young friends to empty the contents into the river.

Javed Iqbal was a fatherly, friendly looking little man. But his genial looks hid the cold, stony heart of a monster, intent on taking revenge on society. He did this by raping and murdering one hundred young boys in a five-month killing spree in 1999.

The horror of Iqbal's crimes is bad enough but is only equalled by the horror of realising that as these boys, street urchins mainly, disappeared one by one, no one noticed and certainly no one cared. Only when Iqbal confessed did the crimes come to light and Pakistani society felt ashamed of itself.

Javed's base of operations was in the market square that surrounds the dramatic Mina-i-Pakistan monument in Lahore. Describing himself sometimes as a journalist and on other occasions as a social worker, he would wander through the markets and often find teenage boys whom he would take home to his three-bedroomed apartment to work as servants. Some of them would end up in his bed, but he insisted that he was not out looking for sex when he strolled through the market. He claims to have just been lonely and liked having the boys around him at home doing housework and preparing food.

As for the boys, as kids living rough on the streets of Lahore, they were delighted to have a roof over their heads for a short while. There were thousands of them swarming around the city, begging and looking for someone to be kind to them. Iqbal provided that.

However, some took advantage and one incident, in particular, would serve as the catalyst for the killing spree that was to follow. Javed was badly beaten and left for dead by a couple of the boys he had taken home with him. He claimed that he had suffered a severe head injury that left him with an impaired memory and that he had had to go into hospital to undergo several operations. To pay for his healthcare, he had to sell his house and car and, tragically, his mother, upset by what her son was going through, had died. Then, when he took the matter to the police, they merely accused him of sodomy and refused to investigate the matter. Four young friends looked after him, boys identified only as Nadeem, Shabir, Sajid and Ishaq Billa. They were the only friends he had in the world and he decided to get them to help him avenge the death of his mother.

Of the one hundred victims of Javed Iqbal, number fifty-seven was a boy named Ijaz, a good-looking lad in a torn white shirt and with an iron ring around his ankle. He was probably around fifteen and was always to be seen with his younger brother, Riaz. Ijaz worked as a masseur in the market square, carrying around a small box of scented massage oils. He made about 20 rupees, 26p, on a good day.

Early in November 1999, he was approached in the square by Javed and two of his young helpers. When Javed offered him 50 rupees for a massage Ijaz and Riaz jumped at the opportunity. They were led to Javed's small house in Ravi Road where, as it was getting dark, Ijaz sent his brother home. Riaz would never see his brother again.

When there was no sign of Ijaz that night and by morning he had still not appeared, Riaz went back to Ravi Road. They told him that his brother had left shortly after him the previous night. The truth was, of course, that he had never left the house and Riaz would next see his face much later in a smiling photograph taken at the house by Javed, Ijaz wearing a new blue shirt. On the back of the photo was written 'Number 57'. The number was wrong, however, and according to the list that Javed later provided to the authorities, Ijaz was actually the ninety-seventh boy to die.

It is likely that Ijaz had been drugged like all the other boys and Javed will then have begun quizzing him about his life. He carefully documented the lives of each one of his victims, perhaps, some suggest, in order to disarm them and lull them into a false sense of security in order to make his task easier. Other, more cynical voices claim, however, that it was just another part of the deadly ritual he went through with each of his victims. He claimed later that he was actually preparing an indictment against Pakistani society for the neglect of its children.

Once he had claimed his one hundredth victim,

he sent a copy of his confession to a newspaper, having already delivered a copy to the police. He kept the remains of his last two victims, dissolved in barrels, at his house in order to prove that what he was saying was true. It is hard to imagine, but the police ignored his confession. Only when they heard that a copy was with a newspaper did they spring into action and go to Ravi Road.

They found a charnel house that filled even seasoned policemen and reporters with horror. The walls and floor were stained with blood and the iron chain lay there, a gruesome reminder of the terror that must have been experienced within those four walls. The walls were decorated with the photographs of his victims, some as young as nine and almost all smiling, just minutes from a horrific death. In the corner was a bag that brought home the scale of the carnage – it contained eighty-five pairs of shoes and items of children's clothing. Javed had pinned a placard to the wall on which he had written: 'The bodies in the house have deliberately not been disposed of so that authorities will find them'.

It emerged that the police had actually arrested Iqbal three times for sexually abusing young boys but he had got off by bribing officers and no charges were ever brought against him. At the time, his neighbours had ganged up on him, trying to get him to control his lust for young boys, but he had simply moved to a house in another part of town.

There was no sign of Iqbal. A note said that he was going to tie a rock to himself and throw himself into the river, but when the river was dragged, nothing was found. It seemed that it had been written merely to put the police off his scent.

The biggest manhunt in Pakistani history was launched and his four accomplices were soon found attempting to cash traveller's cheques for 18,000 rupees in Sohawa. A few days later, one of them, Billa, died in custody, according to the police, after he had thrown himself from a third-floor window. There was public outrage as no one believed the story, used a little too frequently when a suspect died in custody. There was a widespread shake-up of the Lahore Police Department afterwards.

Javed was nowhere to be found and the police did not seem to have a clue as to his whereabouts. Meanwhile, pressure grew as grieving parents came forward, splashing their grief across the pages of the nation's newspapers. Sadly, they had not been so upset when their children had been living on the streets of Lahore.

It ended suddenly on 30 December 1999 when Javed Iqbal simply strolled into the office of the newspaper *Jang* and gave himself up. Two months later, he and his three surviving accomplices appeared in court, the boys giggling when they saw pictures of themselves in the newspapers. It was, inevitably, a media circus.

Javed claimed that he was the victim in this case, that whatever he had said had been distorted and that everyone believed him to be insane. He made a strange, rambling statement in which he claimed he had not actually killed anyone, that everything had been staged to highlight the plight of 'runaway children of poor families who become victims of evil people'. The missing boys were actually alive, he said, and he challenged the police to go out and find them. He claimed that his confessions to the police and to the newspaper were made under duress and he described his fear of suffering the same fate as Billa.

The trial was gruelling, especially for the families of the victims, some of whom collapsed in the corridors outside the courtroom. Eventually, however, Javed and his accomplices were convicted of murder. Two of the boys were sentenced to life imprisonment but Javed and twenty-year-old Sajid were sentenced to death. The judge stated that they should die in a way appropriate to the nature of their crimes. They would be strangled with the same chain that they had used to kill their victims. Their bodies would then be dismembered and dissolved in hydrochloric acid.

There was outrage around the world as human rights officials reacted with horror at the sentence. Even within Pakistan there was criticism. The case was sent to the Lahore High Court on appeal but this court denied that the case came under its jurisdiction. Instead it was sent to the religious court, the Sharia. But on 8 October, before it got the chance to issue its findings, the authorities at Kot Lakhpat Prison announced that Javed Iqbal and Sajid had been found dead in their adjacent cells. They had been strangled with their bed sheets. The prison authorities claimed they had committed suicide, but police investigators and others suggested that this was not the case and, indeed, there was evidence that they had been beaten before being strangled.

The streets of Pakistan's cities still teem with hordes of street kids trying to survive as best they can.

YOO YOUNG CHUL

Yoo Young Chul blamed it on the rich. They were to blame for the things that had gone wrong in his life and he was going to take terrible revenge. He made a plan to kill over a hundred of them.

He was born in 1970 in the village of Waha in South Korea's North Cheolla province. He had not been planned by his parents and his grandmother later told him that his mother had considered killing him at birth. When his parents separated, he moved in with his grandmother and then, at the age of six, with his sister, he went to live with his father in the South Korean capital, Seoul. His father had squandered most of his large military pension on poor business decisions and was now managing a comic bookshop.

Living conditions in the poor district of Mapo were harsh, with no running water or electricity. Their stepmother was cruel to the children, beating Yoo's sister, but never laying a finger on him because he unnerved her by staring at her for hours on end. He hated her.

At eight years old, Yoo and his sister ran away to live with their mother who also lived in Mapo. He attended school where he is remembered as quiet and polite, but the family were desperately poor. Yoo hated it and was often mocked at school because of their poverty. It was at that time that he began to cultivate his loathing for the rich.

In 1988, while he was a student at a technical high school, he fell foul of the law for the first time, breaking into a neighbour's house and stealing a guitar and a cassette player. He was arrested and sent to a juvenile detention centre and never graduated from his high school.

Three years later, he was in trouble again when he was arrested for the theft of money and a camera. This time he went to jail for ten months but was inside again in 1993 after stealing a car. The year 1998 saw him in trouble again, this time for forging documents and impersonating government officials.

In the middle of all this, in 1991, he married and had a son, but when he was arrested for the rape of a fifteen-year-old girl in March 2000, his wife divorced him. His life was a disaster. He was thirty years old, had lost his wife and child, and his long criminal record of fourteen convictions had resulted in him spending eleven years, more than a third of his life, behind bars. Released from prison in September 2003, he began to make money by extorting it from prostitutes and pimps in Seoul's red-light districts, using a police identity card that he had made himself. He earned enough money to set himself up in a studio apartment in the area in which he had grown up, where his neighbours found him to be quiet and respectable.

They were unaware that a vicious serial killer was in their midst.

He practised with stray dogs, rounding them up and clubbing them to death. Then, on 24 September, he was ready.

The first house he picked looked easy to get into, with a wall behind which was a small garden. Best of all, there was no security system. He watched it and noted that the only people living there appeared to be an elderly couple. He clambered over the wall, wearing a pair of gloves, and entered the house through the unlocked front door. He had brought with him a hammer that he had made himself and a knife with a six-inch blade.

The occupants were seventy-two-year-old Mr Lee, an honorary professor at Sookmyung University in Seoul, and his sixty-eight-year-old wife. Yoo went upstairs to make sure no one else was in the house. Coming back down, he went into the master bedroom and stabbed the elderly professor in the throat. Mrs Lee screamed and as she reached over to her dying husband, Yoo rained blows on both of them with the hammer, smashing their skulls.

Having locked the bedroom door, he left by the front door, trying to clean the blood off his trousers with a towel he had taken. Suddenly remembering that he had left the knife inside, he went back for it, having to kick open the locked bedroom door. He had to wipe his bloody footprint off the door before leaving again. He also opened a wardrobe and scattered the contents around the room to make it appear as if the Lees had been murdered in the course of a robbery.

Not long after, he struck again. It was a similar house with a walled garden and no security system. He was soon creeping across the gravel and entering the house. He immediately encountered an eighty-five-year-old woman whom he hit three or four times with the hammer. A sixty-year-old woman who appeared on the stairs was kicked twice in the stomach and he asked her who else was in the house. After she told him that her husband and son were upstairs, he smashed her skull with the hammer. He ran upstairs to find the woman's thirty-five-year-old son emerging from a room, trying to discover what the noise was. Yoo made him kneel down in front of him and shattered his skull with eight or nine blows of the hammer. Unable to locate the woman's husband, he left after opening a safe and scattering its contents around the room, again making the crime look like a robbery gone wrong.

His next target was the house of a millionaire, located in the Samsung area of Gangnam district, one of the wealthiest neighbourhoods in Seoul. When a sixty-nine-year-old woman came out to collect the morning post, Yoo followed her down the path and into the house. He grabbed her, holding his knife to her body, and asked if anyone else was home. She told him she was alone and he dragged her into the bathroom where he killed her with the hammer. Again scattering things around to confuse the police, he made sure he had wiped up all his footprints and fingerprints before leaving by the front door.

On 18 November he was in Hyehwa-dong, looking at a house from which there was the sound of a baby crying. He climbed the wall and went through the front door. Climbing to the second floor, he did not find anyone, but as he came down he bumped into the fifty-three-year-old housekeeper, Mrs Bae. He threatened her with his knife and led her into the master bedroom where the eighty-seven-year-old owner of the house was lying on his bed. Yoo battered the old man with the hammer. The terrified housekeeper was holding the baby that Yoo had heard in her arms. He took it from her, placed it on a sofa and covered it with a blanket. He then used the hammer to kill Mrs Bae.

As he tried to open a safe on the second floor, he accidentally cut himself. Worried that he could be traced from the DNA in his blood, he attempted to set fire to the room and, wearing a stolen jacket to cover his bloodstained clothes, left the building, where he stood a distance away to watch it burn. However, nothing seemed to be happening, and when a woman walked up to the front door of the house, he fled.

He had made mistakes, however. There was a set of bloody footprints in the house and he had been caught from behind by a security camera.

In January 2004 the police had him in custody after picking him up for theft at a sauna. However, they failed to check his criminal record and let him go, thinking he was just an opportunistic thief and not a man who had spent eleven years in prison for a variety of crimes.

Around this time, he lost interest in killing the rich and moved his attentions to women working in South Korea's flourishing sex trade. His wife had been a masseuse and had divorced him, and he had recently been rejected by a woman with whom he had been having phone sex. He wanted revenge.

On 11 February he accosted a twenty-five-year-old woman he thought looked like a prostitute in front of a restaurant and asked her where she was going. He flashed his forged police ID at her and asked her if she would go to a bar with him. When she told him she did not believe that he was a cop, he was furious and lunged at her. She tried to get away, almost making it to the door of the restaurant, but falling down before she reached it. As she screamed for help, he stabbed her five times in the chest.

In March, he called a phone sex parlour and had a woman sent over to his apartment. As soon as she arrived, he bludgeoned her with the hammer and then cut up her body. He disposed of the eighteen sections into which he had cut her in a grave near a mountain track behind Seogang University.

Not long after, he used his fake ID again with a man who had sold him fake Viagra pills in a market. He bundled the man into his own van and killed him. He then left the van in the underground car park of a local hospital and went home to wash off the bloodstains. Returning to the vehicle, he drove it to Wolmi Island, twenty-five kilometres to the west of Seoul. He sawed off the man's hands and tossed them off the pier in a plastic bag. He then set fire to the van and took a taxi home, changing cabs en route because he feared the first driver might remember him.

He continued to order up women from sex parlours. They turned up at his door like lambs to the slaughter, and between April and the middle of July he dispatched ten of them, the last on 13 July. They either came to his apartment or he would arrange to meet them somewhere before bringing them back. There he would kill them with the hammer before cutting off the head and then dismembering the rest. He never had sex with them, for fear of DNA tracing, and he always shaved the skin off their fingertips as all citizens in South Korea have their fingerprints taken. He would then clean the apartment from top to bottom, scrubbing long into the night. The body parts were put into plastic bags and carried in a backpack to a place close to Bongwon Temple – each body taking two trips – where he buried them in shallow graves. It would be all over by around four in the morning.

Panic began to stalk the streets of the capital and women were leaving work early. Sales of pepper spray, gas guns and security alarms shot through the roof as women clamoured to protect themselves. Prostitutes were especially careful. But the police investigation was struggling, even though they again had the killer in custody when he was arrested after beating up a prostitute at a 'love hotel'. He pretended to have a bad leg and to be suffering from epilepsy. When they took off his handcuffs out of sympathy for him, he escaped.

The pimps who ran the phone sex parlours got together and worked out between them that when a certain number called for a woman, the woman always disappeared. Their information was passed to a police officer who advised them to let him know next time that number called.

In the early hours of one morning, a call came through from the suspect number. A woman had been sent but had been rejected by the caller because, he said, she was too old and too ugly. He requested a younger, better-looking woman. The pimps told him they would send her but it would take a little time. They were buying time so that the police could get themselves organised.

Yoo had given a spot behind the Sincheon Grand Mart as a meeting place. A woman was sent there, but the police were right behind her. At four in the morning, as she waited, her mobile phone rang. Yoo gave her directions. Ten minutes later, as the police fanned out across the area, he stepped out of an alley and was apprehended.

In custody, he confessed everything, telling them

where the bodies were. They took him out to Bongwon Temple and he showed them where to dig. As they did so, he looked at a television news camera and said, 'Women shouldn't be sluts, and the rich should know what they've done'.

He pleaded guilty to twenty-one murders and in court said they could add another two to that tally. He later added another five. He was put on suicide watch and almost succeeded in killing himself on 3 October, using electrical flex removed from an electric wall-mounted fan.

He was sentenced to death on 13 December 2004 and now waits on death row with about sixty other condemned men.

FUTOSHI MATSUNAGA

Japan is a country whose people are reluctant to expose their innermost feelings, where etiquette and decorum are everything, and to bring shame is the most heinous of sins. To bring shame on one's country is, of course, one of the greatest sins of all. It may have been for that reason that many elements of the Japanese media were reluctant to publish details of the crimes committed by Futoshi Matsunaga between 1996 and 1998; the horrific murders of seven people, including two children. They refused to believe that such horrific crimes could have been committed by a Japanese citizen.

Matsunaga had been born in the Kokurakita-ku in the city of Kitakyūshū in Japan's Fukuoka prefecture. He was something of a paradox as a child – a charming boy who did well at school but still had disciplinary problems. He was eventually forced to leave the school he was attending after becoming involved in a relationship with a junior high school girl. At nineteen, he married and his wife gave birth to a son.

His marriage did not stop his serial womanizing, however, and he continued to have relationships with women other than his wife, around ten, it has been estimated. One of these was Junko Ogata, a girl he met in October 1982. He proposed marriage to her in 1984, but her mother Shizumi did not approve, mainly because Matsunaga had, on occasion, been violent towards her daughter. He responded by seducing Shizumi as well. As a result, Junko tried to commit suicide in 1985 and Matsunaga used this to persuade her that her family hated her, succeeding in creating a rift between them and her.

In 1993, he began to kill.

His first victim was a married woman with three children, who he persuaded to leave her husband and run away with him. He managed to explain away Junko by saying she was his sister. One of the woman's children died in mysterious circumstances in September 1993 and she herself would die in similar circumstances six months later. It was a lucrative relationship for Matsunaga, however; he succeeded in defrauding her of 11.8 million yen, about £80,000.

In 1994, he began a campaign of intimidation and blackmail of thirty-two-year-old Kumio Toraya, who lived in a condominium in Kokurakita-ku with his daughter. Toraya had told him about his criminal past, even admitting to crimes that he had not actually committed.

In 1996, Matsunaga imprisoned Toraya and his daughter in a freezing bathroom while spraying cold water upon them. He also tortured Kumio by electrocuting him and forcing him to eat his own faeces. His daughter was forced to bite her father and Matsunaga forced them to punch each other; when they did not do it to his satisfaction, they would be given a painful blast from a stun gun. Kumio would die in February 1996 from the injuries he received.

Matsunaga made a stew from the dead man's body parts and forced the daughter to drink it. He convinced her that she had murdered her father and she and Junko were tasked with disposing of Kumio's body. They chopped it into pieces and threw them into the sea close to the Kunisaki Peninsula.

Matsunaga soon found another victim, a woman who he promised to marry. Instead, he took her for 5.6 million yen, about £40,000. He invited her and her daughter to his room where they were taken captive like his previous victims. The woman managed to escape in March 1997 and had to seek psychiatric help. Her daughter was released unharmed.

Matsunaga continued his abuse of Junko but, in the meantime, also seduced her sister Rieko.

He extorted 63 million yen, almost half a million pounds, from Junko's family and then held them captive, during this time horrifically electrocuting Rieko and Junko in their vaginas. He controlled the family completely as if they were members of a cult of which he was the centre. He would soon use the power he had over them to order the series of increasingly horrific murders that would shock the Japanese nation.

On 21 December, he forced Junko to electrocute and kill her own father. Meanwhile, tiring of Junko's mother Shizumi, who was beginning to lose her mind, he ordered Rieko and her husband Kazuya to strangle her on 20 January 1998.

Rieko was next when she began to go deaf. Horrifically, while their ten-year-old daughter Aya held her down, Kazuya strangled her. It was Kazuya's turn next, however. He was imprisoned in a bathroom where he starved to death on 13 April.

Matsunaga next ordered Junko, Aya and Kumio's daughter, who was still under his control, to strangle Rieko and Kazuya's five-year-old son, Yuki.

It was later said by Kumio's daughter at the trial that Matsunaga and Junko had tortured Aya by electrocuting her, a claim that was denied by Junko who maintained that the girl was making it up in mitigation of the fact that she had murdered Aya by strangling her on 7 June 1998. Matsunaga would blame everything on Junko.

Of her entire family, she and her two children were the only ones to survive.

Of course, there was the problem of disposing of so many bodies, a task made more difficult by the fact that they lived in a city. Matsunaga and Junko's solution was to dismember the bodies and boil the pieces in a large pot. They were then disposed of in washrooms or tossed into the sea. Of course, the other inhabitants of the condominium had been hearing strange noises from Matsunaga's apartment, and the smell of the boiling body parts was very unpleasant.

He was still free to continue with his evil deeds, however. In 2000, he seduced another woman with the prospect of marriage and in 2001, she gave her twin children to Matsunaga and Junko. They then persuaded her to hand over 20 million yen, around £138,000. They would need it, they said, to bring up her children.

This incredible story was eventually brought to a conclusion on 6 March 2002. Kumio's daughter had already escaped on 30 January but Matsunaga found her again a couple of weeks later. She paid for the escape by being tortured by him. When she got away for the second time, however, she went to the police and told them the whole unbelievable story. By this time she was seventeen and had been a prisoner of Matsunaga since the age of nine.

Matsunaga and Junko were arrested and the twins and their own two children were taken into police protection.

Initially, the media were reluctant to deal with the true horror of the case. They presented it as similar to another case of kidnapping, that of Fusako Sano, a girl who had been abducted aged ten by Noboyuki Sato and held prisoner for more than nine years. Soon, however, the full extent of the crimes of Matsunaga and Junko became clear and were presented in detail to a horrified public.

They were charged with seven murders, Junko having already confessed to the part she played in them. Matsunaga maintained that he was innocent, however, insisting that the women had made up stories to implicate him. It was difficult for the Japanese police as no human remains were discovered – they had all been disposed of – and there was absolutely no physical evidence. All they had to go on was the testimony of Kumio's daughter and Junko's confession.

On 28 September 2005, the bloodthirsty couple were found guilty on six counts of murder and one of manslaughter – that of Kumio – and sentenced to hang. They appealed and in 2007 Matsunaga's sentence was upheld, while Junko's was commuted from death to life imprisonment on the grounds that Matsunaga had such power over her that he was able to coerce her into killing.